"I love the Word of God, and I _____ _____ doubts that its exactly that—God's Word. Yet when I read what Kurt Wise has written, I love it even more. My heart is warmed; my passions for God are stirred—my mind delights in the new dimensions of knowledge and understanding it gives me. I want to run out as a teacher and share what I am learning, the insights that come as the prism of truth throws new light on my ancient treasure. I am amazed at this brilliant man's ability to speak to my heart and mind in such a perspicuous way!

Whether you want a fresh touch from God—or you are not really sure about God's role in creation—*Faith, Form, and Time* is a book for you. The teaching staff at Precept Ministries International will recommend it to all our students. Even if young-age creationism is not an issue, this book causes its reader to stand in awe of God and assures him he can truly take God at His Word from Genesis 1:1 on—without apology or embarrassment in the face of those who believe otherwise."

KAY ARTHUR
Author, Co-CEO
Precept Ministries International

FAITH, FORM, AND TIME

FAITH, FORM, AND TIME

WHAT THE BIBLE TEACHES AND SCIENCE CONFIRMS ABOUT CREATION AND THE AGE OF THE UNIVERSE

KURT P. WISE

BROADMAN
&HOLMAN
PUBLISHERS

NASHVILLE, TENNESSEE

0-8054-2462-8

Published by Broadman & Holman Publishers,
Nashville, Tennessee

Subject Heading:
CHRISTIAN LIVING / PRACTICAL LIFE / SCIENCE AND FAITH

2 3 4 5 6 7 8 9 10 06 05 04 03 02

To Mom,
Rocking an ear-pained son late into the night
Tolerating a room that "moves"
Cherishing forest critters
Loving without asking for return

CONTENTS

Part 5: From Noah to the New Earth

Bio-Evolutionary Evidence Boxes

PREFACE

The Garage

When I was rather young, my father built a stand-alone garage in our back yard. Several images from this episode are deeply inscribed in my memory. I remember the pride I felt wielding a hammer alongside my father, as if I was doing something as important as he. But there were some surprises to my inexperienced brain that made even deeper impressions. I remember, for example, when the work began that my father explained we were building a garage. I can remember being excited, as I knew something significant was going to be built that was not there before. This would be a large building (huge to a young child) into which we could actually drive a full-sized car, not just one of my toy cars.

I also remember that it seemed as though ages passed while we were digging a hole rather than building a building. It seemed to me that we were going in the wrong direction! Then after the concrete had come with the associated flurry of activity to prepare for it just right, I recognized that this was the foundation of the building my father planned to build. At that time I did not comprehend the importance of that slab. Years later, when a fire burned down the garage, that slab remained. In fact, that concrete foundation remains to this day, as it became the slab upon which another garage was built.

When I saw how easily that first structure was destroyed, I began to recognize a bit of the importance of the time we took building the foundation. Nevertheless, when we finished the foundation and Dad seemed so proud (and I with him, of course), I remember laying my head down in the grass of the lawn and looking across the garage site seeing nothing at all! We (well, mostly Dad of course) had done so much work, but nothing could be seen of this building that was purportedly being built.

I then remember nailing two-by-fours. One part of me was excited because this was surely part of the promised structure, but another part of me was very disappointed. We cut, assembled, and nailed those boards together on the ground! There was one wooden structure laid out on one end of the concrete slab, another on the other end, and one on each side. But after what seemed like an eternity of time, after we were done with what Dad insisted were the walls, I still—with head upon the ground— could see no building . . . nothing at all!

Then there was the construction of the huge wooden triangles that Dad said were for the roof. But alas, once again, after building so many of these, the "garage" was invisible from a bunny's eye view.

I began to seriously question whether I understood what a garage was. Then came the day—a Saturday—when neighbors were invited over, and one of the most wonderful things I had ever seen occurred before my very eyes. We had spent so very long doing "nothing"; yet in the matter of a few minutes the walls went up, the roof went on, and lo, a garage stood before us.

Building the Big Picture

The history of young-age creationism has been very much like my experience with the garage. Young-age creationism is built upon the foundation of God and His revealed word. Thousands of years of divine revelation and thousands of years of study have built an understanding of God and His creation that lay out a solid foundation for theories of earth history. Believers through the centuries have been building walls and trusses, doors and windows to fit into that structure. There have been countless observations and theories of history that seem to make a good fit between the observations of the created world and the claims of divine revelation. However, the young-age creation model of earth history has never seemed to rise from the dirt. Good volumes and papers have been written from time to time on young-age creation geology or biology or physics or chemistry or theology or ethnology, but there seems to have been some reluctance to put the walls together so everyone could see the model.

This book in its own small way seeks to push up and nail together those walls and tresses put together by so many people over so long a period of time. There is hardly anything original here, for "there is nothing new under the sun," but it is hoped that the picture that emerges will encourage some. Before the raising of our garage, I got tired of nailing boards together because I had lost the vision. All that changed as I watched the raising of our garage. I pray some people will be similarly stimulated to continue with renewed vigor in the construction of the framework of young-age creationism.

Another discovery occurred as I watched the garage being raised: I suddenly recognized the work that still had to be done. I recognized the need for windows and where they should be put, the need for doors and where they should be placed. I recognized where the siding was needed, where the electricity should be housed and the shelves built. I pray that this book will stimulate people to continue the building. I pray that they will recognize where their talents and gifts can be utilized—whether it be in Hebrew studies or Greek studies, systematic theology, epistemology, philosophy, physics, chemistry, cosmogony, astronomy, geology, biology, ethnology, archaeology, comparative religions, linguistics, or any of a host of other disciplines. We need researchers, but we also need writers, data entry people, secretaries, and people who can contribute resources.

With the building of the young-age creation model comes the building of an entire Christian synthesis. God's truth should be used to interpret—to *properly* interpret—all the data of the universe. All the stars of the universe, all the rocks of the earth, all the organisms on its surface must be reinterpreted, as well as all the world's literature, philosophies, and religions. They can and should be reinterpreted from a Christian perspective so all these things can be taken captive under the mind of Christ. It's a grand vision that I pray this book contributes to in some small way.

What This Book Is—and Why

This book is inadequate—partly by intent, mostly because of failure. The book was very much limited in length so that it could be written—so that some sort of structure could be raised. However, much is lacking because of its brevity. Many evidences and good theories have not been included. Myriads of good references have not been listed. Just as Charles Darwin said of *The Origin of Species,* this is only intended to be a meager introduction to the subject. The real volume—the complete work—should be expected in the future.

The unintentional inadequacy of this book has many causes—not the least of which are the limitations of the author. I am a paleontologist. I am not professionally trained as a theologian, or a philosopher, or a physicist, or a chemist, or an ethnologist, or a linguist, or any of a host of other disciplines touched upon in the pages of this volume. Furthermore, I am not a writer. Or at least I have not been trained to write for normal people. As a scientist, I have been trained to write for scientists (and we are certainly not normal people). This has undoubtedly resulted in unintentional errors. It is hoped that future volumes will be written not by individuals but teams of experts. The best structure is assembled from the combined efforts of many different people, each trained in different disciplines.

Another source of inadequacy is the changing nature of the field. Experience tells me that by the time this book goes to press, I will have changed my perspective on the framing of some of the structure's walls. Young-age creationism is a young discipline. As such, it changes rapidly. In five years I expect many of the walls to look substantially different. Though the biblical foundation will remain, in ten years I expect the superstructure built on top of it to be substantially different. This is the nature of the sciences—especially the most interesting of the sciences.

It is important also to assert that this book assumes the veracity (the truthfulness) of God and His Word. It does not seek evidence for the veracity of God or Scripture, because such evidence would then have a higher status than God and His Word. This book starts with the assumption that the God described in Scripture exists. What He requires of us is faith—complete dependence upon Him. If we could fully reason our way to God or fully pave a road to Him with proof, then faith would not be required. Thus, there is no way to enter the house of faith by reason or proof; it must be by faith.

This book, then, begins with faith and is written for those already in the household of faith. Although Scripture, language, and logic are used from page 1, this book does not establish the reliability of any of those until chapter 2 and beyond. This is because the ultimate object of Christian faith is God. It is the nature of God that provides reliability to all things reliable.

This book, then, begins with God. So if this book is only to "preach to the choir," what value is it? I pray that its value is to aid each of us as believers in taking captive every thought of the mind and in enlarging our understanding of God to fully encompass all that is known and all that is. In short, I pray that this book offers a small hand of aid and issues a tiny encouragement to the believer's everlasting quest to know God.

KURT P. WISE
Dayton, Tennessee
November 2001

Acknowledgments

Innumerable people have contributed to this book. Conversations with scores of people, oral presentations from hundreds more, as well as countless writings have contributed to the volume that follows. There is nothing new in this volume—all has been borrowed from others. The information from myriads of sources has been chewed and swallowed, partially digested, and regurgitated on the pages of this book in a form that is uniquely mine. Many people have contributed, but the errors and misconnections, the stupid suggestions, and the wrong theories are all my fault and not those of any others. For repeated, long, informative discussions, I want to thank people like W. Gary Phillips, David M. Fouts, John Mark Reynolds, Danny Faulkner, D. Russell Humphreys, Larry Vardiman, Stephen A. Austin, Andrew A. Snelling, John R. Baumgardner, and Todd Wood. There have, of course, been many others.

PART 1

God's Word on the Matter

CHAPTER 1

CREATION FROM A TO Z

Origins is the study of beginnings. Where does a person begin when examining beginnings? The Bible, logically enough, begins at the beginning of all beginnings. The Book of Genesis (which means "beginning") starts with the words, "In the beginning God created." This verse refers to the beginning of all beginnings. Aside from time (which had just begun) there was only God[1]—Who has no beginning. The where, when, how, why, and who of the beginning of everything that began is God.

Can I Get a Witness?

Reconstructing the events of the past is always challenging. In criminal court cases, which often focus on trying to reconstruct past events, eyewitness testimony is highly valued. Events that precede a potential witness's existence, however, are not knowable by eyewitness testimony. The past is no longer occurring; it cannot be replayed or repeated. As humans we cannot revisit an event, once done, to witness it for ourselves.

The simple fact is that we were not there when God first created. Individual human lifetimes are shorter than the age of the creation by at least an order of magnitude,[2] and humanity itself arose after the beginning of the creation. Man was not present at the creation of anything created before man himself was created.[3] And since humans were created late in the creation (Day 6 in a six-day creation), many origination events occurred before man was present. Humans, therefore, both individually and corporately, have time constraints that make them poor eyewitnesses for origins studies.

But a person must be more than just present to be a good eyewitness. The individual also must be capable of accurately observing the pertinent aspects of the event, correctly remembering the information, then reliably passing on that information. Humans have limitations at each level: (1) We can detect only a limited range of sights, sounds, tastes, and smells. (2) Our senses receive more perceivable information than they can detect and transfer to the brain. (3) Our brains can process and store only a finite amount of information. (4) We have physiological limitations, such as blind spots in the eye. (5) The finiteness of language further limits our ability to express information.

Even before the Fall, the above inadequacies would have been in place because man as a physical being is finite in time, space, perceptivity, knowledge, and communicative ability. Yet other limitations have beset humans since the Fall and have further compromised man's reliability as a witness. Some of these imperfections are physical: Diseases have lessened the acuity of the senses, dulled the agility of the brain, and crippled the quality of communication. Another condition that the Fall probably intensified is the loss of information that occurs each time it is transferred from one place to another.

Besides the physical consequences of the Fall, man's moral condition also compromises his ability to be a reliable witness. Humans can choose to perceive or believe inaccurately and can choose to deceive others. "Man is born unto trouble, as the sparks fly upward" (Job 5:7). We are prone to error. Unbelievers run from truth, are blinded by Satan (2 Cor. 4:4), and cannot understand spiritual truths (1 Cor. 2:14).

Therefore, humans make very unreliable witnesses—both inadvertently and on purpose. So even though we can agree that humans were not present for many of the events we study in origins, we must further admit that *even if they were,* they would not make very good eyewitnesses.

God Is Our Witness

God, however, suffers from none of these limitations, making Him the perfect eyewitness of these original events. Since there is only one God (Deut. 4:35; Isa. 44:6), and since there always has been and always will be only one God (Isa. 43:10b), then He was the only one present at the first beginning. By definition all created things (including angels) are temporally constrained. They have origins after the beginning and thus cannot be eyewitnesses of it. So if there was any witness of the creation, God was it:

- He existed at the beginning of time (John 1:1–2). Actually, He and only He existed *before* the beginning of time—before the beginning of everything that had a beginning (Col. 1:17a).[4]
- Unlike humans and other created beings, God is present everywhere in the universe. He is not constrained by space (Prov. 15:3; Jer. 23:24).
- He is the Creator of all things (John 1:1–3; Col. 1:16). Therefore, He had direct experience of every aspect of every beginning.
- Since God is eternal (Ps. 9:7; 1 Tim. 1:17) and unchanging (Mal. 3:6; Heb. 13:8), He has been in existence throughout the entire history of the universe for all subsequent events.
- God is sustainer of everything (Col. 1:17b; Heb. 1:3), therefore He had direct experience and all knowledge of every event in the history of the universe.
- God's wisdom is without limit, and His understanding is complete (Ps. 147:5; 1 John 3:20). He accurately observes, understands, and remembers all aspects of all events.
- Since God is unfallen and in fact instituted the curse on the creation, He is outside the effects of the Fall. Since He is truth and is uncompromised by sin, God is not only the sole eyewitness of the past, but He is also the only fully reliable witness.

He was not just present at creation—not just a *witness* of creation— God actually caused all beginnings to occur, both physical and spiritual. So if a person seriously wanted to know anything about origins or history,

God is by far the best source of such information. He is the *only* eye-witness of many things. And He is the *best* eyewitness of everything because He was not only there; He caused it and sustained it—and continues to sustain it. He fully understands, does not err in His comprehension, does not lose any information in the course of time, and cannot tell a lie about what He knows. Since God created man and man's capacity for language and understanding, God as the Word (John 1:1) would be expected to be able to pass on information to us about the creation of man in reliable fashion. So as long as God is willing to divulge information about the nature, history, and origin of things, this information will definitely be the most reliable source of such information.

Common Knowledge

There is nothing that God does that is not a consequence of His nature. The *way* things came to be, the *order* in which things came to be, the *form* things assumed at their origin, the *pattern* things assumed at their origin, and the *timing* of their origin—all these were consequences of Who God is. If God had been different, the origin of things would have been different. There would have been a different mode, a different order, a different form, a different pattern, a different timing to the beginning of things. Likewise, all events subsequent to the creation—both physical and spiritual—have occurred according to His nature, as permitted and sustained by God.

It may well be that a perfect understanding of the nature of God would have permitted a perfect prediction of the history of everything.[5] The obverse may be true as well: If we had a perfect understanding of the mode, order, form, pattern, and timing of the origin of things (both physical and spiritual), we would have a perfect understanding of the very nature of the Creator Himself.

But since perfect understanding of God and perfect understanding of the creation is outside the grasp of humans, how much understanding of either one—God or creation—do we need in order to better understand the other?

Surprisingly, the Bible's answer to this question seems to be "not much." In the first three chapters of Romans, Paul (under inspiration of the Holy Spirit) presents a threefold argument for the universal depravity of man—reasons why all humans deserve God's judgment.

Argument #1: All humans are sinners. "All have sinned, and come short of the glory of God" (Rom. 3:23). The Old Testament law was given to convince us we could not keep it (Gal. 3:19–24). The law shows us we are sinners. If, however, sinning against God's law were the only condemnation of man, some people might argue that God would have no right to condemn those who had never encountered the Bible. The next two arguments close this loophole.

Argument #2: Romans 2:14 refers to people who, although not familiar with the law of God (the Bible), still do the things required in the law.[6] This passage suggests that God implanted within the existence of all humans something that convicts them of sin. This "law written in their hearts" (Rom. 2:15) might be the "knowledge of good and evil" (Gen. 2:17) acquired by humans after the Fall. It might also be what many people call the "conscience." It is that voice deep down inside that lets us know when we are doing wrong. Since everyone has done something their heart's law (or conscience) told them was wrong, everyone has been convinced that they are sinners, even without the direct claims of Scripture.

Argument #3: Romans 1:18–21 claims that everyone also has been convinced that God is Creator (v. 19). God has done this by means of the things He made—by the physical creation. In fact, not only are humans convinced that God is Creator, they are convinced of His eternal power and Godhead (v. 20)—that is, they are convinced of the nature of God. They are so convinced, in fact, that they are "without excuse" (v. 20).

We can see, then, that from these three arguments from Romans 1–3, every person in the world has already been convinced that he is a sinner and that there is a Creator. From these two facts, a person can deduce that—as a sinner—he is accountable to someone (the Creator) for that sin.[7] Thus, even without the direct claims of Scripture all people are already convinced that they are guilty and in trouble. They know they have no chance at all unless they throw themselves on the mercy of the One to Whom they are accountable.

So while these extra-biblical evidences do not identify the way of personal salvation through trusting in the work of Jesus Christ, they are at least sufficient to convince people of their need and to prompt them to seek a solution. As indicated in Psalm 19:1–4, the creation speaks of God and His attributes to *all* people—to all languages, all places, all ages, all mentalities, and all times. If this were not true, there would be no justification for condemning all who do not believe. And since many of these people have only a rudimentary understanding of the physical creation, it is evident that even a very imperfect understanding of the creation is sufficient to allow a strong inference about the nature of the Creator. All people know enough about the creation to have some understanding of the Creator. Not much maybe, but enough.

It seems, then, that not only is the physical universe the direct result of God's nature, but it is created in such a way that even a basic understanding of it can lead to an understanding of God. This, in fact, is evidence of God's nature. It shows His desire to know man.

An artist can be better understood by studying his or her art, and the art can be better understood by studying the artist who created it. The universe can be seen as God's work of art, so that studying the physical creation can allow a better understanding of God, and studying God can lead to a better understanding of the physical creation. Here is a further reason to suggest that a proper understanding of the physical creation— its origin, its history, and even its present nature—must begin with God and an understanding of Him.

It All Starts with God

It makes sense, then, why the Bible itself begins with God: "In the beginning God . . ." (Gen. 1:1). God is the starting point in history; therefore, God should be the starting point in the *study* of history. He is the "Alpha and the Omega, the beginning and the ending" (Rev. 1:8)—the A and the Z.[8] But because He also *sustains* His creation, He is everything in between; He is A *through* Z. In a proper dictionary of all things, God would be central to the definition of everything. He is the effector of, the sustainer of, and the One to be glorified by every entity of creation. This is why origins studies must begin with God, end with God, and center on God.

God should not be relegated to the inference or conclusion of creation studies.[9] God should be both the beginning and the end of creation studies. We should not be seeking evidence of God or of God as Creator (thus pushing Him off to the conclusion of the study and setting the evidence as a higher authority than God). Rather, we should be seeking a greater understanding of both the creation and the Creator based on the starting point that God is Creator and that the creation is created.[10] This kind of approach produces many benefits. For example:

It deepens our understanding of God. For believers, the goal of origins studies should not be the discovery of evidence that God exists or that God is Creator. These issues should already be accepted by faith (Heb. 11:3), with the full expectation that whatever findings we uncover will enhance our understanding of God. With our thoughts focused on Him, we glorify Him. As we know Him better, we are compelled to worship Him, to stand in awe of Him. Greater knowledge of God results not only in a greater understanding of the creation but a greater understanding of *everything.* A greater understanding of God leads also to a heart more similar to God's heart. Knowing more about God improves our relationship with and our service to God and others.

It improves the accuracy of our knowledge. Inferring truth from two good sources is better than inferring truth from one source alone. Considering information about God's nature should improve our understanding of the physical world. Considering information about the creation should improve our understanding of God.

It provides a powerful teaching and synthesis tool. If the attributes of God are responsible for the origin, history, and structure of the creation, then any of His attributes are likely to have resulted in a wide spectrum of consequences. By understanding Who God is and what He is like, a person might expect to see corresponding physical effects, biological effects, moral effects, psychological effects, and spiritual effects in the creation. It is likely, then, that the attributes of God will allow for the systematization of a large amount and wide range of human understanding. In this fashion a systematic study of God can become the systematizing core of all human thought. Educationally, a systematic study of the attributes of God can be used to organize a corresponding systematic study of all human disciplines. Systematic theology, then, can become the core of systematic academics. In this sense (and this sense alone) theology can once again be restored to the "queen of the sciences."

It tends to encourage the adoption of the best possible ethic. Since God is a God of truth and the standard of all morality, His central position in such studies should encourage us to adopt ethical standards reflective of God Himself. This will guide us in deciding what types of study we will and will not engage in. It should guide us in prioritizing the disciplines of study and the specific projects we explore within them. It should guide us in the proper allocation of our resources. And, of course, it should encourage us to set the highest possible ethical standards as we develop the methods of study and presentation of results.

What's Next?

Throughout this chapter the Bible has been referred to over and over again. We cannot go far in the study of the creation and its Creator without consulting the only eyewitness account we have of the creation. The next chapter discusses the critical role that Scripture plays in the study of the creation and its origin.

CHAPTER 2

THE BIBLICAL STANDARD

Because the Bible is the key element in our first understanding of the creation, we must take a moment to consider what gives the Bible its authority and what we can expect it to say—or not to say. In order to understand its message, we must try to grasp God's intention for giving us His Word and get an idea of what He expects us to do with it.

The Lies We Believe

Although God reveals Himself in those things He has made, and even offers Himself as mankind's Savior, God does not force Himself on us. After the passage we discussed in the first chapter—Paul's argument that God reveals Himself through His creation (Rom. 1:18–20)—Paul goes on to say (v. 21) that man often rejects this truth. Thus, although God offers truth to us, He does not force us to accept that truth. In fact, the freedom He allows us goes much further than that.

Think about the Garden of Eden. God not only gave man a choice either to accept or reject His commandment—to say yes or no—but also the freedom to accept an alternate truth—to believe the serpent's lie that the fruit of the tree had the power to make a person wise. But as Romans 1:21–23 suggests, God's leniency doesn't end there. Sometimes man doesn't just accept alternate truth but actually constructs alternate truth without receiving it from anyone else: "For although they knew God, they neither glorified him as God nor gave thanks to him, but their thinking became futile and their foolish hearts were darkened. Although they claimed to be wise, they became fools and exchanged the glory of the immortal God for images made to look like mortal man and birds and animals and reptiles" (NIV).

God even allows us to put the disobedience into actual practice. So God has placed enough flexibility in His creation to permit us not only to reject truth but to create, accept, hold to, and act out non-truths.

What in the nature of humans and the creation makes these freedoms reality? Is this kind of flexibility inherent in the nature of things, or is the flexibility forced upon it by the contrary nature of man or some force of evil?

It's true that man's depravity is probably the biggest culprit in many of his deviations from the truth. But human depravity may not be an entirely satisfactory explanation. Eve, for example, was able to arrive at some erroneous conclusions in her mind even before the Fall.[1] She presented to the serpent an altered version of God's commandment. She said it was forbidden not only to eat the fruit of the tree but even to touch it.[2] It may be that Eve added the "do not touch" clause for safety purposes—to help her stay as far as possible from temptation and sin. But we must admit that if the commandment was given to man with as little explanation as we are given in Genesis 2:16–17, there was much room for discussion on precisely how it was to be obeyed. The commandment was somewhat ambiguous.

Other examples of ambiguity in God's Word include prophecies that bear fruit in multiple fulfillments as well as parables with multiple meanings. God apparently intended some of the prophecies found in the Bible to address more than one specific situation. Others were not only to address specific situations but also to have larger, less obvious, more long-term implications.

Ambiguity, therefore, appears to be intentionally built into God's Word. Not everything about the Bible is easy to understand. We might even say that ambiguity could actually be built intentionally into the very nature of the creation—for a purpose greater than our understanding of creation.

Could You Be a Little Clearer?

Hebrews 11:6 indicates that in order to please God, a person must come to Him in faith. If God provided man with everything he needed in order to come to God by logic and/or physical evidence, man would be able to come to Him without faith. This would be like getting into heaven without Christ. So how could God provide just enough information or physical evidence to encourage man to come to Him, yet not enough for him to get there without faith?

The answer is *intentional ambiguity*—which prevents us from getting to God without faith but at the same time encourages us to accept Him and His Word by faith. Since faith is required in order to come to God, and since we have the freedom to reject it, and since this was true even before the Fall of man, it appears that God chose to create the universe with inherent ambiguity. In a sense, man's freedom of choice is built into the very fabric of the creation.

So we come to one of our first big questions: Why is it impossible to prove that God exists? It is because of intentional, inherent ambiguity—thus the failure for anyone to prove God's existence definitively in spite of the many and varied "proofs" that have surfaced through the centuries. It is also impossible to prove God created because the Bible says, "*Through faith* we understand that the worlds were framed by the word of God" (Heb. 11:3, emphasis added). It turns out that undeniable, conclusive proof eludes all human investigation.[3]

Another example of creation's ambiguity that has strong application in the sciences is found in 2 Peter 3:3–7. This passage predicts that people will reject Christ's return (v. 3), claiming that "all things continue as they were from the beginning of the creation" (v. 4). Phrased differently, these people believe in unchanging natural laws, processes, rates, and conditions. When such a person tries to infer anything about the past, he assumes the past looks like the present, so he studies the present to reconstruct the past (a method called *uniformitarianism*).

However, verses 5–7 tell us that these kinds of conclusions are invalid because of one thing: God intervenes in history, such as in the Creation, the Flood, and the judgment to come. So the ambiguity of the creation results in the failure of strict uniformitarianism, which might explain the long-term response to the uniformity of natural law, process, geological rate, and geological condition believed and advocated by Charles Lyell in the early nineteenth century. The uniformity of geological condition seems never to have become popular even in Lyell's day. The uniformity of geological rate, popular in the geological community for one and one-half centuries, has gradually been rejected.[4]

God Speaks, Man Responds

Does this ambiguity mean that God does not wish for us to come to Him? Truly, many people have doubted the existence of God because of the absence of logical and evidential proofs—because God hasn't just come out and said so. Yet even though this ambiguity is placed in the creation for a reason we have already discussed—because God requires faith—He does place intriguing evidences of Himself in the creation and offers faith to all who seek it.

The amazing reality is that God desires relationships with human beings. This is why He created mankind in such a way that he is capable of participating in the relationship God offers. Since a relationship is possible only when similarities exist between two individuals, man had to be created with certain similarities to God. Perhaps these are the traits that collectively make up the "image of God" placed in man at creation.

One of these similarities is our capacity to communicate. Just as communication is important for relationships among people, so God also considers communication important in His relationship with humans. The fact that one of God's names is the "Word" (John 1:1) indicates that God is a communicator. Confirmation of this is seen in how soon God spoke to man after creating Him, as well as in the frequency of phrases such as "God said," "the Lord said," and "Jesus said" in the Bible. Man was created as a communicator, both to reflect God's character as a communicator and to receive and respond to God's communication to him.

Because of His desire to communicate with man, God sent His Word to man in several different ways. First, God spoke directly over time to many different people. Second, God gave man the Bible—His written Word. Third, the Word Himself became incarnate in the form of man—Jesus Christ. So whether speaking about the oral Word of God, the written Word of God, or the incarnate Word of God, we know that the Word indeed comes from God, and we would expect it to be true and to possess the attributes of God. The fact that God designed His Word to be written down emphasizes the truth standard He had for the Bible.

Relationship, however, is more than just a monologue. God requires and expects man to respond to the Word. This suggests several things: (1) The general, overall message of Christ as well as both the oral and written Word should be easily understood by human beings. This doesn't mean that *everything* the Bible says is crystal clear but that what a given person needs to know at a given point in time is understandable by him at that time. (2) In order to respond to God's Word, the Word must be made fully available to us. This suggests that the Word in all its forms should bear the attributes of God (such as truth, life, power, and wisdom) when originally presented to man. (3) Additionally, since God is timeless and just, He would be expected to present the Word to every person regardless of time, place, or status. This suggests that the attributes of the Word must be true throughout time. It would not be expected that once given to man, major truths of Scripture should be misunderstood on a wholesale manner for centuries on end or that the truth should be lost to them forever.

Yet because man is finite and fallen, he tends to understand imperfectly, and then either intentionally or unwittingly passes on the truth imperfectly. So during the period of history before the written Word of God, when man was passing down the truth orally through the generations, how did God preserve the accuracy of His message? While direct oral communication from God is reliable, too many oral transfers from one person to another would degrade the information.

In a young-age creation model (taking a straightforward reading of Scripture), the progression of God's Word from oral to written form as well as the length of the time lag between them is understandable and does not allow for massive misinterpretations of the truth. Before man's fall, for example, when he could live forever in perfect form, there was no need for the written word. Once understood, God's Word would have presumably been maintained in human minds forever without degeneration. The Fall of man, with its attendant degeneration, would necessitate the writing of the Word—but not immediately.

Accepting the text at face value,[5] the people listed before the Flood lived for more than nine centuries—probably longer than any texts would survive, making the written Word an impractical device for that time period. And though the length of years would tend to make us question the reliability of information handed down over so long a period of time, the unusual length of the pre-Flood human lifetime made the transfer nearly seamless.

For example, Adam died only 126 years before Noah was born, when Noah's father, Lamech, was 56 years old.[6] This provided Noah with—at the most—thirdhand information of God's oral word to Adam. It also provided—at worst—a thirdhand account of all human history. If Adam and Lamech had direct contact, then decades of repetition were potentially available to make sure that Lamech had acquired the information accurately. Then Lamech had 590 years to pass the information on reliably to Noah. Suddenly the massive time expanse from Adam to Noah seems more like a hand's breadth.

After the Flood, Noah died two years before Abram was born, when Abram's father Terah was 128 years old.[7] Abraham himself, then, potentially had fifthhand information of even the oldest events of earth history. Abram overlapped with Jacob by fifteen years, and with Jacob's father Isaac for seventy-five years.[8] Jacob thus potentially had sixthhand information (or seventhhand at worst). We don't have to track it much farther. Jacob overlapped a minimum of seventeen years with his grandson Kohath[9] and something on the order of five or six decades with Kohath's father Levi.[10] Kohath, then, potentially had seventhhand or eighthhand information. And since Kohath's life almost certainly overlapped with Moses,[11] then Moses had access to eighthhand or ninthhand information of the beginning of time.

Eight or nine transmissions of God's Word—not nearly as many as one would expect—combined with the emergence of a much shorter life span[12] and a substantial change in the social and political structure of God's people. These factors make it reasonable for Moses to be the person called upon by God to write down the creation account and the intervening earth history.

The problem of accumulated transmission error may also help explain why the Bible was presented in a series of steps. As the potential for accumulated error increased with time, there would be reason for more and more written revelation. The culmination of this potential for degeneration might also explain, in part, why the Word became incarnate so late in earth history, and—again, in part—why, when Jesus returned to heaven, the Holy Spirit (the Author of Scripture) was sent to man in a way distinctly different and more personally than was the case before the incarnation of the Word. All this would cumulatively counter transmission and translation errors that occur even in the light of supernatural preservation of the words of the Bible. In this way the total truth available to man could have been kept at least roughly constant from Creation to the present—consistent with God's justice.

How Do We Interpret This?

Now that we have seen God's desire to communicate to man through His Word, we must ask ourselves how we are to interpret what He has said to us. According to Scripture, God is the true Author of the Bible. Among His reasons for writing it is the complete development of every believer (2 Tim. 3:16–17). So if all believers are to apply the Bible's teachings to their lives, Scripture must be able to be understood by all believers. It would be reasonable to assume, then, that to accomplish this end most efficiently, the Bible was written in a straightforward fashion—in the very way in which it is to be understood. We say the Bible is *perspicuous*—that is, it is written the way it is to be understood and is understood the way it is written. The straightforward (or natural) understanding of Scripture is to be preferred over any other understanding.

Approaching the Bible in this way allows us to use certain strategies in understanding it.

Consistency. The assumption of a single author for the Scripture suggests that a consistent hermeneutic (or method of interpretation) should be used throughout the entire Bible, and that the interpretation of one section must be consistent with all other sections of Scripture.

Context. As a result of the consistency of biblical information, context makes up an important part of identifying the meaning of a word or phrase in the Bible. Furthermore, words must not only be understood in the context of phrases, but phrases must be understood in the context of sentences, sentences in the context of paragraphs, paragraphs in the context of books, and books in the context of the entire Bible. An understanding of even the smallest portion of Scripture must be consistent with the message of the entire Bible and not inconsistent with any other portion of the Bible. Scripture should be used to interpret Scripture.

Language Study. God has seen fit to communicate using words, and He created us in such a way that we are able to understand and respond to those words. He also placed His Word in written form. Therefore, words are important. And careful language study should be used to determine the meanings of Bible passages. Study of words, semantics, grammar, syntax, literary structures, and genre are all appropriate components of Bible study.

In current culture, a postmodernist would suggest that meaning is whatever you wish it to be; meaning is not absolute. A postmodern philosophy in biblical studies[13] would separate biblical words from their true meanings. Such a philosophy also is likely to separate the Bible from the "Word of God." But the very existence of a written Word from God seems to suggest that this philosophy is not applicable to the Bible. Instead, the most common and consistent understanding of a word is very likely to be the intended meaning of that word in the Bible. Combined with the constraints that are determined by context, a particular word's meaning can usually be identifiable with relative ease.

Authorial Intent. Postmodernism would also suggest that the intent of an author is not important in order to discern properly the meaning of a piece of literature. The opposite is true for the Bible. God had intent in authoring it, and He created man to understand this intent. Furthermore, God gave particular portions of Scripture to specific people as they needed His truth in their unique situation. Therefore, understanding the setting and the people to whom a particular section of the Bible was first presented can often be critical in properly understanding that passage.

At the same time, God intended all Scripture to be profitable to us (2 Tim. 3:16) at every stage in the history of mankind. Therefore, the Bible, truly unique in literature, must be understood to have intended meaning not only to the first recipients, but to all human beings throughout history. Biblical passages must be expected to apply to events and times throughout human history to follow. Therefore, for example, Genesis addresses creation myths from those of the Canaanites, to those of the Greeks and the Romans, and even the creation myths of the intellectuals of the twenty-first century!

Approaches like these line up with what is called the "historico-grammatical" interpretation of the Bible, which is the traditional hermeneutic of the church—the natural or default hermeneutic that is utilized by all people in all situations unless there is sufficient reason to use another one. And truly, this seems most in line with the nature of God. We are told that we must come to God with the simplicity and purity of a child—not simple-mindedly, but in a trusting fashion. And the historico-grammatical, straightforward interpretation of Scripture is the hermeneutic of children. Children believe what they hear, see, and read. Before being jaded to act otherwise, they do not seek ulterior motives or meanings that distort the text. The nature of God, then, leads us to approach Scripture in this way—to humbly seek the truth He has for us without seeking what we wish the text to say.

An Appeal for Authority

Still, many people will want to ask these questions:

- How important should the claims of the Bible be considered? And why?
- How should the teachings of the Bible be related to the teachings of man?
- Should one have authority over the other, or should they be given equal authority—perhaps in different arenas?

Those who choose to disagree with the assertion that the Bible is authoritative in all matters of faith and practice may continue to remain unconvinced. But one thing must be affirmed by all of us: the Scripture certainly makes that claim of itself. It tells us that the Bible is God-breathed and thus should have higher authority than the claims of man. This seems confirmed by the fact that the Bible is used by God to transform man and build man's relationship with God. If in fact the Bible is the preserved issuance from the mouth of God and carries some of the attributes of God in its basic essence, then it seems only natural to give it authority over any claim of man.

Let's look at a few biblical examples of this.

The Garden of Eden. Even before the Fall of man, the Word of God had priority over the reasoning of man. Adam was told not to eat of the tree of the knowledge of good and evil. So during the entire time that the serpent tempted Eve, and that Eve considered the serpent's claims, and that both Adam and Eve reasoned things out, it was still wrong to eat the fruit—because eating the fruit was a violation of the direct Word of God. The serpent may well have used some very powerful and persuasive arguments. For example:

- God loved Adam and Eve; He would never do anything to hurt them. Human reason would think it inconceivable that God would create a tree with deadly fruit and place it right in the middle of the garden.

- Further evidence that God meant no harm was in the beauty and aroma of the fruit. It was no less beautiful or sweet-smelling than any other fruit in the garden, so human reason might conclude it couldn't be any less healthy than any other fruit that had been given to man to eat.

- The serpent might have pointed out that God was teaching Adam and Eve new knowledge every day and that this knowledge was a good and desirable thing. And since the forbidden tree was called the "tree of the *knowledge* of good and evil," it might be reasoned that the knowledge that would come from eating it would also be a good and desirable thing.

Satan may have used these kinds of arguments and others similar to them. Throughout the entire discussion, however, it remained wrong to eat of the fruit from that single tree. No matter how reasonable the argument and no matter how well evidenced the claims, it continued to be wrong to disobey God's Word. And ultimately, Adam and Eve were condemned for nothing other than disobeying God's Word.

The Temptation of Christ. Here the same person who had tempted Eve thousands of years before was tempting Jesus. In Jesus' situation, however, He not only resisted the temptation but responded to each temptation with a quotation from the Bible. He was the incarnate Word of God, quoting *from* the written Word of God. Jesus did not try logical argument or evidential justification to defend His positions; He merely quoted Scripture because it had divine authority over Satan and his methods.

The Rich Man and Lazarus. As Jesus' story is related in Luke 16, the rich man insisted that Lazarus be sent to evangelize his brothers, because (he reasoned) his brothers would surely listen to one who had come back from the dead. Abraham responded by declaring that if they rejected Moses and the prophets—the Word of God—they would not believe even if they saw with their own eyes someone who had been raised from the dead. This places Scripture over even spectacular observations.

The Apostle Peter. In 2 Peter 1:15–21, the apostle affirms this same principle when he says that even though he (Peter) was both an eye-witness and earwitness of the transfiguration of Jesus, a more sure Word is available to man in the form of Scripture.[14]

As these examples show, the Word of God ascribes to itself authority over the reasoning of man. And if, in fact, it had this authority before the Fall—before man was blinded by Satan, before man purposely sinned, before his interpretations and sensory perceptions became even more corrupted and less reliable than before—how much more should God's Word have such authority now . . . *after* man's Fall? And because the Word is so intimately associated with the One Who created both us and the physical world about us—the One Who defines what is right and true—this suggests that the Bible should be authoritative in all matters: all matters physical, spiritual, psychological, and moral.

Straightforward statements of Scripture should be considered truth, whether they refer to the physical creation, the spiritual creation, or to man. The Bible's authority should not be limited to morality and lifestyle, or to spiritual matters alone. Nor should it be used to answer only certain questions such as "Who?" or "Why?" Because of the nature of God and the fact that Scripture is the Word of God, the Bible should be understood to be authoritative on all matters it addresses. Biblical claims should have priority over any interpretation of extra-biblical data that contradicts them.

Extra-biblical data such as reason, experience, or physical world data can certainly be used to aid in interpreting the Bible. But the rule should be that extra-biblical data should never be used to reinterpret the Bible.[15] Proper interpretation of the Bible can be used to determine the meaning of a biblical text, following the principles of the historico-grammatical hermeneutic outlined above. But reinterpretation involves altering or replacing the interpretations that are natural to the text with interpretations that in fact are not natural to it. If the best interpretation of the extra-biblical data would force an unnatural or contrived meaning upon the biblical text which is contrary to the text's perspicuity, grammar, or genre, then we should reinterpret the extra-biblical data, not the Bible.

So can extra-biblical data ever be properly used to interpret the Bible? Yes—in at least two ways. First, if there are several interpretations of a biblical text that are possible in a natural reading of the text, extra-biblical data can be used to choose one of those. Second, the extra-biblical data might suggest an interpretation of the text that had not previously been thought of but that does fit within a natural reading of the text. This would be acceptable because the new interpretation is not due to an unnatural reading of the text.

Here's my favorite example of this: Revelation 3:15b–16 reads, "I would thou wert cold or hot. So then because thou art lukewarm, and neither cold nor hot, I will spue thee out of my mouth." The context of the passage indicates that it is being said to believers—the believers of the church in Laodicea. But what are the categories "hot," "cold," and "lukewarm" supposed to mean? If this refers to spiritual "temperature," it would seem that God is preferring spiritual coldness over spiritual lukewarmness. Although this is possible, it seems less than satisfying! I puzzled over this for years until archaeology produced an interpretation I never suspected.

Archaeological investigations of the city of Laodicea suggest it was a Roman resort city in the first century A.D. Apparently it had two different water sources. One of these came from mineral-laden hot springs that were popular because of their therapeutic value. But the hot spring water was not good for drinking, so the Romans brought in drinking water through aqueducts from the cold springs of the distant mountains. The overflow of the two water sources—one cold and good for drinking, the other hot and good for physical therapy—when mixed, produced a lukewarm mineral-laden water good for nothing other than inducing vomiting.

This imagery suggests another possible meaning for Revelation 3:15–16: God desires that we be productive by using one gift or another. But—alas—the Laodiceans were producing no meaningful work at all and were to be rejected from God's service. This interpretation is allowed by a natural reading of the text but was not thought of (at least by this author) until the non-biblical data was presented.

Why Believe the Bible?

It is not uncommon these days for believers to claim they believe in the truthfulness of the Bible for a variety of reasons. A best-selling book argues that Scripture is to be believed because it is well-substantiated by manuscripts. So, the argument goes, if we assume the validity of many historic works when only a few late manuscripts of it have survived (for example, Julius Caesar's Gaulic Wars), then why not believe the Bible, which probably has more manuscripts and manuscript fragments dating closer to its original writing than all others of its age? Utilizing criteria in history to authenticate historical documents, the Bible should be considered an authentic historical document.

Another common argument for the authenticity of the Bible comes in the consistency that is found in the message of the Bible's sixty-six different books authored by forty different writers from a variety of socioeconomic backgrounds spanning more than fifteen hundred years. Such consistency would not be expected unless (as the Bible claims) the human writers were inspired by a single Author.

Yet another argument for the Bible's authority was made popular by a best-selling book by Keller, who asserts that following the Bible's dietary laws would, in general, result in better health. He states that this is most surprising because the healthfulness of these practices would not be recognized by human medicine until well into the nineteenth and twentieth centuries after Christ—more than three thousand years after the writing of the laws. Since humans could not have known about the health benefits of such laws, Keller argues this shows that Scripture was inspired by God.

One of the most popular arguments for the accuracy of the Bible is from fulfilled prophecy. Most presentations of this argument begin by documenting a prophecy from the Bible and the way it was fulfilled. The long delay between the prophecy and its fulfillment and the great detail in the fulfillment argue strongly for the supernatural knowledge that was required. The many examples through the entire length of the Bible suggest that the Bible was in fact inspired by God as the Bible itself claims.

Yet another popular argument for the Bible's authenticity comes from biblical archaeology. Throughout its pages the Bible makes hundreds of verifiable cultural, architectural, and artifactual claims. In spite of the fact that many archaeologists do not have religious reasons for believing the Bible and many of the claims seem quite incidental to the biblical text, many of the biblical claims have been verified by archaeological excavation—sometimes in unexpected, spectacular ways. The repeated archaeological confirmation of Scripture argues for a unique level of authenticity for Scripture among ancient texts.

A final example of Bible authenticity arguments centers on the discovery of the Dead Sea Scrolls. Before 1947 the oldest known manuscripts of the Bible dated from after A.D. 1000, well over one thousand years after the writing of Old Testament texts. Centuries before the printing press, Bibles had to be copied by hand. This must have occurred many times between the original authorship of Scripture and the transcribing of the manuscripts we actually have today. Since errors tend to enter handwritten texts each time they are transcribed, it seemed impossible that the Bible of our day was close to its original form.

Beginning in 1947, however, the discovery of the Dead Sea Scrolls changed all that. A number of biblical texts, including the entire Book of Isaiah, were found among the Dead Sea Scrolls, giving us portions of the Bible more than a thousand years older than the oldest, previously-known manuscripts. The differences between the texts are far fewer than would be expected, suggesting that the Bible's accuracy has been supernaturally preserved. Once again, this provides evidence that the Bible is reliable.

Each of these arguments suggest that we should believe the Bible because of *evidence* that the Bible is truthful and reliable. This type of argument provides an unbeliever reason to place initial trust in the Bible. However, this is not sufficient reason for a believer to *continue* to believe the Bible is true. We should understand the Bible to be true by faith. The Bible was true as originally given because its Author is truth. The Bible was preserved supernaturally because God is unchanging and just. So, in answer to the common reasons for belief just mentioned:

- It is because the Bible is true and trusted and valued by so many people that so many manuscripts survive from it.
- It is because the Bible is authored by one unchanging God with one purpose that consistency can be found among so many books written over such a long period of time by so many diverse writers.
- It is because the Bible is written by a caring God with all knowledge that its laws were so wholesome ahead of their time.
- It is because the Bible is authored by an all-knowing, truthful, faithful God that it is so full of fulfilled prophecy.
- It is because the Bible is true that its archaeological claims are so dependable.
- It is because the Bible is preserved by an all-powerful, just, unchanging God that manuscripts separated by multiple centuries are so similar.

The Bible is not reliable because evidence exists that it is; evidence exists that it is because the Bible is reliable. Evidence can encourage unbelievers to place their faith in Christ, but ultimately Christian faith can grow only as Christians rely upon faith and not evidence. The Bible is preserved, reliable, and true because of the nature of its Author. It should be believed over observation and evidence.

What's Next?

If the Bible is to be believed over observation and evidence, is there value in making observations and collecting evidence? Should believers assemble what has been observed and reasoned about a subject to create a synthetic understanding—to create a field of study? Is it appropriate for followers of Christ to pursue an academic discipline? This author believes that each of these questions can be answered in the affirmative, and the next chapter explains why.

CHAPTER 3

THE GREAT SYNTHESIS

Several centuries ago, theology or the study of God was considered the queen of the sciences. This was because all disciplines of human thought were considered with reference to God. Theology lost that status in what has been called "the great divorce." But we need to renew our focus on God once again and base all of our academic disciplines upon God and His truths. This synthesis—somewhat the reverse of "the great divorce"—I call "the Great Synthesis."

I would suggest that the Great Synthesis is what we as believers should band together to accomplish. It will take all of us to make it happen because we need the diversity of gifts, training, and expertise of the church to bring it to pass. But if successful, such a synthesis would once again restore God to the center of human thought. So before we begin to dive into the specific thoughts and theories of young-earth creationism, it's important to take a broader look at the foundations of science and all academic disciplines in general. We need to see what could be accomplished if truth were again given an opportunity to reign supreme.

Why We Do What We Do

The word we use to classify a field of study in higher education—*discipline*—is derived from the same source as the English word *disciple*. A discipline is a carefully defined and trained (or discipled) way of thinking about something.

All disciplines have certain things in common. They have a subject of study and a particular understanding of what is true and what is not true about that subject. They have carefully defined rules about how the subject is to be studied and understood. Academic disciplines, in fact, are full of rules—rules about what sort of training is necessary to study the field, rules about how to study and learn about the field, rules about how to organize ideas, rules about how and where to publish those ideas, and on and on it goes. These rules of the field make up the methodology of that particular academic discipline.

But one must look even further than the methodology of a discipline to discover where the thinking about a field begins because the rules of a field reflect an ethic and an associated group of values that are upheld by those who study the field. The rules of a field also reflect an understanding of what is thought to be ultimately true about the subject of study and how that truth is acquired (that is, an epistemology). Values, ethics, epistemology. Put all of these components together, and you can begin to define the foundational philosophy of a field.

As an example of this, let's use the field of education. In this discipline there are many rules: rules about who can educate, what is to be taught to whom, what is to be taught at each age, how that education is to be done, and so forth. But these rules that make up the methodology of education are based on certain assumptions, values, and claims, such as the basic understanding that people have the ability to learn, that there is something worth learning, that something can be taught, that it should be taught, and that it should be taught correctly. Collectively, these ideas make up the philosophy that is foundational to the discipline of education.

But before a person can properly practice any academic discipline, he must consider the answer to this basic question: Is the foundational philosophy of this discipline based upon the *correct* ethics, values, and truth claims? Many of the practitioners of a field are unaware of the foundational philosophy that underlies what they do. These philosophies are simply accepted—often *blindly* accepted—and are often so deeply buried in a field's methodology that many people never consider whether their claims are correct or not. Sadly, Christians have done little to check the correctness of the ethics, values, and truth claims of the various academic disciplines. Such basic questions as which academic disciplines should we as believers study and what methods of study are ethical for believers to engage in have generally not been systematically examined by believers. There is a need for this to be done for and within all the disciplines. But how should we go about such a project?

Where the Bible Comes In

As the special revelation of God, the Bible provides truth in all areas—areas that it addresses *directly* and areas that it addresses *indirectly*. Therefore, Scripture should be the first source consulted for an evaluation of academic disciplines. This consultation should not just be a search for key words of a field. All scriptural principles and standards should be considered in the light of how they would impact a field. Each important question of a field—for example, Should this field be studied? or What should and should not be studied in this field?—should be considered carefully by examining the Scripture methodically for answers. The entire philosophical foundation of a field should be systematically reexamined in the light of scriptural claims and principles.

Foundational to the philosophy of every discipline is an ethic and a set of beliefs about truth. Scripture itself advocates an ethic—not just an ethic, but the only right ethic. Scripture also tells us about truth—the truth of God. From Scripture, then, we can define, identify, and characterize truth. This in turn can be developed into a complete epistemology, or way of gathering knowledge. This epistemology, combined with an ethic and a set of values—all derived from Scripture—should be the basis upon which all foundational philosophies are grounded. Once these foundational philosophies are established, scripturally-consistent methodologies can be established in each respective discipline. In this manner a truly Christian worldview can be established.

Let's return to our example of education for a moment. Scripture tells us there is truth and that truth is God Himself. Scripture also tells us that we can know the truth, that we can be taught the truth, that we can teach the truth, and that we should seek to know and teach the truth. Scripture thus provides a proper foundation for a philosophy of education and can lead to developing the correct rules and methodologies for practicing it.

But before we can do any of this, we must understand an important concept. Neither foundational philosophies nor rules and methodologies are actually a *part of* the respective disciplines. They define issues about a particular field but are actually *outside* the field. The hands-on practitioners of those fields are not adequately trained to engage in such an endeavor without help from those who are properly trained. This is why there is a great need for Christian theologians, ethicists, and philosophers to team together with Christian practitioners of the various fields to produce Christian foundational philosophies. When believers in each discipline work together with others to develop a proper Christian ethic, epistemology, foundational philosophy, and methodology for each discipline, a complete academic synthesis can be achieved. Such a synthesis would improve our understanding of God. A better understanding of God would improve our pursuit of Him. And all of our academic disciplines would become more fruitful as a result.

Reinventing Science

The remainder of this chapter provides a rough outline of what a Christian foundational philosophy might look like. The philosophy of science has been chosen as an example because of the author's scientific training and experience. What follows is only a partial and embryonic suggestion for such a philosophy. The development of a proper and complete philosophy of science should be the collective activity of a team of Christian theologians, philosophers, and scientists.

The discipline of science studies the physical world. Some of the most foundational of questions for a philosophy of science should include, Does the physical world exist? and Should the physical world be studied?

Scripture begins with the words: "In the beginning God created the heaven and the earth" (Gen. 1:1). Implicit in the very first statement of Scripture is the claim that the physical world does indeed exist. This statement also contains truth about the creation and in turn passes that truth on to human readers. Thus implicit in this statement is the claim that truth about the physical world can be known and should be known. The first words of Scripture provide some shadow of hope that a study of the physical world is not only possible but should be done.

Properly developed, a philosophy of science should be constructed in a systematic fashion. We might begin with a why: Why should we study the physical world? Once that question is answered, we might then wish to know enough about the nature of the physical world to determine how to study it most effectively. We might then wish to identify the values and characterize the ethic that should guide us in the study of the physical world. We might then conclude by developing the rules that allow us to study the physical world most effectively.

Why Study the Physical World?

An examination of Scripture suggests at least three biblically-based purposes for the study of the physical world: to know God better, to serve God better, and to minister to others better.

To Know God. According to Scripture, God shows Himself in the things He has made (Rom. 1:19–20). It would seem that studying the creation would lead to a better understanding of God. There is inherent value in knowing God, and knowledge of God is foundational to all understanding (Prov. 9:10). This means there is value in studying the physical creation to gain some of this understanding.

To Obey God. There is also value in studying the creation in order to serve God better and to follow His commands. First of all, Scripture encourages us to seek wisdom and understanding (Prov. 4:5–13). Understanding permits us to make sense of acquired knowledge, and wisdom permits us to utilize that knowledge properly. Therefore, the effectiveness of our respective ministries is hindered if there are limitations in either understanding, wisdom, or knowledge. So if the study of the physical world has the potential of providing knowledge, we can use this knowledge to give godly wisdom and understanding something to act upon.

Second, we are given dominion over the creation (Gen. 1:26–28; Ps. 8:4–8), a responsibility to care for the animals and plants. In order to provide proper care for something, we first need to understand it—to know what nourishes it, imperils it, and heals it. A study of the physical creation can provide us the knowledge we need to execute our dominion responsibility properly.

Third, we are commanded to maintain our bodies properly as the temple of the Holy Spirit (1 Cor. 3:16; 6:19; 2 Cor. 6:16). A study of the human body has the potential of providing knowledge that will be useful in the proper upkeep of our bodies.

Fourth, we have a responsibility to be good stewards of what we have been given (Matt. 25:14–30; 1 Cor. 4:1–2; 6:20). We will have to give account for the efficient use of everything over which we have been given authority, including the physical resources of the earth and the capabilities of our bodies. A study of the created world can provide the knowledge we need to utilize it most efficiently.

Fifth, we have a responsibility to act rightly in everything we do (Lev. 11:45; 2 Cor. 7:1; 1 Pet. 1:15–16). This means we need to decide how to respond to such concerns as nuclear energy, artificial intelligence, pollution, logging, extinction, famine, disease, infertility, cloning, and overpopulation, as well as many other issues and concerns. Studying the physical world can provide knowledge that is essential to creating correct responses to each of these questions. Once again, divine wisdom and understanding must be combined with proper knowledge to arrive at the correct decisions.

Finally, we are not to be afraid of man (Deut. 1:17; Prov. 29:25) or human ideas. It is common for Christians to capitulate to the ideas and claims of scientists as if their claims had more authority than the Bible. A study of the physical world has the potential of demonstrating that the conclusions of science are tentative truth at best—nothing on par with

Scripture. Study of the physical world might also yield reinterpretations that would not only counter incorrect claims but provide understandings that confirm and enhance our understanding of God and His Word.

To Minister to Others. There is also value in studying the creation in order to better serve other people. First of all, we are to be salt and light (Matt. 5:13–16) and to evangelize the entire world (Mark 16:15). All believers are called to lead Christlike lives and to share His Word. This gives believers another reason to study the physical world—to engage with others who are studying the physical world and to share the truths of God with them.

Second, we also have a responsibility to love one another by serving people (Gal. 5:13–14). Studying the physical world has the potential of providing knowledge that we can use to meet the needs of others (to treat disease, to provide food crops, to advise in bioethical dilemmas, etc.).

Third, the study of the physical world can broaden the knowledge base and experience of believers. This can provide common ground for understanding and communication. This in turn can lead to opportunities for ministry and evangelism.

The Presuppositions of Science

So there is considerable biblical justification for studying the physical world—for practicing science in the most general sense—but more must be known or believed about the physical world in order to study it most efficiently. The opening words of Scripture suggest that the physical world does exist and that information about it can and should be known. Each of these three statements—that the physical world exists, that information about it can be known, and that information about it should be known—must be true in order to justify the study of the physical world. If any one of the claims were false, the study of the physical world would be unjustified and impossible. But none of these claims are knowable by studying the physical world itself. They are assumptions or values that must be accepted as true in order to study the physical world and justify the study of it. We call them *presuppositions*.

What other presuppositions about the physical can be derived from Scripture? The Bible says that every human being will stand before God "without excuse" (Rom. 1:20) because God has revealed Himself as Creator to all humans through His creation (Rom. 1:18–20; Ps. 19:1–6). So God has apparently created the physical world in such a way that all people—no matter where or when they lived—have become convinced of the existence of God and His attributes. Several presuppositions flow from this simple doctrine of the Creator.

- The physical world exists (so God can show Himself through it).
- The physical world has a reliable structure and order (so man can infer from this structure and order the nature of an unchanging God).
- The structure and order of the physical world is understandable by humans (so man can see God in the creation).
- Knowledge can be gleaned from the study of the physical world (for example, the knowledge that God created it).
- Knowledge *should* be gleaned from the study of the physical world (God wishes for us to know Him).
- Physical world patterns should remain constant through time (so the same unchanging God is seen by all people regardless of when they lived).
- Physical world patterns should remain constant through space (so the same unchanging God is seen by all people regardless of where they happened to be located).
- Physical world patterns should be discernable in the course of a single human lifetime (so individuals can come to know Him).
- Human senses and reason are reliable enough to discern truth about the physical world (so people can reliably infer the nature of the Creator from the physical world).
- Human language is capable of describing, understanding, and teaching the truths about the physical world (so the Word can be known by man and information about Him can be passed on to others).

- Truths about unseen things can be inferred from the study of observable things (so we can infer the nature of God from things that are made).
- Physical world patterns are likely to be connected in consistent and simple ways (to point to a single Creator God).
- Observable things have causes (so that among other things, we infer the ultimate cause—God—to those things that are seen).

Even though most scientists are not conscious of them, most of these claims are assumptions that are believed implicitly by every scientific investigation. Science is the process of inferring the structure and order of the physical world. If the physical world did not exist or did not have a consistent pattern that makes it understandable to humans or did not have consistent rules in space and time—or contained no truth at all—studying the physical world would be a futile exercise. If human senses were not sufficiently reliable or human language was incapable of accurately characterizing the nature of the physical world, people could not hope to do any science at all. If people could not infer the nature of reality in a single lifetime, it would require generations to understand physical world truths and perhaps numerous generations more to convey those truths to others. If there were no causes for the things we see, or if the unobserved could not be inferred from those things we can see, scientific discoveries would be limited and there would be little reason to strive for complete understanding.

These claims—these presuppositions of science—are things that must be true for science to be done and that, if wrong, would make science senseless. The doctrine of the Creator (that God created the physical world so all people everywhere through all time could come to know Him through it) is the foundation for all the presuppositions of science. Science, then, is founded upon presuppositions that are themselves founded on the truth of Scripture—and thus on the nature of God.

Outside of Scripture there is no known foundation or justification for the presuppositions of science. If postmodernism is true, there is no absolute truth. There is no reason to believe that the physical world truly exists or—if it does—that it is consistent enough to be studied or that it is perceived the same way by all people. If, as is argued in many forms of transcendentalism, the physical world is not true reality, science would be the study of nothing at all. If the world is controlled by multiple, warring gods—such as was popular in many past cultures including Egyptian, Greek, and Roman—there would be no reason to expect any unity in the creation or consistency in the rules of the physical world. Science would produce meaningless claims in the face of constantly conflicting whims of divine beings. All other non-biblical worldviews (deism, atheism, transcendentalism, and others) provide no good reason to believe in the presuppositions of science.

The presuppositions of science are assumptions. They cannot be proven; they can only be taken on faith. How can you prove whether or not the physical world exists? What experiment can be performed to test the existence of the physical world when every experiment must by definition be part of the physical world? What scientific test can determine the adequacy of human reason or senses or language, when success or failure is perceived, inferred, or interpreted by using human senses, language, and reason? The Bible provides the only known justification or foundation for the presuppositions of modern science.

It should not be surprising, therefore, to learn that modern science was born in the context of Christianity, because science would not be a reasonable deduction from any non-biblical worldview—and in fact is contradicted by several. It follows that both the study of the physical world and the presuppositions of science are justifiable *only* in a biblical worldview. And because the Bible is true, it should not be surprising that science has been so successful in understanding the world. Outside of a biblical worldview, this measure of success is probably the only justification for continuing to do science at all.

It is likely, then, that if non-biblical worldviews continue to dominate the academic world, science as we know it is likely to become extinct. Unless believers can restore the value of the study of the physical world as a means of knowing the Creator, it is likely that only the useful or pragmatic sciences—applied sciences such as medicine and engineering—will survive in the next few decades.

The Ethics of Science

With purposes and presuppositions clarified, now we turn to the values that should be cherished in the study of the physical world. Since God is truth and requires truth in our service to Him and others, truth should be one of the highest values in any study of the physical world. Rather than helping us to know Him better, obey Him, and minister to others, physical world studies that lead to non-truths will become the foundation of misunderstandings of God.

If a person studying the physical world sincerely values truth, he will approach the study of the physical world with excellence. He will strive to receive the best training and use the best resources to examine the physical world at the highest possible proficiency. During the years of formal education, apprenticeship, and professional position, the believer who studies the physical world should be working for God, not man (Col. 3:23). With truth as a driving value, quality education and experience should be embraced, not avoided.

Yet the finiteness of man poses a challenge to any acquisition of truth. Even with the best training, a person can understand only a small part of all truth. A person studying in isolation will not be able to understand all that can and should be understood about his own field of expertise, much less all the truths about other fields. This suggests that collaboration and academic humility should be valued in a believer's study of the physical world. Collaboration can come in the form of coauthors, reviewers, and consulted publications and experts. If truth is valued, scientists will study all relevant literature, enlist coresearchers and coauthors, and seek the best referees for their papers.

Furthermore, if truth is valued, the opposite of truth must be avoided. The Bible says that man is imperfect, prone to error; he is fallen, running from God and truth. This makes the fallen state of man a critical consideration in our approach to science and helps us establish methodologies of science in spite of the depravity of man. The rules of science should be developed so scientists submit their ideas to as many truth standards as possible. God standardized His revelation to a fallen and decaying humanity by putting it in written (physical) form. His written Word as well as the world He created are physical standards of truth against which the ideas of man can be tested. Particularly in science, which is supposed to be the search for truth about the physical world, the ideas and theories of man must correspond with the data of the physical world. Regardless of how elegant, logical, or mathematically plausible a theory might be, if it is contrary to physical world data or the statements of Scripture, the theory must be rejected.

Two other scientific controls against human depravity come from the fields of law and government. In Old Testament law, a murderer was not condemned unless guilt was established on the testimony of two or three witnesses (Deut. 17:6). This minimizes the likelihood of human error in the legal arena. Science can establish an analogous standard by being especially dubious of any results that are not duplicated from the physical world by at least two independent researchers.

In the political world, democracy protects itself against human depravity by depending upon it. In their fallen state, all people seek to advance their respective causes. Each person pulls in a different direction, but it is hoped they will balance each other out. In the same way, if scientists send papers to several other experts for review—especially scientists with high standards—it is hoped that the quality of the papers will be improved and human depravity will be curbed. Such a review process also provides assistance to publishers so they can be protected against papers of poor quality.

With truth as a value, honesty must also be valued. Education, degrees, positions, and professional experience must be reported accurately. The results of any study of the physical world must be reported fairly and accurately. All data, illustrations, and ideas should be properly referenced. Plagiarism should not be tolerated. Popularizers of science don't have to defend the ideas; they can defer criticisms to the people who can defend them.

Summing Up the Great Synthesis

The Bible provides purpose, presuppositions, and values for science. Therefore, Scripture can become the foundation of a complete, biblical philosophy of science—and for every discipline of human thought. When Pontius Pilate asked the question of the ages—What is truth?—the answer in the form of Jesus Christ Himself was standing before Pilate. And even now, when we ask What is truth? we have before us God and His revealed Word. These ought to be the starting and ending points for all disciplines. In an effort to know God better, believers ought to engage in the systematic construction of a biblical worldview. For such a Great Synthesis to occur, the collective activity of a large number of Christian scholars from a wide spectrum of fields is required. And since the union of diverse beings is reflective of the nature of the triune God, such a collaboration has great potential for bringing glory to God.

What's Next?

A study of God's creation, if done properly, can glorify God and teach us about Him. With proper caution in evaluating human observation and reason, there is value in constructing a history of the creation—an account of its origin and its nature through time. The remainder of this book proposes such a history—or at least a brief outline of how such a history might look. We begin with what might be considered in many Christian circles the most contentious part of such a history: the question of time. How old is the creation? In the next two chapters we will address this issue—first from the Bible and then from science.

PART 2

THE DATING GAME

CHAPTER 4

How Old Are Things?

There is no doubt that God knows exactly how old everything is. There is also no doubt that if He chose to tell us how old things are, He would tell the truth. If such information was revealed in His Word, the nature of God would guarantee the accuracy of the information. The real question, then, is whether He has chosen to provide that information in His Word.

If taken at face value, the Bible seems to contain the information necessary to determine the age of things—as well as the information necessary to fairly accurately locate *all* the important events of Scripture on a time line running from the beginning of time through the earliest history of the church. Therefore, we should be able to conclude that the answer to this question is yes.

So in this chapter we will trace the steps of history from the beginning of time through the days of creation, from creation to the Flood, from the Flood to Abraham, and from Abraham to Christ. And we will see why all this historical information is about much more than dates and numbers.

The Creation Week

If we were to walk chronologically through biblical time, the very first step would be to examine the creation of things. How long did it take God to create the universe? How much time elapsed between the beginning

and the end of God's creation? The sequence of six creation days in
Genesis 1 followed by the ending of His creative acts on the seventh day
(Gen. 2:2) would suggest that the creation was done in a single week.
Confirmation of this is found later in Scripture in the midst of the Ten
Commandments, inscribed in stone with the finger of God. Scripture tells
us, "Six days shalt thou labour, and do all thy work: but the seventh day
is the sabbath . . . for in six days the LORD made the heaven and earth, the
sea, and all that in them is, and rested the seventh day" (Exod. 20:9–11).
The clarity of these passages, combined with the straightforward understanding we expect from both the Word and character of God, suggests
that the creation really was completed in a single (human) week.

But should the Genesis account be taken at face value? Is it intended
to convey history? What qualifies the Book of Genesis as historical narrative literature?[1]

Genesis lacks many characteristics of non-historical Hebrew literature.
Characteristics common in Hebrew allegory, such as storytellers, inter-
preters, interpretations, and a non-physical-world focus are absent from
the Genesis text. Most of the terms of the text (like birds, plants, stars) do
not seem to be symbolic. The characteristics of Hebrew poetry with its
parallelism of juxtaposed couplets and metrical balance are also absent
from most of the text.

*Genesis does have many of the characteristics common in Hebrew histori-
cal narrative.* It contains genealogical lists, for example, as well as narrative with interspersed poetic lines, an emphasis on definitions, frequent
use of the direct object sign and relative pronoun, a list of sequential
events separated by the special Hebrew phrase called a *waw consecutive*
(*waw* is pronounced *vahv* and is usually translated "and" as in "And God
said . . ." or "And the earth was . . ."), plus an abundance of geographic,
cultural, and other verifiable details. Included are a number of other features that in Western literature may indicate non-historical, even poetic
narrative (such as numerology, figures of speech, textual symmetry, and
phenomenological language) but that are commonly found in Hebrew historical narrative.

The historical texts in Genesis contrast with non-historical narrative. For the most part, seamless connections join the various Genesis accounts, including those widely accepted as historical. But the short, non-historical passages within the Genesis account—for example, Adam's response at seeing Eve (Gen. 2:23) and the song of Lamech (Gen. 4:23–24)—as well as poetic renditions of Genesis passages found in other places in Scripture (such as in Ps. 104) contrast sharply with the historical flavor of the Genesis text, including the creation account.

Scripture itself refers to Genesis as historical. The remainder of Scripture (Exod. 20:11; Neh. 9:6; Acts 17:22–29) and Jesus Himself (Matt. 19:4–6) speak of Genesis—including the creation account—as if it were to be taken as history. Likewise, most of the Jews and Christians through time have understood the Genesis account to be historical. Since the Genesis account is historical narrative and reliable, its clear claim of a six-day creation should be taken seriously.

Hours in a Day

Next question: If the creation was just six days long, how long was each day?

The most straightforward understanding of Genesis 1 is that the days of creation were twenty-four-hour-long, earth-rotation days. And there is more to favor this position than merely the perspicuity of Scripture.[2] Very often, the first use of a word in the Bible is useful in understanding the meaning of that word. The first use of the Hebrew word *yôm* (translated "day") is found in Genesis 1:5, where God created light and called it *yôm*. The second use of *yôm* is in the same verse, where the "evening and the morning" complete the definition of Day 1. All meanings of "day" throughout the rest of the Bible—including the places where it is used symbolically—are based upon the light portion of an earth-rotation day.

Other observations also support this position. In the hundreds of times when *yôm* is associated with numbers (such as "the third day" or "seven days") in the Old Testament, it always refers to 24-hour earth-rotation days. The phrase "evening and morning" in Hebrew Scripture always refers to twenty-four-hour earth-rotation days. And God's decision to complete His creation over the course of a week as an example to man—along with the clear statement of Exodus 20:11—suggests that the days of creation were the same as the days of man's work week. Exodus 20:11 also suggests that there was no time *between* the days, that the total length of the Creation Week was one week of human time—144 consecutive hours during which all the creating was done and 24 additional hours during which God rested from His creation.

Why a Week?

Next question: Since God would do only what is consistent with His nature, is there any indication in His nature that He would create in the space of six days? At first blush, the answer to this question would seem to be no. God's nature is to create instantaneously,[3] to require no time at all to bring everything into existence—not even a week.

First of all, God is the Creator of time, space, and matter, and is thus independent of all of them. Nothing He does requires time to transpire unless He wishes time to transpire for some reason. If anything, God's normal tempo would be to do things instantaneously. In Scripture this is seen over and over again whenever God seeks to show His true nature. All the miracles recorded in Scripture, for example, seem to be done instantaneously.[4] God's perfection also would suggest that He is completely efficient at whatever He does. In our experience, as long as quality is not sacrificed, human efficiency increases with speed. Since the quality of God's creation is not compromised at any speed, it would seem that the most efficient creation would be one accomplished in zero time.

More evidence of instantaneous creation comes from Scripture's own words. The "let there be" statements of Genesis 1 ("let there be light," "let there be a firmament") are verb forms called *jussives*. Hebrew jussives are either commands (where superiors command inferiors) or requests (where inferiors request of superiors). Since God as Creator is the ultimate superior, the jussives in Genesis 1 are commands. Since scriptural kings who used jussives of command were obeyed immediately (unless they encountered disobedient subjects), the response of the unfallen creation to the King of kings would be expected to be immediate. The commands of the incarnate Jesus (such as the stilling of the waves of the storm) were obeyed instantly; likewise, there is every reason to expect the commands of the Creator Jesus to be obeyed instantaneously.

Further, the Hebrew phrase translated "and it was so" in Genesis 1, when used elsewhere in Scripture (Judg. 6:38; 2 Kings 15:12), suggests completion within the specified time. In the case of Genesis 1, this suggests the completion of the creation within the specified day. Finally, Psalm 33:6–9 warns evildoers that retribution will be visited upon their evil by the same God Who when He spoke creation "stood fast" as a result. The rapid response to sin called for by God in this passage is most consistent with instantaneous creation.

So then, if God's nature is consistent with instantaneous creation, why did it take God so long—even as long as a week? Related to this question, and yet another apparent paradox in Creation Week, is why God rested from His creation. Surely God would not have been weary in the creation. In fact, it's likely that creating delighted Him. If God's nature is to create instantaneously, then He must have had good reason to take six days to create the world; if God's nature is to never need rest, then He must have had good reason to rest.

The only answer provided in Scripture seems to be that God did it as an example to man. In the fourth commandment, man is told to follow God's Creation Week example, to work for six days and rest from His work on the seventh day. When confronted about "working" on the Sabbath, Jesus replied that the Sabbath was created for man, not man for the Sabbath (Mark 2:27). God created over a period of six days and then took a day off to rest from that work not because of His limitations, but as an example to man. A week-long creation, then, is another amazing example of God's stepping out of what we might imagine to be His divine character in order to establish a pattern for man. So the bottom line is this: either an instantaneous creation or a week-long creation can be justified from God's nature and Scripture's claim. A longer creation, however, cannot be so justified.

As Jesus was teaching about divorce in Matthew 19:3–9, He referred to the origin of marriage as having occurred "from the beginning" (v. 8). The creation of Adam and Eve would be separated from "the beginning" by only a few days if Creation Week was only a human workweek in length. The longer the Creation Week is understood to be (especially if it gets into thousands or millions of years), the more difficult it is to see Adam and Eve's creation to be "from the beginning."

A literal week of creation also provides an explanation for the existence of seven-day weeks in pagan cultures. While astronomical indicators provide time markers for days, months, seasons, and years, there is no astronomical indicator for a week. The seven-day workweek seems to be based solely upon a seven-day creation. Biblical evidence suggests strongly that the Creation Week of Genesis 1 and 2 was a human workweek in length—seven earth-rotation days in time, counting the day of rest.

From Creation to Abraham

The second step in walking through a biblical chronology is calculating the time between Creation Week and the birth of Noah. This is made possible by the genealogy of Genesis 5. Genesis 7:11 and 8:13, then, make the third step possible by telling us exactly when the Flood began and ended in Noah's life. The fourth step utilizes the genealogy of Genesis 11 to calculate the time between the Flood and Abraham. Scripture nowhere else summarizes the time between the creation and Abraham or any part of that period, so these genealogies are critically important in developing a biblical chronology. Before we pull the numbers together, let's consider some important points about these listings.

Genealogies are usually only marginally useful for chronology purposes. A list of names, even if it contains a complete list of fathers and sons in the proper sequence, provides only the number of generations. This can be translated into actual time only when the average generation time (the average age of parents at the birth of their children) is known—or guessed—information that is rarely provided in any genealogy. The most common time-type information given in genealogies is the age of people at their deaths. And although this kind of information is somewhat helpful, at least to provide an upper limit on generation time, it does not give us the *actual* generation time. The genealogy that is most useful for chronology is one that provides the age of the parents at the time of the birth of their children. But this is uncommon among genealogies, both ancient and modern.

It is interesting, then, that the genealogies of both Genesis 5 and Genesis 11 do provide the age of fathers at the birth of their sons—exactly the kind of information we need in developing a chronology. Since the words of Scripture are both accurate and economical, the structure of these genealogies suggests a chronological purpose.

A chronological function is further evidenced by comparison of these with other biblical chronologies—and there are many of them (including the genealogies in Gen. 4, 5, 10, 11; Exod. 6; 1 Chron. 1–8; Neh. 7; Matt. 1; and Luke 3). The genealogy of Moses in Exodus 6:16–20 contains the ages of the patriarchs at the time of their deaths. This is more useful than a list of patriarchs but not sufficient to determine an accurate genealogy. Yet at least this brief genealogy does contain some time information—a feature that stands in contrast even with the larger genealogical list in which it is found (Exod. 6:14–29). In fact, aside from the three genealogies of Genesis 5, Genesis 11, and Exodus 6:16–20, none of the many genealogies of Scripture (including genealogies of Genesis 4 and 10) contain anything more than a list of people.

Of all the steps in a biblical chronology from the creation to Christ, only two steps require a genealogy—the time between creation and the Flood and the time between the Flood and Abraham. And guess what? These happen to be the only genealogies that have chronological information!

An accurate and efficient Scripture would suggest strongly that the genealogies of Genesis 5 and 11 were specifically designed for chronology and were intended to be utilized in that manner. Because of their chronological structure and function, these two genealogies in Scripture—and only these two genealogies—should be considered *chronogenealogies* (or, genealogies with time-keeping purposes).

Crunching the Numbers

In order to develop a chronology from genealogies, however, more than the right kind of time indicators are needed. The genealogy must also be complete. If it is a sequence of patriarchs such as that found in Genesis 5 and 11, the sequence must be complete. The patriarchs of each generation must be listed, and only those who are in the direct lineage. There must be no gaps in the list. So are the lists in Genesis 5 and 11 complete?

On the face of it, a comparison of Luke 3 and Genesis 11 would suggest the answer is no, because Luke 3 adds the name Cainan to the list of Genesis 11. Actually, although the name is not listed in the Hebrew manuscripts of Genesis 11, it is listed in the Greek translation known as the Septuagint, a text that was popular at the time of the writing of Luke. But a careful examination of the Septuagint text shows that the numbers associated with Cainan are identical to the numbers for the adjacent name in the list, and the name Cainan itself is found in the list of Genesis 5.

It is not inconceivable, then, that Cainan was erroneously inserted while Genesis was being translated into Greek for the Septuagint. This author suspects that the name Cainan was not listed in Luke 3 when it was originally written but was inserted by a copyist in order to make it conform with the (in this particular case, erroneous) Septuagint text. The Luke account, then, may not provide sufficient evidence to suggest that a gap exists in the genealogies of Genesis 5 and 11.

Even so, while the evidence for gaps in the Genesis 5 and 11 genealogies is weak, the evidence *against* gaps is rather strong:

- First, the narrative makes it clear that Seth was the actual son of Adam and Eve (Gen. 4:25); Shem, Ham, and Japheth were the sons of Noah (Gen. 5:32; 6:10; 7:13; 9:18–27; 10:1); and Abram, Nahor, and Haran were the sons of Terah (Gen. 11:26–31).

- Second, the Scripture indicates that the names of some patriarchs were almost certainly given to them by their actual fathers. This suggests that Seth was the actual son of Adam (Gen. 5:3); Enos was the son of Seth (Gen. 4:26), and Noah was the son of Lamech (Gen. 5:29).

- Third, the distinct way in which the relationship between parent and child is related in Genesis 4:25–26 and 10:25 further suggests that Seth was the actual son of Adam and Eve, Enos was the son of Seth, and Peleg and Joktan were the sons of Eber.

- Fourth, the facts that Noah, Shem, Ham, Japheth, and their wives were the only survivors of the Flood and that Arphaxad was born only two years after the Flood (Gen. 11:10) suggests that Arphaxad was actually the son of Shem.

- Fifth, Jude 14 states that Enoch was the seventh generation from Adam. This suggests that no gaps exist in the Genesis 5 list between Adam and Enoch.

- Finally, the Hebrew name Methuselah is thought by some to mean "when he dies it will come" or "when he dies, judgment." If one assumes that no gaps exist and that the numbers of Genesis 5 are correct, Methuselah's death is found to occur in the same year the Flood began. This suggests that God may have waited for the death of Methuselah ("when he dies") to bring judgment upon the earth ("it shall come"). This also suggests that the ages and years of at least the second half of Genesis 5 are complete and accurate.

When all the evidences are considered, there are very few places in the genealogical lists of Genesis 5 and 11 where gaps could possibly exist. Combined with the fact that these genealogies seem to be designed to be chronogenealogies, the evidence is strong that there are no gaps in the genealogies of Genesis 5 and 11.

So here's the final scorecard, utilizing the numbers found in the Hebrew text:

- 1,656 years elapsed between the Creation and the Flood.
- 342 years elapsed between the Flood and the birth of Abraham.[5]

This means that a period of time close to two thousand years elapsed between the Creation and the birth of Abraham.

Abraham to Christ

The remaining steps in the biblical chronology lead us from the time of Abraham to the time of Christ. These steps include the time between Abraham and the Exodus, between the Exodus and the building of the temple, between the building of the temple and the beginning of the Babylonian captivity, throughout the years of the Babylonian captivity, and finally the time between the end of the captivity and the time of Christ.[6] In the interest of brevity, these calculations will not be presented here in detail. Suffice it to say that this biblical chronology suggests that about one thousand years elapsed between the times of Abraham and Solomon, and about one thousand years elapsed between Solomon and Christ. This would place Abraham at about 2000 B.C. and David and Solomon at about 1000 B.C. Both of these dates coincide with generally accepted archaeological dates.

The fact that a complete creation-to-Christ chronology can be developed from the biblical text suggests that it was written so that such a chronology could be developed. The fact that the chronology was derived from the Word of God suggests that such a chronology should be accurate (as the archaeological dates generally confirm for the second half of it).

From this we conclude that the physical universe is only about six thousand years old.

Because not all the biblical texts specify the exactness of the times listed,[7] there is some flexibility in biblical dating. However, that flexibility is probably something on the order of a few percentage points.[8] Whereas there is substantial biblical evidence for a creation that is six thousand years old, there is little to no biblical indication that the world could be thousands of years older—let alone tens of thousands of years older (or thousands of thousands of years older as suggested by conventional science).

One Hand on the Bible

The non-biblical chronology currently accepted in the historical sciences challenges more than just the age of things. The process of developing this chronology has required that a sequence of historical events be developed and accepted. It is this sequence—and not just the timing—of the origin of things that is contrary to the claims of Scripture. So if you believe the Bible to be the ultimate authority of truth, pause and consider how you can square these discrepancies:

1. Genesis 1 claims that the earth came into being before the sun (compare Gen. 1:1 and 1:14–18), fruit trees before the sea creatures (compare Gen. 1:11–12 and 1:20–21), and flying animals before land animals (compare Gen. 1:20–21 and 1:24–25). The conventional old-age chronology reverses the timing of each of these events.

2. Genesis 1:30 suggests that all the animals before the Fall were vegetarians, whereas old-age chronology suggests there was never a time when all animals were herbivores.

3. Old-age chronology suggests that death, disease, and suffering preceded the appearance of man by hundreds of millions of years. This seems to be counter to numerous biblical claims: for example, God's description of the creation as being "very good" (Gen. 1:31); the strong association between man's sin and animal sacrifice in Romans 5; and the description of heaven in 1 Corinthians 15 as being free from the curse of death that came with the fall of man.

4. Scripture indicates that man was derived from dust (Gen. 2:7) and not from animals as argued in old-age chronology.

5. Scripture indicates that Adam named all the animals (Gen. 2:19–20), something that would not be possible in non-biblical chronology because so many thousands of animals became extinct long before Adam came to be.

6. Eve was created from the side of Adam (Gen. 2:21–22) and not derived from a population of pre-humans as suggested in conventional chronology.

7. According to Genesis 2:10–14, a river flowed out of the Garden of Eden and divided into four rivers, three of which were the Gihon (the ancient name for the Nile), the Hiddekel (the ancient name for the Tigris), and the Euphrates. The rivers currently known by these names are not connected to one another now, and in conventional chronology were *never* connected to one another.[9]

8. According to Scripture, there were no thorns or thistles before man's sin (Gen. 3:18), whereas old-age chronology would have these things preceding even man's appearance by millions of years.

9. Old-age chronology would deny the long life spans of pre-Flood and early post-Flood humans as recorded in Genesis 5 and 11.

10. Scripture tells us that all the land animals and birds were represented on the ark (Gen. 6:17–20), whereas the old-age chronology would suggest that thousands of species were extinct long before humans arrived on the scene and could not possibly have been on the ark.

11. The Bible claims that the Flood of Noah lasted for more than a year (Gen. 7:11 compared to 8:13) and covered the entire surface of the earth over the highest mountains (Gen. 7:19), whereas old-age chronology suggests that there never was a global flood on this planet.

12. Finally, Genesis 11 tells us that at a time when all the humans on earth were united in language and tower-building, God introduced a number of languages to force them to spread across the earth's surface. In old-age chronology, however, humans capable of building cities were never all located in one place, and human languages were generated one by one over a long period.

Old-age chronology and Scripture cannot both be true, and they cannot be reconciled. The time argued for in old-age chronology is thousands of times longer than that indicated in biblical chronology. The dates are not just slightly different, so they cannot be easily modified to make them agree. Not only does the sequence of events in the two chronologies differ, but even the nature of the events in the two chronologies are different. It is only with the rejection of old-age chronology in its entirety—not just the age of things but also the actual events of history and their order of occurrence—that the biblical chronology can be accepted. Alternatively, the acceptance of humanly devised old-age chronology or any variation of it would require the rejection or modification of divinely inspired Scripture. Acceptance of Scripture's clearly understood intent requires the rejection of old-age chronology and the acceptance of a radically different biblical chronology.

High Stakes

Clearly, this is about much more than time and dates. The changes required in order to accept old-age chronology would require a modification of more than Scripture; it would also require an alteration of what Scripture teaches—including its theology.[10]

According to Matthew 24:38–39, for example, Christ will return to judge the earth even as the Flood impacted the earth. If old-age chronology is true, the Flood was not global, so neither should Christ's return be expected to be.

According to Hebrews 4:3–11, believers can look forward to a rest from their labor just as God rested from His work after the creation. Old-age chronology would suggest that there never has been a time when God ceased from His creative activity. This in turn would challenge the traditional Christian understanding of the future reward of believers.

Traditionally, heaven is thought to be perfect, in part reflective of the perfection of the pre-Fall, pre-Curse world (Isa. 65:17). Acceptance of old-age chronology would deny that there was any period of creation's history where perfection reigned. This in turn would challenge the traditional understanding of heaven. The acceptance of old-age chronology would require a substantial modification of Christian eschatology.

According to Scripture, man was created by God in the image of God (Gen. 1:26–27). This provides the foundation for capital punishment

(Gen. 9:3–6) and why swearing at other people is considered sin (James 3:8–10). Old-age chronology strongly suggests that man was derived from animals, not God. Acceptance of such a chronology would undermine the biblical doctrine of right and wrong and would undermine traditional biblical arguments against abortion, euthanasia, and much more.

The acceptance of old-age chronology also would deny the truth of numerous biblical passages. This would undermine the traditional Christian doctrine of Scripture's authenticity and authority.

The traditional Christian position on sin and its consequences is that God created the world and man in a state of perfection and that man fell from this state by sinning. As a result of this sin, death entered the world for both man and animals (Rom. 5; 1 Cor. 15, and the connection between man's sin and animal sacrifice). Man needed a perfect redeemer. Old-age chronology would deny any period of perfection and further suggest that the death of animals preceded man's sin by millions of years. Acceptance of such a chronology would undermine the biblical doctrines of sin, death, and even salvation.

According to Scripture, God established marriage by creating man first, then woman from him. The divine origin of marriage justifies its permanence in God's eyes (Matt. 19:3–9) and explains why the husband is established as the head of the wife (1 Cor. 11:3–10). If old-age chronology is true, Adam and Eve (if they ever did exist) would seem to have been derived from a population of reproducing apes. The acceptance of old-age chronology would require a substantial revision of the Christian doctrine of marriage.

Finally, acceptance of old-age chronology requires a substantial revision of the biblical doctrine of God and His nature. According to Psalm 33:6–9, for example, God is fearsome and quick in judgment because He spoke and the creation responded immediately. Old-age chronology, which denies a rapid creation, would challenge the doctrine of God's justice and His speed of judgment. Accepting old-age chronology would also deny the truth of Scripture, which would in turn challenge the claim that God is truth. With the acceptance of old-age chronology, God is seen as responsible for introducing death, disease, and suffering into the creation hundreds of millions of years before man sinned. This in turn would challenge the biblical claim that God is a God of goodness and mercy (Ps. 100:3–5).

Summary

Scripture seems to be designed in such a way that a biblical chronology can be constructed from it. This chronology suggests that creation's history is only about six thousand years long and features a series of unique events in a particular sequence—all at substantial disagreement with the old-age chronology accepted by many people. Ultimately, all Christian doctrine is based upon the clear understanding of Scripture and the biblical chronology derived from it. The nature of the God of creation requires the acceptance of biblical chronology and the rejection of conventional old-age chronology.

What's Next?

As clear as a youthful creation seems to be in Scripture, it does not seem to be so clear in the physical world. The physical evidence of antiquity is addressed in the next chapter.

CHAPTER 5

How Old Is Old?

A face-value reading of the Bible indicates that the creation is thousands of years old. A face-value examination of the creation suggests it is millions or billions of years old. The reconciliation of these two observations is one of the most significant challenges to creation research. Much more research must be devoted to this question to produce an acceptable resolution. This chapter addresses only introductory considerations of this complex topic.

A Question of Deception

God is not a deceiver. But wouldn't the creation of a universe that looked old at the moment of creation be a deception? An examination of the activity of Christ would suggest that the answer is no. Consider the feeding of the four thousand and the five thousand, for example (Matt. 14:15–21; 15:32–38; Mark 6:34–44; 8:1–9; Luke 9:12–17). Once the fish and loaves had been multiplied and divided so many times, something on the order of one part in four thousand to five thousand of any given fish or loaf was made of the original food. The remaining 99.9+ percent was supernaturally created. The created portion of the fish was fashioned as if it had actually come from a fish from the Sea of Galilee, and as if it had been caught, prepared, and cooked. The created portion of the bread was fashioned as if the wheat had grown in some previous season and was harvested, combined with other ingredients, and baked. Yet none of these events actually occurred.

Since the purpose of creating the fish and bread was to simulate fish and bread for human consumption, that is exactly what Christ did. In the process of creating something with a particular function, Christ created an apparent but non-existent history. The food looked much older than it actually was.

Many of the healings recorded in Scripture are similar to these miracles. The healing of the man lame from birth (Acts 14:8–10) is a poignant example. With his healing came the repair of the malady; the restoration of atrophied muscles (as if he had been walking all along to develop them); as well as the implantation of balance, coordination, and muscle control into the brain (as if he had learned how to walk). All this was done instantly and effectively because we are told that he "leaped" up in response to the command to stand. Since the immediate purpose of the healing was to have the man walk, God created an apparent but non-existent history of learning to walk and walking. It looked as if the man had a longer history of walking than he actually did.

Yet another example is Christ's first public miracle: the turning of water into wine (John 2:1–11). Once created, the wine had the appearance of having been derived from grapes that had grown in a previous season and were harvested, pressed, and sealed to make wine. Since the immediate purpose of making the wine was to provide drink to replace the wine that had run out, Jesus created an apparent but non-existent history of wine-making. The fact that the wine did look as if it were older than it really was is evident in the response of the one person who tasted the wine. He deduced (v. 10) that the wine must have been there from at least the beginning of the feast, concluding erroneously that the wine was much older than it actually was.

Since God is directly responsible for each of these events, we must conclude that God can and does create things that appear much older than they really are. If God's purpose in creating something is fulfilled by creating it with the appearance of age (as was the case in each of the above examples), then He will do it. And as is also evident in each of these examples, He chooses to leave the creation in that state, without physical proof of the true age. To use a term from chapter 2, He provides sufficient *ambiguity* in the creation for humans to conclude erroneously a history that never actually occurred . . . if they so choose. This is apparently because God requires faith of us (Heb. 11:3).

At the same time, however, God does provide the truth and gives us reason to believe it. In each of the above examples, God does tell us the truth. After all, each of these accounts is included in Scripture. Even at the time of each of the events, the truth was made known to the people involved. The four thousand and five thousand actually saw Jesus multiply the loaves and fishes. The lame man and the witnesses were told by Paul that the healing was done by God. The governor of the feast in Cana who deduced the wrong history of the wine had neither seen it being made nor had he been told how it was made (John 2:9), yet Jesus ordered servants who *had* witnessed the transformation to go and present the wine to him. Although the governor did not avail himself of their knowledge, eyewitnesses were sent to him. Testimony of the truth was given in each case. God seems to provide testimony of the creation events that preserves the evidence of non-existent history. It is up to us to accept His Word by faith.

God does not stop there, however. He generously provides encouragement so that we will accept the faith He offers. In each of these cases, there was enough evidence provided to question any alternative hypotheses that described how the miracles occurred. In the case of the feeding of the crowds, for example, the large number of witnesses would make it hard to accept any alternative hypothesis. The many people who had known the lame man to be lame and who saw him in his cured condition would also make alternative hypotheses difficult to accept. In the case of the wine in Cana, the governor of the feast made an alternative proposal—that the wine had been there all along. However, there are problems with this hypothesis.

First, the governor himself noted that saving the good wine for later in the feast would be breaking tradition—and the Jews were strong on tradition.

Second, the governor also noted the extraordinary quality of the wine—especially in light of the fact that it was three days into the feast when people would probably not be able to tell the difference (John 2:10). Even if the wine had been available from the beginning of the feast, it makes little sense that it would have been held back until so late in the feast. It would have been more reasonable for a small part of the wine to have been traded for more of the low-quality wine.

Third, anyone investigating the situation would find it odd that the wine was taken from water purification jars and not wineskins. These evidences do not necessarily prove the truth; they only suggest that something is wrong with alternative claims.

These principles also apply to origins issues. God was the only eyewitness to the entire creation. In His Word He has provided His own eyewitness testimony that He created the universe and the earth only thousands of years ago. It is up to us to accept His Word by faith. Furthermore, even though He does not provide physical proof of this, God has provided evidence against alternative hypotheses. Historically, young-age creationists have found it relatively easy to do this: to locate and expound upon the evidence against alternative hypotheses. What has been much slower in coming is our ability to fill the scriptural gaps with reasonable scientific scenarios about what actually did happen in the past. Much more work is required to answer the numerous questions posed by chronology science.

The Trouble with Dating

Many methods have been devised for determining the age of things in the creation. Many of them yield ages in excess of six thousand years. Each method, however, runs into difficulty with at least some data—not usually enough to falsify the method completely, but enough to question conclusions derived from it. Too many methods exist to deal with all of them in this book, so only a few examples will be given.

The age of the Grand Canyon was calculated by determining the rate of erosion over the last century by comparing century-old photos with the current canyon. This rate was then utilized to determine how long it would take to erode the volume of rock that is missing from the Grand Canyon. Unfortunately for this hypothesis, which suggests the canyon is tens of millions of years old, lake sediments upstream of the Grand Canyon (which couldn't be there after the canyon began to be formed) seem to date from only the last five million years.[1]

Another dating method tried to determine how long it would take to form the successive petrified forest layers of Yellowstone National Park by adding three things together: the time it would take to form the required soil layers, the time it would take to form the mature forests on those soils, and the time it would take to bury each forest. What was actually observed were trees in multiple layers with the same ring pattern, suggesting that they were actually formed at the same time in the same area of forest.[2]

Here's another dating method: since the rate at which salt enters the oceans exceeds the rate at which it leaves the oceans, they have been getting saltier over time. The oceans currently have only about one hundred million years worth of salt, rather than the billions of years of salt they should have if they were actually that old.[3]

Several problems also are observed among radiometric dating methods. First, in the case of potassium-argon (K/Ar) dating, potassium decays over time into argon (a gas). When molten lava flows over the earth's surface, it is generally assumed that because it is a gas, argon escapes from the lava before the lava cools. This should result in a K/Ar age of zero. K/Ar ages are calculated assuming this is true. In actuality, however, recent lava flows have shown that they do *not* lose all their argon. Rather than having an age of zero, they consistently yield K/Ar ages of hundreds of thousands to millions of years.[4]

Second, the relative reliability of radiometric dating methods can be tested by performing multiple radiometric dating analyses on the same rock. If accurate, each radiometric method should produce the same radiometric age. In actuality, however, multiple methods usually yield multiple, non-overlapping ages.[5]

Third, if radioactive decay has been occurring for billions of years (as various radiometric ages indicate), there should be a lot more helium in the atmosphere than there actually is.[6]

And fourth, radiometric isochron dating assumes that the only way a straight isochron line can be produced is when multiple samples are taken of the same age and the same rock. In fact, straight isochron lines can be produced from a group of different rocks with very different ages.[7]

In the case of carbon-14 (C-14) dating, if the earth has had a stable atmosphere for longer than thirty thousand years, as is generally assumed, then C-14 should be in secular equilibrium (that is, the amount of C-14 produced in the upper atmosphere should be equal to the amount of C-14 breaking down by radioactive decay). One also would expect C-14 dates of tree rings to correspond to the ages one gets by counting rings. In fact, the earth's atmosphere is 20 percent out of secular equilibrium, and the tree rings begin diverging from C-14 ages before about 1000 B.C. or so.[8]

The fact that any alternative theory has problems should suggest that something is not quite right with those alternatives. Although these provide insufficient evidence to prove them wrong, they do provide sufficient reason to seek a better explanation. It would be reasonable simply to turn to the reliable Eyewitness and accept His Word for the fact that the creation is actually only six thousand years or so old.

Younger Than It Looks

So why does the world, in so many ways, look old? If God created things that already had the appearance of age, this might account for at least some of what we see in the physical world. But is there any reason to believe that God's purpose in creating necessitated that He create things with the appearance of age?

Careful consideration of the physical world does indeed suggest that creation of an apparent, non-existent history may have been a common part of God's creation. Consider, for example, the origin of plants on Day 3 of Creation Week. According to Genesis 1:29–30, the plants were created to serve as food for humans and animals. For fruit trees to provide food, they would need to have been created with fruit already developed, as if it had developed from the pollination of flowers, resting on branches and stems that would appear to have been developed through years of growth. Those trees also require soil for growth, soil that had to have been created along with the trees. Since soil is sapped of nutrients and eroded away over time, some process of soil production must have been created, a process that derives soil from rocks over a long period of time. Yet since it takes so long to produce soil, every different stage of soil production must have been produced as well—as if it had been produced through this process.

Consider also the origin of the sun on Day 4 of Creation Week. According to Genesis 1:14–15, the purpose of the sun, moon, and stars was to provide light on the earth and to mark off time. And since the unfallen creation was probably created to exist forever,[9] it was probably intended that the lights of heaven would not just shine briefly but persist in their shining. To fulfill their function, then, they should have shined light upon the earth when created. Given also the dependence of things like the photosynthesis of plants on the particular kind of light coming from the sun, the light that was created would have had to look like the kind of light that actually came from the sun—even when it had not actually come from the sun.

Thus, even though the sun was created eight light minutes away,[10] light was probably created—in order to fulfill its function—already having arrived at the earth as if it had traveled the distance from the sun to the earth (when it really hadn't). And since the light was created to persist, there must have been light created at every point between the sun and the earth on its way to the earth. Again, this light would have been created as if it had actually come from the sun, when it actually had not. This, however, would have produced light for only eight minutes. God must have produced some sort of light-generating mechanism in the sun so light would continue to issue from it. If fusion is the source of light in the sun, as is popularly assumed in science, then that light is generated in the center of the sun where fusion's required temperature and pressure exist.

However, photons of light produced in the center of the sun cannot easily escape out of the sun. Because of the density of material inside the sun, the photons bounce around among the molecules of the sun. Because of this, it is thought that light requires something on the order of ten thousand years to make its way from the sun's center to its surface. And since light was to be shining continuously from the creation onward, light must have been created at every point in the inside of the sun from its center to its outer edge—as if it had been generated by fusion in the sun's center and then traveled outward to its present position. This would provide light on the earth for ten thousand years after the creation. For light to continue after that, fusion would have been created in the center of the sun. Even now, some six thousand years after the creation, the light from the sun we are now seeing was not generated by fusion in the sun. It only *looks* as if it were.

Among other examples, consider the organisms created on Day 5 and Day 6. Shelled mollusks (like snails and clams) were probably created with shells. Snails and clams hold on to their shells for their entire life, adding new shell material as they grow. The adult shell, then, contains shell material laid down at every stage of their lives. The shell of a created mollusk would contain shell material that *looked* as if it were formed in the early life of the mollusk, when it actually was not.

If God created coral reefs—which seems likely—then they must have been created with apparent evidence of development that never occurred.

All adult animals formed would have been created with knowledge—knowledge of what to eat, how to eat it, how to behave, and how to communicate. In the case of some organisms, survival of the population may have been possible only with an entire age distribution. Not just adults but also subadults and young must have been created.

In these and countless other ways, God's purpose in creation required the creation of things with the appearance of age. Newly fashioned, the creation would have looked much older than it really was. And even now the creation looks much older than it really is because of how God created it. Although created six thousand years ago, light from the sun, for example, *looks* like it should be at least ten thousand years old. Although created six thousand years ago, photons of light from some distant objects of the universe *look* as if they have been traveling for billions of years. If one thinks the oceans started out freshwater (rather than being created salty) and became salty with time, the oceans *look* like they are tens of millions of years old. If one thinks the universe expanded from a single point (rather than being created at some large initial size), it *looks* as if it is billions of years old.

How Much Do We Really Know?

An incorrect understanding of history might also explain why creation appears older than it really is. For example, if there was a period of higher radiometric decay rates than are measured at present, then radiometric ages would be too old.[11] If the speed of light was faster than is now measured, or if the universe had very strong distortions in the fourth dimension, or if the universe has a sufficiently non-uniform distribution of mass-energy, then light might be able to travel farther than would be expected in a six thousand-year-old universe. Although these ideas are not currently an accepted part of the creation model, they have been and are now being considered.

But even in the current creation model there are processes that can affect age indicators. For example (see chap. 14), precipitation rates and temperatures are thought to have been very high immediately after the Flood and to have decreased exponentially after that. A number of processes used to determine the age of things—such as amino acid racemization, thermoluminescence, and protein decay—are dependent upon temperature and rainfall. Amino acids randomize more quickly in warmer and wetter conditions, and thermoluminescence and proteins decay more quickly in warmer and wetter conditions. Many organisms (such as corals and chalk-producing organisms) also grow more quickly in warmth and higher rainfall bringing nutrients to the oceans. Using current rates in any of these cases yields ages that appear older than they really are.

As another example, the creation model suggests lava was produced at much higher rates and under much more water during the Flood than is believed in non-Flood geology. Less argon gas would have been released under these conditions, leaving the lavas with K/Ar ages that are too old. High precipitation rates in early post-Flood times may also be capable of accumulating the large ice sheets currently found in Greenland and Antarctica.[12] Geocatastrophism and high precipitation rates during and after the Flood would have generated extremely high erosion and sedimentation rates. If estimated using modern rates, these chronometers would result in consistently exaggerated ages.

Here's another: carbon-14, the material used in C-14 dating, is continually being produced in the upper atmosphere as cosmic radiation from the sun (consisting mostly of charged particles) impact nitrogen atoms (the most abundant gas in the atmosphere). The newly produced C-14 combines with oxygen (the second most abundant gas) to produce C-14-containing carbon dioxide. This heavy carbon dioxide (a C-14 atom contains two more neutrons than a "normal" C-12 carbon atom) circulates down through the atmosphere to the surface where plants incorporate it into their structure. While these plants remain alive (as well as the animals which eat them), the C-14/C-12 ratio is maintained in organisms at approximately the same ratio as is found in the atmosphere. After the death of the organism, however, decayed C-14 atoms are not replaced, and the changing C-14/C-12 ratio is used to determine how long it has been since the organism died.

In the current creation model, the earth's initial magnetic field may have been sixteen to thirty-two times stronger than the present field. Such a strong magnetic field would have deflected many cosmic rays, resulting in very low, pre-Flood C-14 production. There also may have been a more stratified atmosphere before the Flood, resulting in less of the heavy carbon dioxide making its way to the earth's surface. There was probably also more carbon dioxide in the early earth atmosphere, with much of it being captured in limestones during the Flood. This would have diluted any heavy carbon dioxide that did make it to the surface. As a result, there may have been very little to no C-14-based carbon dioxide in the pre-Flood atmosphere. Without C-14 in the air, there may have been no C-14 in organisms before the Flood. Current C-14 levels were probably built up after the Flood, explaining why C-14 is out of secular equilibrium. In light of this, C-14 ages will be increasingly too old as the true age gets closer to the Flood.[13]

Certainly, the young-age creation model needs to be developed a lot more in order to reinterpret adequately the age-dating methods that exist. Studies are needed in astronomy, physics, chemistry, geology, atmospherics, climatology, and even biology. Despite the incompleteness of the creation model, however, the inconsistencies with old-age indicators provide encouragement, while the claims of Scripture convince us of the truth.

Pieces of the Puzzle

The creation model is able to do more than poke holes in other people's arguments. There are several physical indications that the creation is as young as Scripture indicates. Supernova remnants provide one possible example. A massive star can explode in a phenomenal explosion called a supernova. Large amounts of material are ejected from the supernova, and these expand away from the remaining core. As the material moves away, it grows thinner and thinner until it is no longer visible to the human eye. If our galaxy is billions of years old, it is reasonable to assume that supernovae have occurred at a constant rate through time. However, even though it is possible to see older supernovae, the only supernova remnants we see are only thousands of years old. This seems to be evidence that the galaxy is only thousands of years old.[14]

Comets provide another possible example. Comets continually lose material as they travel about the sun—especially as they pass close to the sun. It is estimated that they lose an average of 1 to 2 percent of their material on every close pass. Comets that we can see from the earth cannot be much more than two hundred passes in age. At this rate a number of familiar comets have been in the inner solar system for less than ten thousand years. Although distant sources have been proposed for these comets, the sources seem to be inadequate to explain many of the comets we see. The solar system, which is thought to be as old as the comets, would appear to be thousands (and not millions or billions) of years old.[15]

Also in the solar system is a bunch of dust, which is being built up by the breaking up of comets and the colliding of asteroids. But it is also being depleted as it is swept up by the sun and planets and pushed out of the solar system by radiation. The loss rate is so high that the solar system would be cleaned of certain-sized particles in less than ten thousand years. Unless the accumulation rate is extremely high, the solar system would appear to be thousands of years old.[16]

Geomagnetism provides another indication of the youth of the world. Although offered only as a tangential comment, Horace Lamb suggested in the late nineteenth century that the earth's magnetic field could theoretically be produced by a current of electrons circulating in the outer core of the earth. If such a current really was the source of the earth's magnetic field, however, friction would cause a rapid decline in both the energy of the electrons (called *free decay*) and the strength of the magnetic field it generates. By the beginning of the twentieth century, the earth was considered much too old to take such a hypothesis seriously. Alternate (dynamo) theories for the earth's magnetic field that permitted the field to persist for billions of years were developed. These theories were revised to allow for reversals of the earth's magnetic field as per the physical evidence that it has reversed in the past, but such reversals require something on the order of one thousand years to accomplish in dynamo theory.

Lamb's free decay theory was revived by creationist Thomas Barnes and then revised by D. Russell Humphreys to accommodate evidence that the earth's magnetic field has reversed. Reversals in the Lamb-Humphreys model can occur in as short a time as every few weeks. As Humphreys predicted, cooling lava flows ought to make it possible to distinguish between reversal times of one thousand years and those of a few weeks.

A lava flow made of basalt (the type of lava which flows from the Hawaiian volcanoes) that is a couple of feet thick takes a couple of weeks to cool. Iron minerals in the rock that act as little magnets will orient themselves like tiny compass needles as long as the lava is hot. As the lava cools, however (from the outside in), these minerals get "frozen" into position—a position that indicates the magnetic field direction when the lava was still hot. If the orientation of the field at the time the lava flowed reversed *before* the center of the flow cooled, then there would be one orientation preserved in the outer part of the flow and another orientation preserved in the inner part of the flow. This could happen only if the reversal occurred within the few weeks it takes to cool the lava. If the dynamo theories were right, however, such a lava flow would never preserve a magnetic reversal.

In 1986 Humphreys predicted that such lava flows ought to be found. By 1988 such a flow was found, and by 1990 a second had been found. The validation of this prediction seems to suggest that the dynamo theories are wrong and the Lamb-Humphreys theory is correct. If that is true, however, the rate of decay of the field observed in the last 150 years suggests that the magnetic field of the earth is significantly less than twenty thousand years old. And, since there is evidence in some of the oldest rocks on earth that a magnetic field was present at their formation, this suggests that the oldest rocks on earth (and probably the earth itself) are substantially less than twenty thousand years old. If a similar mechanism is responsible for other magnetic fields in the solar system, then the moon, sun, and planets also are substantially less than twenty thousand years old.[17]

Summary

Although there are many different indicators that the universe is old, each one struggles with data that does not seem to fit. Because God created things with the appearance of age, some of the excessive, apparent age is due to the nature of the initial creation. The different history of the creation proposed by creation theory is responsible for some of the excessive age that remains. There are even a few indicators that suggest the creation is only thousands of years old (and not billions as is commonly believed by non-creationists). All of this suggests that it is not unreasonable to accept on faith the claims of Scripture—that the creation is only about six thousand years old. It also suggests that the young-age creation model has some explanatory value among the chronology sciences.

What's Next?

About six thousand years ago, God set creation's time clock into motion. As the hours, days, weeks, and years ticked off on this clock, God's purposes were met and His plan was unfurled. The remainder of this book will step briefly through some of the events on this time clock, more or less in the order they occurred. This will begin with several chapters devoted to the events of Creation Week, beginning with the heavens above, then the earth beneath, and moving on to organisms and finally man.

PART 3

CREATION WEEK

CHAPTER 6

The Maker of Heaven

Scattered among the six days of creation are the beginnings of four different parts of the physical world—the heavens, the earth, organisms, and man.[1] The next four chapters will deal with the creation of each of these things in turn. This chapter will study the creation of things above, which covers portions of three of the six days of Creation Week. We will see what God's intentions were in creating the heavens, why the laws of creation argue in favor of His making the universe with man as its object, and how His nature is revealed in the things He has made—both above us and around us.

With Man in Mind

Before we gaze too deeply into space, we should notice there are several references in the biblical text that indicate man is central to God's creation:

- The organisms created on Day 5 and Day 6—as well as the earth itself—were to be ruled over by man (Gen. 1:28).
- Plants were created as food for humans (Gen. 1:29).
- The lights in the heavens were created to be timekeepers for man (Gen. 1:14).
- Even angels were created to be ministers to the elect (Heb. 1:14).

- According to Romans 1:19–20, God shows Himself through the things He has made. This indicates that God created the physical universe in such a way that man could come to know Him.
- Man is the last (the penultimate) creation.
- Man is the only creation that has the "image of God" (Gen. 1:26–27).
- It is because of man's sin and not the sin of angels, for example, that the creation is cursed (Rom. 8:18–22).
- It is also because of man's sin that the Creator came to earth in the image of a man (Phil. 2:7), and died and was resurrected to provide salvation to man—and apparently only to man because even the angels cannot experience salvation.
- Humans seem to have been especially created to glorify God (Gen. 2:7). The remainder of the creation—including the sky above—was created so man could glorify his maker.

God's focus on man is so much a part of the universe, in fact, that even unbelievers have made note of it. Even to those who do not believe in a Creator, the universe appears as if it were created for man. This is called the Anthropic Principle.[2]

Natural Laws

Characteristics that make a case for the centrality of man begin with some of the most basic characteristics of the creation. Our bodies, for example, are constructed of particles of physical matter arrayed in three-dimensional space. In order for our bodies to operate reliably, they must be made of particles with a consistent nature, they must work according to consistent patterns, and space must hold those particles in a consistent manner.

Thus, God created space with three dimensionality, and He created matter with consistent particles, all operating according to rules that operate consistently in time and space. These consistent patterns of particle behavior are called *natural laws*. Desiring that man should be able to see Him in the creation, God created these natural laws in such a way that we could figure them out—even during the course of a single human lifetime. He even created the natural laws in such a way that they can be represented in simple mathematical form. These are just some of the basic characteristics of the universe God set in place so man could know Him.

More is needed for man's role in creation, however, than a universe that operates in a consistent, understandable pattern. There are very particular patterns that seem to be essential for human life.

The law of gravity is an example. For humans to exist, the earth must remain in proper position with respect to the sun for thousands of years of time. People who are capable of calculating such things have concluded only one mathematical form of the law of gravity would produce a stable earth orbit—namely, that gravitational attraction between two objects decreases with the square of the distance between.

But gravity is more than just a type of attraction between two objects; it is also the absolute strength of the attraction. In the mathematical form of a natural law, there is a number that measures the magnitude of the relationship. In the law of gravity, for example, there is a particular number that defines the strength of gravity in the universe. Since natural laws are generally thought to be unchanging, numbers like this are considered constant. They are called physical constants. Just as the gravitational constant determines the strength of gravity in the universe, the electromagnetic constant determines the strength of attraction between electrical charges. Other physical constants include the charges and masses of subatomic particles like electrons and protons, the speed of light, attributes of space, and so on.

Interestingly enough, not only are particular natural laws essential for life, but particular values of the physical constants are also. If the electromagnetic force constant were just slightly stronger, for example, electrons would be held so strongly to atoms that they would never be shared between atoms. Without sharing electrons, molecules couldn't exist. Without molecules, many things in the universe—from the human body to the earth itself—could never be. If the electromagnetic force constant were just slightly weaker, atoms couldn't hold on to their electrons—again precluding the possibility of molecules. God carefully chose the current electromagnetic force constant of the universe—as well as all the other constants—to make human life possible.

God created a consistent universe that behaves in a consistent manner, ruled by a suite of specially designed natural laws and specially chosen physical constants—all so that humans could live and come to know God.

The Matter of Creation

The design God placed into natural laws He also placed into the particles of the universe. Most of the molecules in the human body, for example, are built upon a backbone of carbon atoms. God designed the carbon atom to have particular characteristics that make it the ideal backbone for organic molecules. In fact, it has been argued that carbon is the only atom that could function like this. Similar arguments have been made for the unique roles other atoms play in organic molecules, such as hydrogen, nitrogen, oxygen, phosphorus, and sulfur.

On the next level of organization, God also designed molecules essential for life. The most abundant single molecule in the human body—water—is not organic at all. It has some amazing characteristics that make it a great place for the processes of life to occur.

- A large number of substances can be dissolved in water.
- Because water is a liquid at normal temperatures on the earth's surface, it makes a good fluid for transporting molecules.
- Whereas most substances of the universe expand as they become warmer, water actually contracts as it warms through a certain range of temperatures. Because this temperature range is around the freezing point of water, ice is lighter than water even though it is colder. As a result, ice floats. If water acted like other substances in the universe, frozen water would sink, and lakes would freeze from the bottom up. Life in water in cold regions would not be possible.

- Another characteristic of water is its tendency to "stick" to itself. The electrical characteristics of a water molecule cause it to be electrically attracted to other water molecules. This causes water to form droplets when it falls and to bead on waxed surfaces. The same quality allows insects like water striders to walk on top of water, and it permits water to be pulled long distances through tubes of small diameter. This capillary action permits trees to raise water many feet upward—from the ground beneath to the leaves above—without expending any work in the process.
- Water's unique ability to carry large amounts of heat—especially when evaporating—permits water to function as an air-conditioning fluid.

Water is truly a spectacular substance.

Another remarkable molecule is carbon dioxide. As a gas, carbon dioxide is made available to plants in abundance, and its greenhouse effects allow comfortable temperatures on the earth's surface. Upon its solubility in water, carbon dioxide produces carbonic acid—another important molecule in the erosion of rocks and the sustaining of acidic solutions. God designed these and other molecules specifically so life could flourish—and this includes human life.

At the next level of structure, many of the molecules of the universe are concentrated in gaseous astronomical bodies (like stars) and solid bodies like planets and moons. God arranged these bodies into larger systems. Moons were arranged around planets. Solar systems were created from such things as planets and comets. Solar systems and nebulae were arranged into galaxies. Galaxies were arranged into galactic clusters, and galactic clusters into superclusters. Superclusters were then arranged into even larger structures.

In His plan for our Milky Way galaxy, God made sure that stars were not placed close enough to our solar system to pull planets out of their orbits. Even though most solar systems have multiple suns, God designed our solar system with a single star so the earth's orbit was stable. Of all the different types of stars in the universe, our star's color was chosen for photosynthesis, and its type was chosen for stability. The earth's orbit is made just the size and shape necessary to produce the appropriate range of surface temperatures. God's consideration of man shows up in the design of the entire universe—from its most basic structure to the largest bodies it contains.

Both the Nice and the Necessary

For those who believe in a Creator, these Anthropic Principle evidences are exactly what we expect to see. The most common explanation of those who do not believe in a Creator is that this is the only possible way it could be. After all, the only way that we as humans could be looking at the universe is if we exist, and the only way we could exist is if the universe is built in such a way that we could exist! Therefore, they say, why shouldn't we expect the universe to have characteristics necessary for human life?

But not all the Anthropic Principle evidences seem to be necessary for human life. Anthropic Principle observations began in the 1940s when particularly large numbers were found to recur in what seemed to be unrelated characteristics of the universe.[3] It is not clear how this initial observation (which appears to be not much more than a mathematical curiosity) is necessary for the existence of humans—or any other life for that matter. And although natural laws seem to be necessary for life, it is not necessary that those natural laws be understandable by humans. Even if the laws were understandable, it is not necessary that they be inferable in the course of a single lifetime, nor that they should be represented in the human language of mathematics. There are, therefore, characteristics of the universe that—although not necessary for the existence of humans—are certainly convenient.

Most importantly, these characteristics permit humans to infer the nature of God reliably from those things created. That is why theistic models are superior to non-theistic models in providing reason for all of the Anthropic Principle evidences—not just those that are necessary for intelligent life. Non-theistic models must appeal to happenstance to explain most of the apparent design of the universe, but the God of creation has sufficient power to accomplish the task. Finally, theistic models provide a purpose for the creation—and for humans themselves. By providing a better explanation, a more capable cause, as well as a purpose for all we see, creationism should be preferred over non-theistic models of origins.

And young-age creationism has a further advantage over the alternate theories. This is because there are many characteristics of the universe that must be designed in a very specific way for life to exist and persist. For every such characteristic, however, there is at least one more that would have to be the way it is for the universe to develop into its current state. In the young-age creation model, God creates the universe in a complete, mature form, meaning the universe did not have to develop into its final form. Because the universe does not have to develop, fewer evidences of the Anthropic Principle have to be explained in the young-age creation model. It is, therefore, a simpler hypothesis. And when two theories are equal on all other points, a simpler theory is preferred over a more complex theory. Young-age creationism provides the best possible explanation of the Anthropic Principle evidences.

Compelling Evidence

According to Romans 1:18–20, God shows Himself and His attributes through those things that are made. Since God requires faith of us (Heb. 11:3), He does not go so far as to provide proof that He is Creator. Compelling evidence, yes; proof, no. The very structure of the universe, then, would be expected to provide compelling, non-conclusive evidence of God and His nature.[4]

Inference of God's nature begins with evidence that the universe had a beginning in time—that it is not infinitely old. On the theoretical level, both Relativity and the Second Law of Thermodynamics indicate this is true. According to the First Law of Thermodynamics, the total amount of matter and energy in the universe remains constant. But according to the Second Law of Thermodynamics, the amount of available energy decreases through time. Every process that utilizes energy loses a bit of it into a form that cannot be used by any other process. If the universe were infinitely old, there would be no usable energy left in the universe and we would not be here. The existence of usable energy in the universe suggests that the universe had a beginning in time. If General Relativity is true—which it seems to be[5]—the universe is constantly changing in size. It is either expanding or contracting. Since neither contraction nor expansion can continue forever, the relativity theory also suggests the universe had a beginning.

Physical evidence seems to confirm this theoretical inference and further suggests that the universe is actually expanding. It has been observed that the farther a galaxy is away from us, the more the light from it seems to be shifted toward the red end of the spectrum. This is called redshift. Since red light has the longest wavelength of the visible colors, redshift represents the lengthening of wavelengths. An expanding universe will not only lengthen the wavelengths of light; it will do more lengthening for objects that are farther away. Because of this, the increased galactic redshift with distance is interpreted as evidence of the expansion of the universe. Since expansion cannot go on forever, the universe seems to have had a beginning.

Since it was a unique occurrence in time, the beginning of the universe was an event. And since in our experience, events have causes,[6] the beginning of the universe would seem to have had a cause. And this is the main point. Various evidences suggest the cause of the universe had attributes we know to be possessed by the God of Scripture.

First of all, the Anthropic Principle observations provide compelling evidence that the cause of the universe had man in mind.

The Second Law of Thermodynamics also provides another clue about the nature of the universe's cause. Just as energy is required to build complex structures, so complex structures contain usable energy. One of the ways in which total usable energy in the universe can decrease through time is with a decrease in complexity. But there are examples where the total usable energy in the complexity of a system increases. The building of a house, the manufacturing of a car, and the growth of an oak tree are examples. What are some observations we can make of each case?

First, whereas the usable energy of a smaller system increases, energy enters the system from a larger system, and the usable energy of that larger system decreases. As a house is built, for example, food is consumed as energy by the construction workers. Those workers grow older and get tired, food resources are used up, and stockpiles of construction materials are depleted. As cars are manufactured, energy in the form of electricity is poured into the factory. The energy sources used to make the electricity are used up, and stockpiles of parts are depleted. As an oak grows, light from the sun provides the external energy. During this time the sun itself loses huge quantities of its own energy.

Second, each system has some sort of mechanism to convert the external energy into a usable form and some sort of plan that makes sure the energy is utilized in the proper manner. As a house is built, for example, food is converted by human bodies into useful activity and guided by the architect's blueprint. As cars are manufactured, electricity is converted into mechanical energy by machines, and the machines are organized according to the design of the factory. As an oak grows, sunlight is converted into chemical energy by photosynthesis, and this chemical energy is used to build the tree according to the plan outlined in the plant's DNA.

If our experience is correct, complexity increases in systems only with an external energy source, a proper energy conversion mechanism, and a design. In light of the Second Law of Thermodynamics, the universe at its origin must have had a lot of usable energy—a lot more than it has now. How did the universe get into such a form? Our Second Law observations would suggest that the universe's energy has an external energy source, that something is capable of converting it into a usable form, and that there was some sort of intelligent plan followed. This in turn suggests that the cause of the universe possessed energy and could convert that energy into a usable form. The cause of the universe was thus very powerful. The cause of the universe must also have followed some sort of intelligent plan. The Second Law of Thermodynamics suggests that the cause of the universe was both powerful and intelligent.

Just how powerful was the universe's cause? A study of processes that transfer energy and information gives us hints. The Second Law suggests that usable energy is lost in every energy transfer. As a result, the amount of energy available in the energy source is always observed to be greater than the amount of energy given away. If the same principle is applied to the origin of the universe, the cause of the universe had more energy than the total amount of energy in all the universe. It also had the ability to transform that energy into a usable form. It thus has the ability to control all the energy of the universe—meaning that it has all power.

Just how intelligent was the universe's cause? In our experience, information is lost in every transfer of information. This means that the amount of information in the source is always greater than the amount of information transferred. Applied to the origin of the universe, the information possessed by the cause of the universe must have been greater than the total amount of information placed into the universe. This would suggest that the cause of the universe had more information than is found in the universe—meaning that it had all knowledge.

Yet another clue to the nature of the universe's cause comes from chaos—*technically defined* chaos. When people hear the word *chaos,* most of them probably think of pandemonium or disorder; when a physicist uses the word *chaos* in a technical sense, he means something quite different. The chaotic systems of physicists do have outcomes that are unpredictable, but the systems are not totally unknowable. Processes that are technically chaotic have been found to operate according to simple rules.

The problem seems to be that there are too many different simple rules that combine in complex ways to produce the ultimate result. It is generally believed that if all the rules were understood, and if the beginning state of the system were fully understood, it would be possible to predict all future states of the system. Unfortunately, it seems that humans are incapable of knowing enough about the system to make such predictions accurately. A small error in the understanding of one small part of the system will eventually lead to wrong predictions.

One example of a chaotic system was given in the film *Jurassic Park*. This involved the path of a water drop on the back of a hand. The exact path depends upon known rules of motion, but it also depends on the mass of the drop, the shape of the surface of the hand, the wind speed and direction, the orientation of the hand, the number and distribution of hairs and their length and flexibility, the oiliness of the skin, the temperature of the air, the drop, the skin, the height from which the drop fell, and on and on. Since each of these things is critical in determining what path the drop actually follows, and since none of these things can be known fully, the exact path cannot be accurately predicted.

The study of chaotic systems has suggested that many—perhaps most—of the systems of the universe are chaotic. Even the path of planets about the sun has been determined to be chaotic, so dependent are they upon the mass, shape, distribution, speed, direction, and balance of every body of the solar system—even the dust! For an accurate prediction to be made about the future of a chaotic system, virtually everything that can be known about the system must be known—at extremely high precision. The Anthropic Principle suggests that the universe was designed so man could exist and persist for thousands of years. This suggests, then, that the universe was designed to persist for thousands of years—in a state known to the designer. This further suggests that the designer would have to know everything there is to know about a huge number of systems in the universe. Perhaps everything would need to be known about every single process in the universe!

The designer, therefore, would have to have all knowledge. But even though predicting the future state of a chaotic system requires great knowledge, being able to determine the future state requires something more. Every starting detail of the system must not only be known; every starting detail of the system must be set up in precisely the right way. For a designer not only to know how the universe comes out but to be certain that it will come out as intended, every detail of the universe must be put in place in exactly the right way. All power in addition to all knowledge is required of the designer of the universe.

Describing the Designer

As currently defined, the universe contains all matter, space, and time. The beginning of the physical universe is the beginning of matter, material space, and physical time. The cause of the universe, then, must have caused the beginning of all matter, material space, and physical time. This means that the cause of the universe was independent of these three things. Since it was independent of matter, the cause of the universe seems to have been non-physical. Since it was independent of space, the cause of the universe seems to be both *outside* the universe and at every place *within* the universe—transcendent, immanent, all-present. Since it was independent of physical time, the cause of the universe seems to be unchanging, always present, and eternal.

Arabians of the Middle Ages classified causes of events into personal causes and material causes. Material causes, like a baseball breaking a window by impact, must exist physically before the event in physical time, and they must make some sort of physical contact with the event to cause the event. For example, the baseball must exist physically before the breaking of the window, and it must follow a trajectory through space before the event in order to bring it into direct contact with the glass and to break it. Personal causes, like a person spontaneously coming up with an idea, do not have to precede the event physically in physical time, nor must they contact the event physically to cause it.

For example, a human soul/spirit (which is not physical) can conceive of a sin or an idea of a painting without having physical contact with the sin or its idea. Since the origin of the universe involved the beginning of both time and matter, the cause of the universe could not have preceded the event in physical time, nor could it have had physical contact with the event to cause it. Our experience suggests, then, that the cause of the universe was a personal cause, not a physical cause. This suggests that the cause of the beginning of the universe was a personal being with a will.

Taking all the evidences from this chapter into account, it seems that the universe is the result of a conscious decision of a personal, immanent, transcendent, immaterial, changeless, eternal, omniscient, omnipotent, communicating being who had man in mind in the process. Being a personal being transcendent to the universe, this inference is contrary to both atheism and transcendentalism. Being immanent, this inference is contrary to deism. Most importantly, this inference is uniquely consistent with the God of Scripture. And—as expected from Scripture—the structure of the universe was designed in such a way that it provides compelling evidence of God and His nature.

The Creation of the Heavens

The Bible says that the heavens were created and then spread out "as a tent to dwell in" (Isa. 40:22). The purpose of the heavens was to provide a place for man to live, to know God, and to glorify Him; and they were created in such a form as to make it possible for man to do these things from the beginning. Natural laws were created already operating with physical constants in place. The universe was created large enough to support life and to house the lights God would place in it.[7] The universe was probably created with subatomic particles, atoms, and molecules already in place.[8]

On Day 4 of Creation Week, the sun, moon, and stars were probably created complete and in place. The moon was created already orbiting the earth, and the earth and moon (along with the other bodies of the solar system, including other planets, moons, and comets) were placed in an orbit around the sun. The sun was already in place within the Milky Way galaxy, which was already located within its local cluster and within our supercluster. All the bodies of the universe were arranged into their largest structures.[9] Furthermore, in order for the bearers of light to fulfill their function at creation, they were probably created not only bearing light but—as argued in chapter 5—with light also created at every point between the light source and the earth.

All of this is consistent with various of the attributes of God. Let's look at a few of these characteristics.

God is one, yet He is also three (Matt. 28:19; John 14:26; 15:26; 2 Cor. 13:14; 1 Pet. 1:2). His internal nature is diverse. It seems that because of this, God loves variety. So when He created the bodies of the universe, He created them in great variety. He created different kinds of galaxies and a variety of stars.[10] He also created a variety of planets, moons, and comets—a variety which has always been challenging to explain in atheistic origins models.[11]

God has great abundance (John 10:10). The universe was created larger than it had to be, and with a greater variety of astronomical bodies than was necessary to accomplish His other purposes.

God's nature is filled with glory. This is reflected in the incredible beauty of the universe. The planets and their moons as well as the galaxies and their stars are majestic in their brilliance. Through the millennia the beauty of the heavens has always created awe in humans.

God is a God of order (1 Cor. 14:33). Early in the history of modern science, physicists and chemists had considerable success at new discoveries by following a symmetry principle. Once chemists had discovered enough elements to determine the pattern we now know as the Periodic Table, further elements were predicted by assuming through symmetry and completeness that the table would be complete. In a similar manner, the principle of symmetry has been used to predict the existence and characteristics of subatomic particles. Even the forms of the natural laws of the universe are elegant.[12]

God is unchanging (Ps. 102:25–27; Mal. 3:6; James 1:17), and He probably intended His initial creation to exist forever. As it stands right now, the Second Law of Thermodynamics would seem to make this impossible. At the same time, the Second Law is essential for the reliable operation of a large number of processes of the universe.[13] It is likely, then, that another natural law operated in the original creation—perhaps a law that relocated heat energy into active energy sources of the universe. This would allow energy sources to persist indefinitely.

So, as we can see, the heavens give us a picture of God's nature. Truly, "the heavens declare the glory of God" (Ps. 19:1).

Why Not the Big Bang?

Not everyone sees it this way, of course. The most popular atheistic theory for the origin of the universe is the Big Bang theory, which leaves God totally out of the picture. Here's basically how this hypothesis works.

It begins with all the space, matter, and time of the universe compressed into infinite or near-infinite density, and then supposes that it expands from there. Very early in its expansion, energy in the form of very high-energy gamma radiation condensed into subatomic particles, most of which collided again to produce gamma rays again. As the expansion continued however, the gamma rays got stretched. Once stretched so far, they lacked the energy necessary to produce more subatomic particles. But the density and temperature for a time was high enough to fuse heavy particles together to produce atomic nuclei—first as deuterium nuclei, then helium nuclei, then boron nuclei, and so on. This continued until the expansion had dropped temperatures and pressures below what was needed for fusion.

During this entire period, the universe's particles were so close together that light could not travel very far before it bounced off them. Not until the expansion separated the particles far enough could the light become free to travel through the universe. Traveling in every direction because of earlier collisions, the light moved ever afterward, going in all directions into space. Billions of years of expansion since this event stretches the original gamma radiation into microwaves. Evidence of such a beginning of the universe would be found: (1) in the large ratio of particles of light to particles of matter, (2) in light elements in abundances inversely proportional to their mass, and (3) microwave radiation coming in uniformly in all directions. Because each of these expectations are known to be true of our universe, the Big Bang theory is well-evidenced. Because the microwave radiation was a prediction of the theory even before it was possible to detect such radiation, the Big Bang theory is even more powerfully supported.

Yet the Big Bang theory cannot be true for the following reasons.

- According to Scripture, the universe is only about six thousand years old; the Big Bang theory requires it to be billions of years old.
- Subatomic particles, the elements, and many of the compounds of the universe were created in a single day of Creation Week; the Big Bang theory has these things developing over billions of years.
- That something is wrong with the Big Bang theory is evidenced by the fact that the microwave radiation has actually been found to be too uniform—more uniform than the distribution of matter in the universe.

Even though the Big Bang theory is wrong, no young-age creationist theory has yet been forthcoming to provide an alternate explanation of its evidences.[14] In its precise form, the Big Bang theory is a mathematical theory derived from General Relativity theory—though actually, that isn't true, because it has not been possible to get from General Relativity to the Big Bang theory without the mathematics becoming so complicated that it cannot be solved. In fact, this happens several times in the process of deriving the Big Bang theory. Each time this happens, the equations are simplified by making an assumption about the universe. Once this happens, further progress is made until once again the equations become too complicated to solve and another simplifying assumption must be made. So a particular sequence of simplifying assumptions has been made in order to generate the set of theories of the universe's origin that have come to be known as the Big Bang theories.

Common assumptions in Big Bang theories include the unboundedness of the universe and its uniform distribution of matter. On the fourth day of Creation Week, God placed the sun, moon, and stars within the "firmament of the heaven" (Gen. 1:14–19). The "firmament" called "heaven" had been created two days earlier (Gen. 1:6–8) to separate the "waters which were under the firmament from the waters which were above the firmament." This suggests that all the bodies of the universe are bounded above by "waters above." If so, the universe is bounded—not unbounded, as often assumed. Also, if matter is distributed as unevenly as it appears to be, the universe is much less uniform than is usually assumed.

It is likely that young-age creation theory (both in the study of the biblical text and the physical world) would suggest a different set of assumptions than is usually assumed in studies of the origin of the universe. If mathematical derivations were made using these assumptions, perhaps a theory could be derived that not only better explained the known features of the universe but was also compatible with biblical claims about the universe's beginning.[15]

Summary

The universe was created full of evidences about God's nature. He created the universe with man in mind, and evidences of that intention were woven into the fabric of universe. This can be seen in such places as the Anthropic Principle. God also created the universe in such a way that compelling physical evidence existed for God having created it. And because God created all things by His Word (John 1:1–3; Heb. 11:3), evidence of language was created throughout the creation (such as the mathematical precision of the universe and the mathematical nature of the natural laws). Because there is only one God (Deut. 6:4; Isa. 45:18; Mark 12:29; 1 John 5:7), the many Anthropic Principle arguments point in the same direction, and the many natural laws and processes of the universe work together to create a *universe* (not a *multi*verse). This also explains why the search for "grand unified field theories" (GUT theories) and "theories of everything" (TOE theories) have led physicists to make progress in understanding the universe.

The universe seems to operate with mathematical precision, and natural laws have a mathematical form. The universal presence of language in the structure of the universe suggests that the cause of the beginning of the universe may be a communicator. The similar conclusions drawn from diverse arguments (such as the intelligence suggested by the universe's design, the Anthropic Principle, chaos theory, the Second Law of Thermodynamics, and the similar conclusion deduced from such a large number of Anthropic Principle observations) suggest that there is only a single cause for the beginning of the universe. The heavens were made by the hand of God.

What's Next?

From the creation of the heavens above us and the air around us, we next turn our focus to the creation of the earth beneath us.

CHAPTER 7

Day 3: The Earth

Much is still not understood about the form in which God created the earth's surface and its atmosphere. We are unclear about how these things were originally arranged, how they operated, or exactly how they existed before the Fall and the Flood. Even today, in fact, because so much of the earth remains inaccessible to us, we know much less about its mysteries than we do about the life that exists upon it. But the findings that do emerge from a study of the earth and its material makeup reveal that it was created to support life and to endure many centuries of wear and tear. And just as we saw in the last chapter on the creation of the heavens, the nature and character of God run through the length and breadth of the earth, revealing its Maker as One Who has immense power, mercy, glory, and wisdom.

Solid Ground for Survival

One of God's purposes in creating the earth was to provide a suitable habitat for man—so man could know, worship, and glorify God.[1] In order to achieve this purpose, the earth was created in a precise manner.

To provide the proper climate, the earth was not just placed in the best possible orbit about the sun. It was also placed at the proper tilt and given the proper rotational rate.

To provide humans, animals, and plants the atmospheric gases they need (like water, oxygen, and carbon dioxide), the earth was created with enough mass so that its gravity could hold on to such gases, and yet not so massive that it also holds on to light, poisonous gases like hydrogen and helium.

To provide protection from deadly charged particles coming in from the sun, the earth was created with a strong magnetic field. Because it was probably created with a strength sixteen to thirty-two times its present strength,[2] the original magnetic field of the earth was probably also strong enough to prevent the creation and accumulation of radioactive carbon-14. This magnetic field was formed by creating a large array of electrons circling the center of the earth. For these electrons to move in consistent circular orbits, the earth was created with a zone that is highly conductive electrically. This resulted in a threefold division of the earth's interior: an inner zone (called the inner core), a zone where the electrons circulate (called the outer core), and an outer zone (called the mantle). Additionally, the mantle was created with a consistency that allows the crust to float on the earth.

On the Surface of Things

By the end of Day 3 of Creation Week, the earth had continents and oceans. Oceans and continents still exist today, of course, and are caused by differences in the rocks beneath. The upper three to five miles of rock beneath the ocean basins is called ocean crust. The upper twenty miles of rock beneath the continents is called continental crust. Since ocean crust is more dense than continental crust, it floats lower in the mantle, just as oak wood floats deeper in water than balsa wood. It is likely that the original oceans and continents were created with the same differences in crustal density. Since the water-to-land ratio on the earth is critical in maintaining optimal surface temperatures,[3] at least three-fourths of the surface of the created earth was probably covered with water.

But exactly where those continents were located at creation is unknown. Certainly, there was a lot of continental motion during the

Flood (see chap. 13), including motion leading up to the creation of a single supercontinent known as Pangaea. Considerable research is needed to clarify the positions of the original continents at creation, but they may have been in the configuration now known as Rodinia.[4] One thing we do know through our understanding of God's nature is this: because of His love of diversity, He probably created great variety into the original continental regions and their topography.[5]

On the third day of Creation Week, according to Genesis 1:9, God commanded the waters to be gathered together into one place to let the dry land appear. The text says nothing more about how it happened than this: "And it was so." The details about how dry land was formed are not indicated. Was a uniform crust divided into continental and oceanic crust on that day? Were continents moved about on the earth's surface? Was continental crust raised out of the water, causing erosion and deposition along continental margins? Were crustal fractures made on this day—locations where earthquakes would happen later? Were there earthquakes? Volcanoes? We simply do not know. In time, however, research may provide the answers to these questions.

On Day 3 plants were created to serve as food for animals and man (Gen. 1:29–30). But before plants could thrive, a large array of characteristics was needed[6]—optimal soils, for example, and a variety of soils. Each soil needed to be stocked with minerals, and it needed a good source of water. So mineral cycles were created to stock the soils with minerals, and a water cycle was created to provide plants constantly with needed water. Just as lightning plays an important role in the maintenance of quality soil on the present earth, the lightning activity on the original earth was created to optimize early earth soils. So the soils could persist through time, the earth was also created with soils in various stages of formation, with all the processes of soil formation already in place.

Most of the cycles of the earth involve bacteria. Since Genesis does not specify when the bacteria of the earth were created, it is possible they were created in association with the earth before the creation of land plants (Day 3 of Creation Week) and animals (Day 5 and Day 6 of Creation Week).

The oceans were created as an environment for sea creatures, and they contained an optimal balance of nutrients, minerals, and salt.[7] Not all the organisms on the bottom of the sea live on rock, so many different sediments were created on the ocean bottom as well. Large volumes of lime mud were probably formed to help maintain the proper pH in the ocean. As on land, cycles were created in the world's seas for the continuous provision of nutrients and minerals. Some of the earth's oxygen cycle and many of the mineral cycles of the ocean involve algae. The Bible does not specify when the algae of the oceans were created. It is possible that they were created with the oceans (on Day 2 or Day 3 of Creation Week).

The same would likely have been true of the earth's lakes and rivers. They would have been created with the bottom sediment and nutrients necessary to provide an optimum environment for the aquatic organisms that would live there.

According to Genesis 1:20, birds fly in the "firmament of heaven." Since a "firmament" called "heaven" was created on Day 2 (Gen. 1:6–8), the earth's atmosphere was probably fashioned on the third day of Creation Week as an environment for the earth's organisms.[8] And again, it was created perfectly for the survival of life.

- The upper atmosphere chemistry destroys methane and ammonia, gases that can mess up organic chemistry and prove fatal if they exist in abundance.
- There is enough oxygen in the earth's atmosphere so animals on land and in the sea can breathe, but not so much that forests would erupt spontaneously in flames.[9]
- There is enough carbon dioxide in the atmosphere to allow photosynthesis in plants.
- There is the right amount of greenhouse gases (water vapor, carbon dioxide, oxygen, and others) to keep the earth's surface warm, but not too warm.
- There is enough ozone in the atmosphere to protect the earth's surface from harmful ultraviolet radiation.

The earth was also created with some sort of water cycle so water would be available to all organisms. Although Scripture provides some clues about this, the exact nature of the water cycle is currently unknown. The seasons referred to in Genesis 1:14 and 8:22 and seemingly reflected in tree rings[10] suggest that the earth was created with a hydrological cycle perhaps similar to the present cycle. On the first day of the Flood, "the fountains of the great deep were broken up." Since "fountains of the great deep" probably refers to terrestrial and oceanic springs,[11] the earth was probably created with springs on both land and sea. Whether these springs were more abundant or of a different nature from current springs is unclear. The springs were created with water issuing from them. Such water or the water introduced from rain may have provided the water for the river of Eden that watered the lands around it (Gen. 2:10–14). As in the present, temperature differences from equator to pole—combined with the earth's rotation—produced consistent easterly and westerly winds. These winds still drive currents that are important in spreading nutrients and organisms throughout the earth's oceans.

Lasting Value, Living Virtues

God did not create the earth to exist forever in perfect form. He knew that man would sin. He knew that He would have to curse the entire creation. He also knew that He would have to judge the earth with a global flood. Both the Curse and the Flood would substantially impact the earth. So the earth was created in such a way that it would not only provide an optimal environment for animals and man in the Edenic world, but that it would survive both the Fall and the Flood and provide an optimal environment after these global catastrophes. The earth has shown remarkable resilience. This incredible ability to survive abuse makes the earth look almost as if it were an organism. Unbelievers have used this kind of evidence to argue that the earth *is* a living organism—an organism with the name Gaia. This Gaia Hypothesis has become popular in some circles.

Just like the heavens, the earth's structure also gives evidence of God's nature.

- His wisdom is evident in the intricate design and interrelated nature of cycles in the earth system.
- His love and provision are evident in how the earth provides for the needs of the creatures that swim, fly, and crawl on its surface, and how it is capable of surviving catastrophic judgments.
- His love for man is implied in how the earth is designed with man in mind.
- His triune nature is seen in the variety of continents, living environments, and ecosystems on the earth.
- His abundance is clear in the variety that exceeds what is necessary for organisms to survive.
- His unity is shown in the interrelated nature of the earth's systems.
- His glory is evident in the earth's beauty.

Everywhere you look on the earth, evidence of its Creator is visible to the naked eye. For those with eyes to see, "the earth is the LORD's, and the fulness thereof" (Ps. 24:1).

What's Next?

We move from the creation of man's physical environment to focus on the origin of earth's organisms—plants, algae, protists, bacteria, and animals.

CHAPTER 8

AFTER THEIR KIND

As our grasp of the biological world expands, we see many evidences of the nature of God and find masterful precision in even the most "simple" of organisms. The miracle of DNA alone reveals a fascinating portrait of its Creator, and we will look at that. In this chapter we also will deal with many of the points where the evolutionists tie their tent of beliefs to the ground—theories with compelling evidence and often a kernel of truth. But through a study of the detailed complexity of organisms, the differences and similarities in species, and various observations on the known characteristics of plants and animals—plus an introductory overview of an exciting, relatively new field of science—we will see that young-age creationism provides the best explanation for this vast array of life on earth: these images of God's glory and power that have been created "after their kind."

The Language of DNA

God is a communicating God. He is the Word (John 1:1), and, in the form of Jesus Christ, "the Word was made flesh, and dwelt among us" (John 1:14). The Word created all things (John 1:3), and by His command all things came to be (Ps. 148:5). Since God seeks to be known in those things that are made, it is not surprising that evidence of a communicating being should be seen throughout His creation. Perhaps nowhere is this more obvious than in the structure of DNA.

All human languages involve at least five characteristics: (1) hierarchal coding, (2) emergent modularity, (3) linguistic structure, (4) sending mechanisms, and (5) receiving mechanisms. Each of these will be considered in sequence.

First, language utilizes a code. In English, for example, twenty-six letters form the building blocks of the language. A particular order of letters will "code" for a word. The building blocks differ in different languages, but in every case they are placed in a particular order to code for some word. Language codes don't just stop there, however. They are also hierarchal. A particular sequence of words is strung together to code for a particular phrase or an idea, and a particular sequence of phrases is strung together to code for a complete thought. Complete thoughts are strung together in a specified way to code for a full argument. At each level there is coding for a higher level.

The DNA molecule has hierarchal coding as well. DNA includes a string of four different nucleotides (guanine, cytosine, adenine, and thymine)—the building blocks of DNA—analogous to the three building blocks of Morse Code (dots, dashes, and gaps). The four nucleotides of DNA are arranged in sequences of three (called *codons*) to code for the twenty or so amino acids used in living organisms—analogous, again, to Morse Code coding for the twenty-six letters of the English alphabet. This characteristic of DNA is so much like language that it is commonly called the "genetic code," and the name *codon* is given to the set of three nucleotides that codes for a particular amino acid.

At the next level up, DNA codons are strung together in particular sequences to code for genes—tens of thousands of them in the human genome. This is similar to the way alphabet letters are strung together in particular sequences to code for words—hundreds of thousands of them in the English language. At an even higher level, just as words can code for a virtually endless array of different concepts, the genes on the DNA are able to code collectively for a vast array of molecules found within created organisms.

Second, language is modular. Letters can be added to the beginning or the end of words to change the meaning of those words. One prefix or suffix can be switched for another to change tenses of verbs, the plurality of nouns, the inclusiveness of adjectives, and so on. Interchangeability of letters and short sequences of letters provide great flexibility to language.

This modularity works at multiple levels. Words can be substituted for other words or added to a sentence. A description can be made more or less precise, a noun can be made more or less inclusive, a verb can be made more or less strong, and so forth. At another level, entire prepositional phrases or parenthetical notes can be inserted, taken out, or replaced. Replacement or insertion can occur at the level of sentences, paragraphs, chapters, and even books. This modularity—especially the kind of modularity that emerges at each level of language's hierarchy—gives language phenomenal versatility. It is this characteristic—called *emergent modularity*—that makes it possible for us to convey an enormous range of concepts.

DNA appears to show this same characteristic. Since four different nucleotides in three positions could code for as many as sixty-four items (4 x 4 x 4) and yet codons in living systems only code for twenty or so, more than one individual codon is assigned to code for a given amino acid. Among other things, this means that an interchange in the nucleotides—especially the third nucleotide in a codon—can at times lead to no change in the protein that is being coded for. Furthermore, of those codon changes that would result in a different amino acid, a small number of them produce a protein structure with no appreciable changes. Other amino acid changes do significantly change the protein structure, but they create proteins of only slightly different function—somewhat like what a suffix or prefix change might have on a particular word.

At another level, a gene can be substituted for another gene, resulting in one protein being substituted for another. Genes can be turned off by means of other genes or short DNA segments. There are even mechanisms to insert or delete genes. At an even higher level, entire gene groups can be substituted for other gene groups by insertion, deletion, or by being turned on or off. This emergent modularity in DNA empowers its extraordinary flexibility and also allows DNA to code for a lot of complexity in a very compact length.

Third, human language exhibits linguistic structure. Words can be classified into different categories (such as nouns, verbs, adjectives, adverbs, prepositions). Linguistic rules determine how words are to relate with other words—both to words in the same category and to those in other categories. A preposition, for example, must be linked with an object of a preposition. An adjective must be linked with a noun. An adverb must be linked with a verb. And so it goes. There are further rules about how the word forms should be in agreement and what the proper order of the different word forms should be. Human languages can differ widely, even when sharing the same alphabet and many of the same words, but they still possess their own linguistic structure.

In DNA there is some hint that a linguistic structure may be present. There are codon sequences that function in turning particular genes on or off. Other codon sequences change the rate at which a particular gene is used—perhaps analogous to our grammatical rules that call for adjectives to modify nouns and adverbs to modify verbs. Other codon sequences, in turn, modify multiple genes. There are also examples of particular groups of codon sequences that must be activated in a particular order before genes can be activated or turned off. At a higher level, there are also frequent examples of sequences (or cascades) of genes that must be turned on in a particular order to achieve the desired result.

It seems, then, that codon sequences are of different categories, that rules exist on how codon sequences relate to one another, and that other rules exist on the order of codon sequences. So far, we have come to understand only a small number of these rules of codon sequence interactions. However, the rules we do understand seem roughly similar to rules of linguistics. Perhaps the similarity is even greater. The Word Who created DNA might well have placed into it a linguistic structure similar to that which He placed within human language.

Fourth, language must have a sending mechanism. Human language is meaningless outside of its proper context. A thought—even if it is thought in the proper letters, words, and sentences according to the proper linguistic structure—is not communicated unless it is somehow expressed. A book—even if written in the proper way—is not communicated if it is not picked up and read. For communication to be successful, the person who is communicating must express the information in a form that is fitting for the receiver.

The information in the DNA of a cell is not in a useful form for the cell. The DNA in complex organisms is close-packed to save space, but the information cannot be read from it in this form. Sophisticated mechanisms exist to unravel and unzip the DNA so it can be read. Yet even this isn't enough. In order to protect its information, most of the DNA is stored in the nucleus, whereas most of the information is needed *outside* the nucleus. Complex mechanisms have been created in cells to copy information from the DNA on specially designed molecules of messenger RNA that carry the information outside the nucleus in a form that can be used by the cell.

Finally, language needs a proper receiver. A perfectly expressed thought in English is not understood by an Indonesian untrained in English. A perfectly written book in English—accurately printed in ink on paper—cannot be understood by an English-speaking person who is blind. For communication to be successful, the receiver must be equipped with the necessary sensory apparatus and training to perceive and understand the information he or she is given.

True, the information on the DNA leaves the cell nucleus on messenger RNA. But most of the cell cannot make sense of the information on the messenger RNA. Sophisticated machinery in the cell is devoted to translating messenger RNA information into chains of amino acids in proper sequence. These chains are folded in proper shapes and tagged for proper location by other mechanisms. They are then transported to the proper locations by still other mechanisms. It is in this final form and position—and only then—that these molecules are useful in making up the cell structure and allowing cell processes to work.

- At every level of structure, DNA uses codes.
- At every level DNA has parts that are designed to be interchangeable.
- DNA's information seems to be arranged according to complex rules.
- DNA is found within a complex cellular system designed to translate DNA information into a form usable by the cell, to create specific structures the cell needs, and to place them in their proper location in the cell.

All these characteristics are shared by human languages. On several different levels and in several different ways, DNA has the structure of language. All organisms on earth—from bacteria to animals, protists to plants, algae to fungi—have DNA. Evidence of language is found in all earth's organisms. Since God created with evidence of His nature, and since God is a communicating God, the language basis of organisms should not come as a surprise to creationists. In fact, it is likely that principles of human linguistics may be helpful in unraveling DNA's language. And since language in our experience is only produced by some communicating intelligence, non-creationists would not expect DNA to be based upon a language.

Biological Complexity

God knows everything (Ps. 147:5; Heb. 4:13; 1 John 3:20), and His omniscience is evidenced by the complexity of the creation. Perhaps nowhere is this complexity more stunning than among living things. Even the "simplest" organisms on earth are remarkably complex. Single cells must be capable of a diverse array of tasks:

- They must identify dangerous chemicals in the world around them and protect themselves from those chemicals.
- They must be able to identify energy sources and needed chemicals in the world around them and move toward them.

- They must be able to take in those things and convert them into usable forms.
- They must be able to build their bodies, repair any damage, and reproduce themselves.

Each of these capabilities requires complex machinery. And all this is packed into a cell so small that it cannot be seen with the naked eye. Some of these tiny organisms thrive in the water of your water heater and essentially freeze to death in temperatures you live in. Other forms live in glacial ice. Some forms live in acid; other forms live on salt. Some forms eat oil, thriving thousands of feet beneath the earth's surface. Some of them get energy from the sun, some get energy from hydrogen gas, and some get energy from sulfur dioxide. Humans and most animals—including horses, cows, and even termites—cannot break down complex plant molecules. So the job of digesting most of the plant material in the world falls on the tiny, one-celled organisms in the intestines of humans and animals.

Most organisms cannot get the atmosphere's nitrogen gas to enter into any chemical reactions. Instead, God created some of the single-celled organisms in the world to be capable of breaking the powerful bonds of nitrogen molecules. In the process they produce nitrates as waste products—wastes that become the needed fertilizer for other organisms. Oxygen—so needed by animals—is actually a waste product of photosynthesis.

A closer examination of a cell reveals complex structures. Cell membranes surround all cells, providing protection and allowing only certain things in and out of the cell. Genetic information for repairs, reproduction, and the building of cellular structure is stored in DNA molecules. More complex organisms have more DNA, and they pack it tightly into specially designed chromosomes. Every cell stores its DNA in a special region. In more complex organisms this region is protected with a specially-designed membrane (a nucleus). Another region of each cell is devoted to producing ribosomes—the machines that construct amino acid chains from messenger RNA. Other regions of every cell are devoted to the folding and tagging of protein molecules. More complex organisms cordon off those sections of the cell with membranes (endoplasmic reticulum and golgi bodies) to increase efficiency of production.

Every cell also has structures designed to extract energy from the environment. More complex organisms—requiring proportionately more energy—concentrate the energy extraction in special structures surrounded by their own membranes and containing some of their own DNA. These include mitochondria for extracting energy from glucose sugar and chloroplasts for extracting energy from the sun.

A closer examination of cells reveals even more complexity. Each of the processes of the cell involves complex chemical reactions. The unwinding, unzipping, copying, rezipping, and rewinding of the DNA requires a complex set of chemical machinery. The process of modifying and transporting the messenger RNA to the ribosomes requires another complex set of chemical machinery. The creation of an amino acid chain, the folding of proteins, the tagging of proteins, the transport of proteins, the selection of molecules to be taken in and let out of the cell, and the processes of extracting energy from the environment—all these require complex machinery. Further machinery is needed for the cell to assume and change its shape, to move, and to ingest items from outside the cell. The complexity, beauty, and elegance of these molecular systems is awesome and stunning.

Furthermore, in virtually every case in each system, a large number of parts must work together. Even when parts that seem unnecessary are taken away, there are usually multiple parts that are necessary to allow the system to work. This minimal or irreducible complexity is difficult to explain in non-creationist scenarios.[1] It is difficult enough to build a complex system when one has the parts or the ability to make it and the plan or the ability to design it. It is even more difficult if one lacks the parts and the ability to make them and also lacks a plan and the ability to design it. Such is the challenge of non-theistic models of origins. Irreducible complexity (complexity that won't function even if one part is missing) introduces even further challenges for these same models. These models usually suggest that complexity was derived in some sort of step-wise manner—one step at a time. It is difficult to imagine how such complex systems could be assembled without a Creator.

Yet complexity is found at every level of biological organization. We find complex chemical systems within complex cells. We find cells in complex tissues, and tissues within complex organs. Organs are located within complex organ systems, and organ systems within complex bodies. Organisms themselves are arranged in complex populations and communities. Even communities and ecosystems are arranged on a global level so that carbon, sulfur, nitrogen, and phosphorus can be cycled through the earth's organisms for a continuous supply. The remarkable complexity found at *any* level is found in *every* level, and the complexity found in each level is integrated with the complexity at other levels. Intuitively, this complexity and integration of complexity seem to be achievable only by design.

An attempt has been made recently to formalize an argument for design[2]—at least certain *types* of design. This approach is commonly called *intelligent design* (ID). Design in the ID sense is limited to complex patterns that cannot be produced by known natural law or process and cannot be generated by randomness (at least as we currently understand it). Among the huge number of patterns that exceed this complexity, ID-type design is limited only to those patterns that would be expected in a designed system—what is called *specified complexity*. By this definition, biologists can specify a particular complexity when they infer a function for a structure found in an organism. This inference may be based upon placement in an arrangement of other structures and/or based upon function that the biologist believes needs to be filled. It need not be made based upon any explicit belief in design.

Implicitly, however, a type of design has been assumed. When the biologist runs experiments on the organism to determine if the part actually has the hypothesized function, he is testing implicitly for design. If the predicted function is verified, the system has the specified complexity. From that, intelligent design can be inferred. Such specified complexity is very difficult to explain in non-theistic models of origins, but it is an expectation of creationist theory.

The Relatedness of Life

Because of His variety, the triune Creator loves variety. This love of variety led to the incredible variety of organisms we see on earth—as well as to the various levels of maturity God created into organisms at the very beginning. Since plants were created to serve as food for animals and man (Gen. 1:29–30), some of the plants in a given population were created already mature, bearing seeds and fruit. Meanwhile, some were probably created already flowering to produce fruit to replace what was eaten immediately, and others were created already maturing in order to bear fruit in a season yet to come. Furthermore, plant populations were probably also created with a normal age distribution of young to old.

As for animals, they were created in only two days. It seems to be God's nature to create something instantaneously and to fulfill His function for it at the moment of creation. This means that animals were probably created in mature populations as well. Since He commanded the swimming and flying creatures to be fruitful and multiply and fill their habitats (Gen. 1:22), God did not at first fill the earth with them. God may have created mature male/female pairs of these animals. On the other hand, certain organisms may have required more than two individuals to survive, so for these organisms God may have created small populations rather than individual pairs. There is no record in Scripture that land animals were commanded to fill the earth. This may be because they were created already filling the earth, or it simply may be that the command was not recorded in Scripture; so we really can't know. But because of the similarity between how they and other organisms were created, land animals may also have been created in small, mature populations and expected to fill the earth—as was the case with flying and swimming animals.

Since a wide diversity of organisms was created instantaneously, the original organisms on earth were not in any way related to one another. Even different members of the same population were not related to one another. Only the offspring of these original populations could truly be genetically related. On the issue of genetic relatedness, many creation biologists have considered the phrase "after its kind" to be important. It is used ten times in Genesis 1, associated in every case with the origin of organisms. Organisms were spoken into existence "after their kind" (vv. 11 and 24), and organisms came into existence "after their kind" (vv. 12, 21, and 25).

Traditionally, the phrase is thought to mean that God created organisms to reproduce "after their kind"—that is, to mate only with others of their own kind. This has been commonly understood to mean that God created each biblical "kind" with built-in genetic barriers that prevented them from being able to reproduce with any organism outside that kind. Such barriers may or may not exist, as Scripture does not demand their existence; but if they do exist, genetic relatedness obviously spread through created kinds as time went on. It would follow, then, that organisms that can successfully interbreed should be of the same created kind. And even if uncrossable genetic barriers do not exist—even if "kinds" are less formally defined (Williams, 1997)—it is still likely that successful crosses indicate which organisms are of the same kind.

Although many species definitions are used in the present, the most popularly taught definition is the biological species definition of naturally interbreeding populations of organisms that under natural conditions do not interbreed with other populations. By definition all members of such species can interbreed successfully, so all members of any such species are of the same created kind. But animals classified in different species are known to interbreed successfully as well. Dogs (*Canis familiaris*), for example, can interbreed successfully with wolves (*Canis lupis*) and coyotes (*Canis latrans*). This means that the biblical "kind" is a broader term than the species of modern classification.[3]

Since "kind" is a term with too many non-technical meanings, Frank Marsh in 1941 recognized the need for a special term for a biblical "kind." He proposed the term "basic type" or *baramin*. Derived from the Hebrew, *baramin* means roughly "created kind."[4] Marsh[5] suggested that successful hybridization could be used to identify species that are actually part of the same basic type or *baramin*. Creation biologists in Germany have used Marsh's reproductive criterion to identify a number of basic types.[6] To facilitate such studies, reports of crosses between different species is currently being assembled into an Internet-accessible database.[7]

What is truly astonishing about lists of crosses between species is how common and widespread such crosses actually are. And this is as true of plants as it is of animals.[8] Among orchids, for example, thousands of interspecific hybrids are known. Some are even crosses among four different genera! Grasses, roses, lilies, and fuchsias just begin the list of plant groups that show common interspecific crosses. Among the 149 species of ducks, swans, and geese in the world, 80 percent of the species, 40 percent of the genera, and 60 percent of the tribes are known to cross with other groups. Cerion land snails as well as numerous birds and mammals begin a long list of animal groups that show common interspecific crosses. The commonness of successful interspecific crosses is not expected outside of young-age creationism.

For two organisms to interbreed successfully, the two must be compatible on many levels.

- Their habits must have the same timing. They must seek mates at the same time of the year and go about their business at the same time of day.
- They must be attracted to one another.
- They must be compatible both physically and chemically.

With such a list of things that must be exact for mating to be successful, it is easy for two organisms to lose their ability to cross. Since genetic mistakes are introduced in virtually every generation in our current world, populations are in a state of constant change. It seems unlikely that two populations separated for many thousands of generations could remain capable of interbreeding. It is much more unlikely that interbreeding would be possible after tens of thousands or hundreds of thousands of generations of separation. Yet those who maintain that the earth is billions of years old suggest that most of the earth's species have been distinct for hundreds of thousands to millions of years.

One noteworthy example is the cama—a cross between a camel and a llama.[9] According to conventional dating, these two species have been separated for at least forty million years. But the successful crossing of a llama and a camel suggests that their separation was much more recent than that. The fact that interspecific hybridization is common among most of the organisms of the world suggests that life's diversity is probably only as old as the thousands of years that young-age creationism suggests. At the same time, the genetic plasticity suggested by the ubiquity of interspecific hybridization is what might be expected of a God Who created organisms in such a way that they would persist (and even thrive) in a changing world.

The Discontinuity of Life

Young-age creationism suggests that within baramins, life is more related than is believed in traditional biology. But young-age creationism also suggests an unrelatedness that is much higher than expected in traditional biology.

Evolutionary theory suggests that all organisms are at least ultimately related. Just as a family tree consists of a group of related humans, Charles Darwin introduced the concept of a "tree of life"—the theory that all organisms are somehow related. But young-age creationism suggests something very different. For example, organisms created by God on any particular day of Creation Week were unrelated to those created on any other day of Creation Week. Genetic relatedness would only exist among organisms that have interbred *since* the creation.[10] The remainder of the earth's organisms would be genetically unrelated.

Thus, the young-age creationist would expect genetic unrelatedness to be a common characteristic of the earth's organisms. Rather than a single "tree of life," young-age creationists expect there to be many "trees of life"—one for each separately created group of organisms. This would be something like an orchard of separately created "trees of life," a creationist arboretum of biological form. The young-age creationist also believes that God placed multiple evidences among living things to show that life's form had separate origins. Not only were they created with breaks or discontinuities in genetics, but probably discontinuities in biochemistry, development, behavior, biological form, and other categories. The young-age creationist expects discontinuity on many levels to be a common characteristic of the earth's organisms. But the young-age creation biologist needs a tool to recognize such discontinuity.

Such a tool comes in the form of baraminology.[11] Just as theology is the study of *theos* (God) and biology is the study of *bios* (life), baraminology is the study of baramins. The ultimate end of baraminology is to identify, name, and classify baramins—God's created kinds.[12] A complete baramin would include both living and dead organisms in the present, organisms represented as fossils, and organisms we can never gain direct access to (such as past forms that were never preserved or have never been discovered as fossils). Baraminology restricts its study to known organisms—living individuals plus the dead ones we know about because we have actual bodies or fossils. It is only after conclusions are drawn about known organisms that speculations about entire baramins can be made.

The group of all known organisms that shows continuity within but that is discontinuous from any other group (all known members of a baramin) is called a *holobaramin* (fig. 8.1). The first goal of baraminology, then, is the identification of holobaramins. Holobaramins are discovered by building up smaller groups called *monobaramins* (fig. 8.2) and breaking up larger groups called *apobaramins* (fig. 8.3).

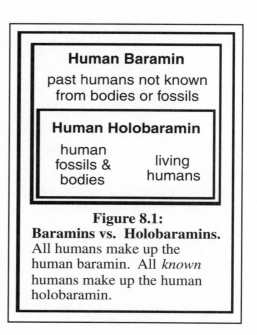

**Figure 8.1:
Baramins vs. Holobaramins.**
All humans make up the human baramin. All *known* humans make up the human holobaramin.

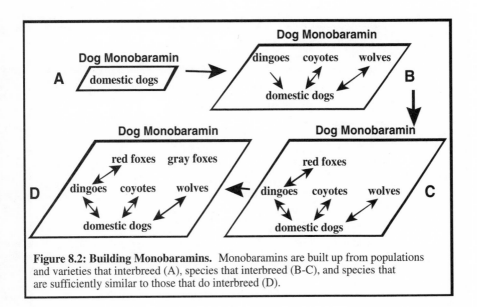

Figure 8.2: Building Monobaramins. Monobaramins are built up from populations and varieties that interbreed (A), species that interbreed (B-C), and species that are sufficiently similar to those that do interbreed (D).

Monobaramins are groups of organisms that are believed to show continuity within but that may not include all the organisms continuous with them. As organisms are added to a monobaramin, it grows in size, approaching the desired holobaramin (fig. 8.2). Domestic dogs, for example, would comprise a monobaramin because all of them can interbreed. Because wolves, coyotes, and dingoes can interbreed with domestic dogs, they can be added to the dog monobaramin. And because certain foxes can interbreed with dingoes, they can also be added to the dog monobaramin. The foxes that are not known to interbreed can still be included because of their high similarity to foxes that do interbreed with dogs. The holobaramin, therefore, is a group at least as large as the largest included monobaramin. The holobaramin containing dogs, for example, includes at least coyotes, wolves, dingoes, and foxes.

Holobaramins are also identified by dividing apobaramins into smaller apobaramins (fig. 8.3). An *apobaramin* is a group of organisms believed to be discontinuous with all other known organisms. All humans and known land animals, for example, would make up an apobaramin, because all these organisms were created on a separate day of creation

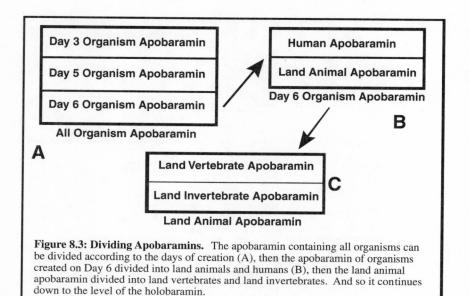

Figure 8.3: Dividing Apobaramins. The apobaramin containing all organisms can be divided according to the days of creation (A), then the apobaramin of organisms created on Day 6 divided into land animals and humans (B), then the land animal apobaramin divided into land vertebrates and land invertebrates. And so it continues down to the level of the holobaramin.

from all other organisms. And because humans were created separately from land animals (Gen. 2:7), all humans would comprise one apobaramin, and all land animals would comprise another. Since all humans are descendent from Eve (Gen. 3:20), all humans also make up a monobaramin. At some point a successively divided apobaramin becomes the same as a monobaramin as it is built up. At this point the holobaramin has been defined. The group of all known humans, for example, is both a monobaramin and an apobaramin. It is thus a holobaramin. All known humans combined with all unknown humans would comprise the human baramin (fig. 8.1).

Different Streams of Thought

The most significant challenge of baraminology is deciding when to add to a monobaramin and when to divide an apobaramin. When one organism is found to hybridize successfully with a member of a known monobaramin, that organism is added to the monobaramin. Hybridization, then, is a criterion for adding to monobaramins; it is an additive criterion. An organism might also be added to a monobaramin if it is sufficiently similar to one of its members. Sufficient similarity, then, is another additive criterion.

In a sense, conventional evolutionary theory would claim that additive criteria exist to unite all the organisms of the earth into a single monobaramin. Young-age creationists think differently. Young-age creationists are currently in the process of debating and evaluating which additive criteria are appropriate for the building of monobaramins.

Subtractive criteria are used to divide apobaramins. These criteria identify discontinuity. Conventional evolutionary theory would claim that true subtractive criteria do not exist. But such criteria not only seem to exist; they seem to *abound*. Just as thinking about how tall we want to be cannot increase our height (Matt. 6:27), there are certain things about organisms that seem inherently distinct and unchangeable. Let's look at a few.

Ribosomes, for example, are one piece of machinery in the process that makes chains of amino acids from the information on the messenger RNA. These machines are so basic to the way a cell works that disaster in cells would almost certainly result if they were changed. Yet three different groups of organisms have been found to possess distinctly different ribosomes: two different groups of bacteria (*archaebacteria* and *eubacteria*) and all other organisms (*eukaryotes*). So different are these ribosomes that evolutionists have suggested that the three different groups diverged from one another all the way back at the beginning of life. But the structure of ribosomes seems to suggest that these three groups are simply apobaramins and thus were independently derived.

Yet there are things in a cell that are, in a sense, even more basic to the existence of a cell than ribosomes. The machinery that copies the information from the DNA and puts it in the form of messenger RNA must also be constructed carefully in order to convey the proper information to the ribosomes. The machinery created to copy the DNA must also be designed carefully to minimize the errors that are transmitted to the next generation. A comparison of organisms on the earth shows there are some differences in these processes in different organisms. It is likely that some of this diversity is evidence of unrelatedness and can be used to define apobaramins.

Yet even more basic than the machinery that is used to interpret the information of the DNA is the structure of the language itself. The genetic code is basic to everything else. Even the components of each of these processes and the structure of ribosomes themselves are built from the genetic code. Just as the dividing of languages caused catastrophic failure of human social structures at the time of Babel, it would seem that the dividing of genetic codes should result in catastrophic failure of living systems. A change in the code, if not accompanied at the same time by a change in the complex machinery that interprets the code, would seem to lead to a cell that would not work. Yet the machinery itself is built from the same code and, therefore, wouldn't work if the code were changed. Several organisms, however, have been found to possess slightly different genetic codes. Since all organisms have not yet been examined for distinct genetic codes, there may be more diversity in genetic codes than is presently recognized. Each group of organisms with a distinct genetic code would seem to be an apobaramin, and therefore would have been created separately.

At a slightly higher level of organization is an organism's metabolism. This is how the organism gets energy from its environment. The diversity of mechanisms for extracting that energy is truly astounding—at least among the bacteria. Protists, animals, and fungi extract their energy from the organic molecules (food) that they are able to find in the environment. True algae and plants, of course, get their energy from the sun through the complex process of photosynthesis. (Actually, they use a particular form of photosynthesis with a particular set of pigments to grab the light, and a particular set of chemicals and devices stores that energy into particular high-energy chemicals.) The separate creation of plants (on Day 3 of Creation Week) and animals (on Day 5 and Day 6) in part reflects the fundamental differences in the way these organisms extract energy from the world around them.

Whereas all non-bacterial organisms in the world get their energy in only one of two ways, the bacteria have a great variety of energy-extraction mechanisms: (1) Some of them extract energy from organic molecules in ways similar to how animals do it. (2) Other bacteria get their energy from the sun—some with a photosynthesis pathway similar to plants, others with different types of photosynthesis. (3) Other bacteria get their energy by breaking apart molecules of nitrogen from the atmosphere. (4) Others get their energy from hydrogen gas. (5) And still others derive their energy from hydrogen sulfide gas. The origin of diversity in such fundamental processes of organisms seems difficult to explain by evolutionary process. One assumes that these bacteria are doing exactly what they are supposed to be doing, since energy is needed for any cell to survive and it would seem necessary for these organisms to have their energy-producing mechanisms functioning well. The distinct metabolisms used by bacteria have been used to divide the bacteria into phyla,[13] but they are also reasonable justification for dividing bacterial phyla into distinct apobaramins, presenting us with likely evidence of the distinct origins of these groups.

There is additional reason to separate algae, plants, protists, and animals from even the bacteria with similar metabolisms. Those who believe that all of life is related would claim that these "higher" groups had separate origins from separate groups of bacteria. But if this were the case, the characteristics shared among the "higher" organisms and not by bacteria would have had to come into being separately. Besides differences in individual components of the cell possessed by higher organisms and not the bacteria, there are also organelles of the cell such as the nucleus, the endoplasmic reticulum, and the golgi bodies. Even more fundamentally, however, sex must have come into being independently in the different groups. On the level of the organism, there is a need to get genetic information from the two parents together in the nucleus of the developing offspring. This requires a special design and machinery of its own.

Furthermore, on a finer level, there also must be a mechanism that permits the combination of the DNA in a way that still permits the organism to survive. Then there must be a different kind of process than is found in bacteria that divides the cell and copies and divides the DNA. Somehow all of these complex processes ended up the same in the different higher groups. If these groups arose separately, somehow these complex processes would have had to arise more than once—and identically! If on the other hand these groups arose from one bacterial group, then the separate origin of at least one identical metabolism must be explained. Either way, it does not seem possible to derive the diversity in metabolisms by natural process. This all seems to argue that groups of organisms with distinct metabolisms had separate origins—that they are different apobaramins—and probably that they all had separate origins from the other kingdoms of biology.

Another amazing set of differences among different bacterial groups—even among those with similar metabolisms—are those that permit the organisms to survive in what humans consider extreme conditions—conditions that would prohibit the survival of humans or any plant or animal. For example, some bacteria thrive in extreme temperatures; several live in temperatures close to the boiling point of water. These are called *thermophiles* (they are "heat lovers"). Other bacteria persist in very salty conditions—some even directly on salt crystals. These are called *halophiles* ("salt lovers"). There are also *acidophiles* that love acid conditions and *barophiles* that thrive miles beneath the earth's surface. In each of these organisms, the basic machinery of the organism has to be specially designed for those conditions.

For most organisms, high temperatures unravel the critically needed structures of the cell's machinery. In fact, the human body generates a fever to unravel the structures of invading organisms. At the same time, a prolonged high fever is to be avoided because it will eventually unravel the machinery needed in our own bodies. A high temperature does not just unravel a single necessary structure, it unravels hundreds of necessary structures and cellular machines. Similar problems arise in conditions of extreme pressure, salinity, and acidity. God has designed special chemical structures and cellular machines that can survive (and even thrive) in each of these extreme conditions. For each extreme environment God has equipped the organisms with the entire complex group of special structures and cellular machines needed by them.

If the organisms were not specially created, however, they must be derived from one another or from organisms that live in non-extreme conditions. Each individual structure must be changed in so many different ways to make this happen that it seems unlikely that such a transition could occur under natural conditions. Besides, such transitions must be made in each of an entire group of structures and cellular machines—not just one.

When all these issues are considered—genetic codes, ribosomes, metabolisms, extremophiles—the bacteria can be divided into scores of apobaramins. There is reason to believe that discontinuity is a very common feature among the bacteria. The other biological kingdoms (protists, algae, fungi, animals, plants) are divided into subgroups (called phyla) according to the most fundamental differences in the way they reproduce and develop. This is yet another level of biological organization that seems to show differences suggesting independent origin.

- The fungi-like protists are divided according to how DNA from the two parents is combined to produce the next generation.
- The algae are divided according to the pigments used in photosynthesis and, like the protists, by how cells divide to produce the next generation or produce the larger organism.
- The plants are divided according to how they reproduce.
- The animals are divided according to how they reproduce and how they develop, including the development of body symmetry.

Differences in any of these things are fundamental enough to suggest that they would be difficult to derive from one another or from another organism. It is likely that upon careful consideration, powerful evidence exists to suggest that each phylum currently defined is an apobaramin with a separate origin from the hundreds of other known phyla of the earth. As young-age creationism expects (and evolutionism does not), evidence of unrelatedness seems to abound among the earth's organisms.

Biology with Maturity

As we have discussed in previous chapters, God created things in a mature form, fulfilling function at the moment of creation. This has a number of interesting biological consequences.

Common Characteristics. Since God desires that we would be able to look at the creation and deduce that He is a single God, He separately created organisms with similar characteristics. Common characteristics across life (such as DNA) are a consequence of a common Creator Who desires to be known as such. If on the other hand the similarities are postulated to be due to common descent, then evolutionary trees can be developed. All a person has to do is assume that similarity is due to a common origin, not a common Creator. But this would be similar to the assumption made by the governor of the feast at Cana (see chap. 5). He assumed that since the wine he tasted was in so many ways similar to any other wine he had drunk, it must have come about in a similar manner (that is, it had been created by humans, not specially created by God).

Assuming that similarities in organisms are inherited from a common ancestor rather than having been specially created by God allows "family trees" of organisms to be created. More similar organisms are connected to one another by short branches, and less similar organisms are connected to one another by longer branches. But since we deduce that all organisms are created by the same God, then all organisms have similarities. Thus, all organisms can be placed successfully on a family tree— or what others call an "evolutionary tree" or "phylogeny" (fig. 8.4). Young-age creationism understands that things have been created in such a way that the data God placed there as evidence of common creatorship can also be reinterpreted as evidence of evolution.

Complete, Precision Design. The expectations of young-age creationism go even further. Since God was interested in creating mature organisms, He designed the machinery of those organisms so they could maintain themselves, repair themselves, and reproduce. DNA, for example, was created to carry information that the organism needed. Duplicational, transcriptional, and translational machinery were created to interpret and copy the DNA information effectively for the purpose of developing and maintaining the adult form. Cellular machinery, the cells themselves, tissues, organs, organ systems, and the entire organismal body were created with the same thought in mind. Whereas evolutionary theory suggests

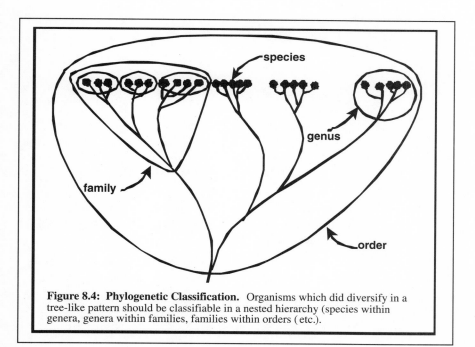

Figure 8.4: Phylogenetic Classification. Organisms which did diversify in a tree-like pattern should be classifiable in a nested hierarchy (species within genera, genera within families, families within orders (etc.).

that we have the characters we do because of the evolution of our DNA and that we are the sum total of all our parts, young-age creation suggests that we have the DNA and the parts we do because of who we are and what God created us to be.

This has many implications. It would seem, for example, that we are much more than a sum of our parts. In the "nature vs. nurture" debate, it appears that God has created us with some potential to reach beyond our parts, to overcome predispositions of nature, nurture, and even sin. This in turn seems consistent with the common scriptural claim that Christ is victor and that we can take part in His victory in a variety of ways.

Broad Similarities, Different Details. God created organisms with similarities, and He created processes of development in those organisms that were designed to generate the adult forms of those organisms. He also created organs and organ systems, tissues and cells, and even special molecules in such a way as to generate those adult forms. It might be expected, then, that similar chemical, cellular, tissue, organ, organ system, and

Bio-Evolutionary Evidence:

Homology

Homology: Similar structures in similar positions in different organisms that may or may not have very different functions.

In bio-evolutionary theory all organisms are ultimately descendant from common ancestors. Because of this, organisms should share some of the characteristics inherited from their common ancestor even if they use those characters differently. In other words, homologies should be common. Since evolution is thought to be ongoing, the more recently two organisms shared a common ancestor, the more similar they ought to be. If all organisms did evolve via the "tree of life" from a common ancestor, homologies can be used to reconstruct that tree. Thus, the fact that homologies are common and that they can be used to construct a tree-like pattern of similarity is evidence that all life evolved from some common ancestor.

developmental designs were created in organisms that are similar in their adult forms but nonetheless separately created. Further similarities might be expected because of how organisms were designed to interact with other organisms in complex ways.

Plants, for example, must be created in such a way that they create molecules that animals can break down for energy. In the same way, decomposers must be designed to break things down and create wastes that can be used as fertilizers and other necessary chemicals needed by other organisms. In like manner, for carbon, water, vitamins, and minerals to be cycled in such a way that they are never depleted, organisms all over the earth have to be built of structures, machines, and chemical processes that permit them to share such resources.

In young-age creation theory, God created all the kinds of organisms. They also were created with the capacity for substantial change. Because they are created by the same God, similar structures might be expected in similar positions (just as the same computer company makes similar keyboards for different computer models). God, however, has a form that cannot be described by a simple hierarchy (*e.g.*, although Jesus submitted to His Father's will, He was also one with Him). Reflective of this, a creationist would expect organisms were created with homologies contradicting the *single* hierarchal tree expected in evolutionary theory. Homologies also would be expected within baramins that diversified after the creation. Creationists, then, would expect abundant homology. They also would expect that homologies could be used to create hierarchal trees. In fact they can be used to make *multiple* hierarchal trees—each with homoplasies (similarities that contradict the tree).

With the common use of computers in the last few decades, it has become possible to count how many different homology trees can be made and to count how many homoplasies there are for each tree. These methods have shown that multiple trees and numerous homoplasies are the rule rather than the exception—just as young-age creation expects and evolution does not.

All of this would be expected to result in similarities of development and chemistry that reflect the similarities found in adult forms. Therefore, trees of similarity of adult organisms should then be roughly similar to trees of similarity of development as well as trees of similarity of many different chemical structures. On the other hand, God created a variety of organisms, and He created in such a way to suggest that He created them, that they were not genetically related. One might then expect that the trees of similarity built from adult forms, the trees built from ways of development, and the trees built from chemicals might be different in detail even if they are similar in a broad sense. If then, one assumed that similarity is due to common descent rather than common creation, separate phylogenies could be produced from adult forms, or from modes of development, or from any of a variety of chemicals. The young-age creationist would expect that these phylogenies should be similar in the broad sense and different in the specific sense.

Not surprisingly, then, phylogenies built in this manner are similar. And this similarity is often used as evidence of evolution. The argument typically goes that they are separate evidences of evolution and thus would not be expected to be similar unless the organisms actually did evolve from one another. These similar phylogenies would be expected with either evolutionary theory or young-age creationism. What is not expected in evolutionary theory are the many differences in the details of these trees. Yet such differences do exist. In fact, a comparison of any two phylogenies will show differences in details that are difficult to explain in evolutionary theory, but that would be expected in young-age creation theory.

The Fossil Record. These important findings form another consequence of the creation of adult forms. No created organism was derived from any other created organism. The only true transitions in earth history would be those that occurred after the creation. If God created genetic barriers to change, then transitions would be restricted to stay within those barriers (within baramins, for example). Given the short earth history in young-age creationism, transitions that took longer than the time available would not have occurred even if they were theoretically possible in a longer earth history. Additionally, for there to be fossil evidence of any transition that did occur, fossil-forming processes must have been fast enough to preserve the transition and they must have occurred at the right time and place in order to record the transition.

A few such possibilities exist in the young-age creation model (see chaps. 13 and 14 for details), but they are few in number. The young-age creation model would expect very few transitions to be evidenced in the fossil record, both because of the rapidity of the Flood and because God created organisms in their adult forms. In contrast, evolutionary theory requires that millions of such transitions must have occurred to produce the many different kinds of organisms that exist and have existed in earth history. It is also believed that the fossil record has been preserving snapshots of earth history more or less continuously for billions of years.

If most species living in the present are known as fossils, and if species have persisted for millions to tens of millions of years, it is reasonable to expect that a fairly large percentage of the millions of transitional species that have existed in the past would have been preserved in the fossil record. The rarity of transitional species in the fossil record seems to fit the expectations of young-age creationism better than it fits the expectation of evolutionary theory (see also the fossil record discussion in chap. 13).

This is especially true among the shallow marine invertebrate animals. Something on the order of 95 percent of the fossil record is of shallow water marine invertebrates, and most of those are found in just a handful of phyla. Yet there seems to be a complete absence of transitional species among these animals—even though these are the best represented animals in the fossil record! On a higher level of biological organization, the young-age creation model would also expect communities to appear suddenly in the fossil record. In the initial creation, God created mature communities. The Flood may have buried some of these communities in their entirety. Both of these expectations should result in the sudden appearance of organismal communities without much apparent development of those communities over time. And in fact, organismal communities do seem to appear suddenly in the fossil record—an observation difficult to explain in conventional theory.

Organismal Development. This particular implication of the creation of adult forms is also one of the most popular yet controversial evidences used to defend evolutionary theory. God designed organismal development in order to develop the desired adult organism most effectively. Each step in development must be capable of surviving, but each step must also be capable of generating the next step as well. The smallest unit of an organism that is capable of surviving and reproducing itself or some variation on it is the cell. It is not surprising, then, that God chose to begin the developmental pathways of most organisms with

Bio-Evolutionary Evidence:

Embryological Recapitulation

Embryological recapitulation: the stages of an organism's development (ontogeny) from a single cell to an adult that look similar to (recapitulate) the stages in the evolutionary ancestry (phylogeny) of that organism from a single cell over billions of years. In short, when ontogeny recapitulates phylogeny.

In bio-evolutionary theory, one way an organism can change is by adding stages to its development. If this happens, the adult form of an ancestor will look like one stage in the development of its descendant (*i.e.,* ontogeny will recapitulate phylogeny). Examples of embryological recapitulation should be as common as this form of evolution is.

In young-age creation theory, intrabaraminic diversification can include the insertion or deletion of developmental stages already programmed into organisms. However, if they exist at all, examples of true embryological recapitulation should be restricted to changes within baramins. Young-age creationism would expect *general* similarities between the development of an organism (God-designed development of the organism from a single cell) and the phylogeny of that organism (man-conceived evolution of the organism from a single cell). Alongside those general similarities, however, the young-age creationist expects differences in details of ontogeny and phylogeny.

Almost all examples of embryological recapitulation break down when examined in detail. There is compelling similarity between development and phylogeny in general appearance, but the differences in detail suggest the similarity is not because of embryological recapitulation. The claimed evidences of embryological recapitulation are better explained by young-age creation theory than by evolution.

a single cell. In evolutionary theory, with its assumption of natural derivation of complexity, it is assumed that the first organism on the earth was a simple one, albeit a single cell that exhibits a high level of complexity. In evolutionary reasoning, nevertheless, all organisms evolved from a single cell.

In truth, organismal development was created by God to efficiently derive the adult form of a given organism from a single cell (see fig. 8.5A). But evolutionary phylogeny proposes that, since natural process is most likely to take the easiest path, organisms developed by following an efficient pathway from a single cell to the organism of interest (see fig. 8.5B). Since this is true, the young-age creationist might expect that many times the development of an organism indeed passes through a series of steps that are roughly similar to the series of steps proposed for that organism's evolution. In other words, development should be generally similar to evolution (fig. 8.5). But at the same time, the general similarity might be expected to be contradicted by differences in the specific steps. For example, God's love of diversity might be expected to generate a wide variety of developmental details unexpected in natural process. Because of His desire to be known, He might have added even further variety.

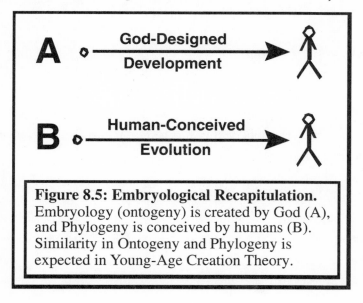

Figure 8.5: Embryological Recapitulation.
Embryology (ontogeny) is created by God (A),
and Phylogeny is conceived by humans (B).
Similarity in Ontogeny and Phylogeny is
expected in Young-Age Creation Theory.

General, compelling similarity is found to exist between an organism's development (also called its *ontogeny*) and that organism's proposed evolutionary history (also called its *phylogeny*). This similarity led Erst Haekel in the nineteenth century to propose a biologic law that "embryology recapitulates phylogeny" (also known as *embryological recapitulation*). The similarity is strong enough that it appears in many textbooks as evidence of evolution, even to this day. This is in spite of the fact that many evolutionary biologists reject embryological recapitulation. The reasons for the rejection vary, but they range from theoretical problems with the principle to abundant differences in the details between embryology and phylogeny[14]—exactly what would be expected in young-age creation theory. The similarity (and dissimilarity) between ontogeny and phylogeny is better explained by young-age creationism than by evolutionary theory.

Beauty and Perfection

Just as we saw with the heavens and the earth in previous chapters, God's nature and character are seen in other ways in the organisms He has made.

God's Glory. As clearly as God's majesty is seen in the huge objects of the universe, it is recognized even more universally in the biological creation. The beauty of butterflies and birds in the sky, corals and diatoms in the sea, flowers and fungi on the land, as well as countless other organisms have inspired the pen and brush of poets and artists for thousands of years. The beauty of the biological world testifies of the glory of its Creator, though even in its depths and ranges of beauty it can only begin to approach His splendor.

Those who believe in a Creator God have no problem with this principle. But biological beauty is challenging to explain in evolutionary theory. Organisms usually generate their beauty at some cost to the organism. Either complex chemical pigments are required or cleaver mechanisms are employed for the diffraction of light. Either way, energy is invariably expended by the organism to create and maintain its beauty. In evolutionary theory, anything that requires an investment of energy on the part of the organism should have come about only because it was necessary for the organism's survival. But the beauty of organisms—even that which is utilized by the organism for mate choice, defense, and so on—does not seem to be necessary for organismal survival. It seems to fulfill a function beyond survival: to show the abundance and glory of God.

God's Perfection. This would include His perfection in all His attributes (His perfection in beauty, holiness, knowledge, etc.). The original creation is likely to have reflected this perfection in a variety of ways. For example, it is likely that the genetic material of created organisms lacked errors. There were originally no mutations in the DNA of the earth's organisms. In the young-age creation model, all mutations have come into being since the Fall (see chap. 11). This leads us to conclude that *mutational load* (a measure of the total number of mutations possessed by an organism) started out at zero and has grown to its present level only in the last few thousand years.

Alternate models of earth history suggest that organisms have been in existence hundreds of thousands of times longer than is suggested by young-age creationism. They claim that hundreds of thousands of times more mutations have occurred in the history of life than is suggested by young-age creationism. But in these long-age models, mutations have been accumulating for so many years that unless some mechanism for cleaning out mutations exists, all organisms would have died out long ago from catastrophic errors in their DNA. No such mechanism has been discovered. It is also difficult to conceive of a way to design a system that could prevent such failure in the course of billions of years of earth history. Yet organisms do not seem to be going extinct because of high mutational loads. This suggests that organisms possess the low mutational loads expected in young-age creation theory rather than the much higher genetic loads expected in alternate models of earth history.

Because of the current revolution in genetic studies, it is now becoming possible to measure organismal mutational load directly. The young-age creation model predicts that those loads will be much smaller than expected in conventional theory—small enough to suggest that life on earth has been here only for thousands of years, not millions or billions of years.

God's Omniscience and Wisdom. Another expectation of a perfect Creator is optimality in His initial creation. One would expect the original organisms He created to have been complex (to reflect God's omniscience and wisdom) and to contain evidence of design (to showcase, in addition to His other characteristics, the Creator's provision). But out of the many potential designs that would show both complexity and design, we would expect only the best of the designs to actually be created—at every level of biological complexity and organization.

As straightforward as this expectation seems to be, however, we face two challenges in demonstrating and measuring optimality. First, there is a problem of human limitation. We simply don't know enough. A wise, omniscient God, when considering an optimal design for a particular item (let's say, the thumb of a panda) would consider optimality in all dimensions of space and time. Capable of understanding how every detail of the universe fits together with every other detail, an omniscient God would consider the optimality of the part as it relates to the whole of the entire universe, not just by itself. He would thus, for example, not necessarily give a panda the best of all possible thumbs; rather, He would give the panda the best possible thumb for what the panda *does* with the thumb. Since as far as we know, the panda utilizes his thumb only to strip leaves from a bamboo branch, an optimal thumb for a panda might be substantially different (including less complex) than an optimal thumb for a human, who uses his thumb for a greater variety of complex functions.

God also is capable of foreknowing all the conditions that will be met by organisms through time. Because of this—and in order to use them to reveal His nature to man through time—God might be expected to design organisms in such a way that they would *persist* through time. Organisms, then, would not just be created to live in the original, uncursed world (see chap. 11). They would be created in such a way that they could also live in the fallen world and in the radically different and changing world that followed the Flood. Because of this, God probably created organisms with

Bio-Evolutionary Evidence:

Suboptimal Improvisations

Suboptimal improvisations: biological structures that
are less than optimal variations on structures characteristic
of a larger group of organisms.

In bio-evolutionary theory, natural selection chooses from among the best variations available, but the direction of change (to produce variation) is random. Evolution cannot think ahead. It can only work with what is currently available and can only improve it if change just happens to go in the right direction. Because evolution is continuously occurring, there should be numerous examples of structures that are not as optimal as they could be, but are rather suboptimal—suboptimal improvisations on the structures of their ancestors.

In young-age creation theory, God optimally designed all organisms, taking into consideration the entire universe through all of time. Subsequent to the creation, however, mutation has introduced deviation from optimality, and intrabaraminic variation has produced change not optimally designed for the environment organisms find themselves in. Given that most of the biological forms were predesigned, very few if any of these suboptimal forms would be expected to be true suboptimal improvisations. Young-age creation would expect more optimality than evolutionary theory and very little, if any, suboptimal improvisations.

Very few suboptimal improvisations have been proposed (Stephen Jay Gould's panda thumb is the most famous example), and the fact that they are truly suboptimal is dubious (*e.g.,* according to conventional theory, the panda's thumb has been adequate for millions of years). The biological world seems to be more optimal than evolutionary theory expects.

a great potential for change—the ability to survive in changing world conditions. The challenge that all of this poses to us is that we as humans struggle to calculate the optimality of even a *small part* of biological design, let alone the optimality of the entire system—and even less so, the optimality of that entire system through time.

A second challenge to measuring optimality in the initial creation comes with the changes that have occurred since the creation. The consequence of God creating organisms capable of changing is that they actually did change as the world changed. An extraordinary amount of change probably has occurred among organisms since the Flood (see chap. 12). Returning to our example of the panda for a minute, it is likely that the panda species arose after the Flood—from some bear or bear-like organisms in the original creation. It is thus most likely that bears in the original creation were not created with thumbs at all.

Another source of change came with the Fall. It was because of the Fall that genetic errors (like mutations) entered the system for the first time, sprinkling the creation with imperfections. But some of these transformations may not have obliterated evidence of previous forms. Remnants of previously utilized or more fully utilized structures might be expected in currently living organisms. In fact, remnants seem to exist in the form of vestigial organs and genetic throwbacks (see chap. 14).

Our understanding of organisms and earth history is still too rudimentary to estimate the true nature of change that has actually occurred among organisms since the creation. At this point, young-age creation theory predicts *near optimality* in the present creation with an unknown amount of deviation from this. Evolutionary theory claims to predict something similar. It seems reasonable to assume that when given a choice between two structures, natural selection will tend to select the one that works better and to eliminate the one that does not. Thus, if optimal or near-optimal structures can somehow be generated (which is a substantial challenge for evolutionary theory), evolution will select the more optimal structure. Yet as Charles Darwin pointed out, history may deal an organism a less than optimal hand.

Evolution, then, expects that the world should be near perfect with an unknown amount of imperfection sprinkled in. Although neither theory can yet quantify how far organisms should be from perfection, one might figure that young-age creationism would expect the world to be closer to perfect. The rarity of arguments for imperfection seems to suggest that the world is closer to perfection than would be expected in evolutionary theory—or in any theory that suggests a very long history for life.

It's interesting to note that biologists do, in fact, study organisms as if they were designed for efficiency and perfection. When an organism is studied and found to have a bunch of parts, the biologist tends to want to know what the parts do. Therefore, the biologist is assuming that the parts are actually arranged in an integrated system, and that each part of the system fits into that system's function, as if it were designed perfectly. This approach is generally used not because the systems are *believed* to be designed (most biologists insist that organisms are *not* designed), but simply because the approach works so well. Invariably, the parts of organisms are found to have function and to fulfill that function well—as if they were designed perfectly for the larger system. Much of the active research going on in the science of biology involves the deduction of biological function and thus biological perfection.

Netted Hierarchy

We will close this chapter by looking at organisms through another attribute of God—the attribute that causes the greatest challenge to a human understanding of God: His triune nature. It has always been difficult for humans to understand how God can be both three *and* one, rather than three *or* one. How is it, for example, that Jesus can be one with God the Father and yet submissive to the Father's will? How is it that Jesus could be an "only begotten Son" yet exist without a beginning, being one with the Father? How could there be one God and yet Jesus could be baptized while the Holy Spirit descended as a dove and God the Father spoke from heaven?

On and on our questions could continue. Mankind has struggled with such questions for thousands of years—in fact, probably from the

Bio-Evolutionary Evidence:

Hierarchal Classification

Hierarchal classification: organisms are grouped by similarities into successively larger groups—extremely similar individuals being grouped into species and similar species grouped into genera, genera into families, families into orders, orders into classes, classes into phyla, phyla into kingdoms and realms.

In bio-evolutionary theory, the first organism is thought to have evolved step-by-step into all the organisms on earth today. This process involved the change of organisms and the splitting of populations into different species. Successive splitting events should cluster groups of species together into larger groups and those groups into larger groups, and so on. The hierarchal classification of species into genera into families into orders into classes into phyla into kingdoms is exactly what evolutionary theory would expect.

In young-age creation theory, God created organisms to reflect His nature. God is three distinct beings, united into one. Reflective of that nature, He created numerous distinct beings with similarities. At the same time, there is something of a hierarchy in the Godhead (*e.g.,* Christ sends the Holy Spirit to speak of Jesus, and Jesus submits to the will of the Father). One might expect, then, that the similarities God created would allow classification into a hierarchal pattern. Yet, just as the unity of the

creation. What is the structure of the Godhead? On the one hand, there is evidence of different levels of authority (Jesus' submissiveness to the Father, for example, or the Father's sending of the Holy Spirit to elevate the Son). On the other hand, the members of the Godhead are one.

An examination of the authority structures that God set up among humans suggests similar difficulties. On the one hand, there is evidence of different levels of authority (such as the husband being head over the wife, positions in the church having authority over other positions, believers being

Godhead contradicts a simple hierarchy, God created similarities to contradict simple hierarchies. This will allow the construction of *multiple* hierarchies—each with homoplasies (similarities that contradict the tree).

With the common use of computers in the last few decades, it has
become possible to count how many different hierarchies can be made
and to count how many homoplasies there are for each tree. These methods have shown that multiple hierarchies and numerous homoplasies are
the rule rather than the exception—just as young-age creation expects
and evolution does not.

Because humans were created in the image of God, a picture of how
God created can be seen in how humans make things. In many houses,
for example, one can find several different "species" of spoons that can be
classified in the spoon "genus." The spoon, fork, and knife "genera" can
be classified in the silverware "family." The silverware, dish, kitchen, linen,
and condiment-ware "families" can be classified in the tableware "order,"
and so such classification can continue. Although the items did not evolve
from a common ancestor (they were separately created), they still can be
classified in a hierarchy. At the same time, this is not the only possible
classification (*e.g.,* it can be according to what they're made from, what
store they were purchased from, etc.) Furthermore, in the first classification, there are very strong similarities between the cloth napkins in the
tableware "order" and the towels of the linen "order," placed among
forks of the tableware "order" or among the grilling instruments of the
cookware "order," and so forth. The multiple hierarchies and frequent
homoplasies encountered in the classification of man-made objects is
what one might expect in the classification of God-created objects.

commanded to be submissive to governmental authorities). On the other
hand, there is evidence that seems to contradict that (such as each spouse in
marriage having authority over the body of the other spouse, every person in
the church submitting to everyone else). As great as the human desire might
be to discern a simple structure in God's creation, the creation does not seem
to be that simple. This seems to reflect the nature of God Himself.

With the structure of the Godhead and His created institutions being
so incomprehensible to humans, it should come as no surprise that the

structure of God's biological creation is also difficult to characterize in a simple manner. The Bible, for example, classifies organisms in a variety of ways—a variety of apparently *contradictory* ways.

- In Genesis 1, organisms are classified according to the day they were created—plants vs. flying and swimming creatures vs. land animal creatures.

- In Genesis 2, organisms are classified into creatures to be named by Adam (flying creatures and some of the land creatures) vs. creatures not to be named (presumably everything else).

- In Genesis 6, organisms are classified according to those that need saving on Noah's ark (land and flying creatures that breathe air) vs. those that do not (swimming organisms and land animals that do not breathe air).

- In Leviticus 12, organisms are classified according to those that are clean for eating vs. those that are not.

Each classification was made to fulfill a different function. If applied in a strict manner to the classification of life, they produce conflicting classifications. It appears that God created organisms in such a way that they can be classified in a *variety* of hierarchies, based on the needs of the classifier. This suggests that God created organisms with a complex multidimensional network of similarity.

Evolutionists, however, suggest that organisms and the characteristics of organisms arose in a particular sequence. It has been traditional to believe that evolution occurred only once—that there is only a single phylogeny or "tree of life." It also has been traditional to believe that once organismal groups have arisen, they do not recombine with other groups or trade a lot of information. In other words, the branches of the tree of life do not fuse with other branches after they have branched. If this is true, it should be possible to group organisms together in increasingly larger groups, just as smaller branches on a tree can be grouped together with other similar-sized branches around the larger branch from which they sprang. Evolution would predict that only one such grouping would be the correct one—specifically the one that groups organisms according to how they actually evolved on the "tree of life." Evolution also predicts that such a grouping should be relatively easy to discover and should stand with few ambiguities. There should be few to no apparent branch fusings.

The fact that biologists have grouped life into successively larger groups (species within genera, genera within families, families within orders, orders within classes, classes within phyla, phyla within kingdoms) should yield powerful evidence for evolution and against the expectations of creation. And in the minds of many people, it does. But a closer look suggests otherwise. Ambiguities in biological classification not only exist; they seem to be very common.

A character that suggests a relationship different from what other characters are suggesting is called a *homoplasy.* In the popular classification method known as *cladistics,* so many homoplasies exist that computers that are running cladistics programs commonly generate not just a few, but literally thousands of equally good trees of similarity (called *cladograms*)—even when attempting to classify only a few dozen species. As we have become capable of identifying the detailed nature of genetic material, similar patterns have been recognized at the level of DNA. Because of this, it has become increasingly popular to suggest that the genetic homoplasies are somehow traded and shared among organisms (a phenomenon called *lateral gene transfer*).

As we have learned more and more about organisms, we have come to recognize that homoplasies are a very common feature of biology, both at the level of the organism and at the level of its DNA. Such ambiguity seems to be reflective of the multiple classifications of life given in Scripture. Organismal similarity seems to be arranged in a complex multidimensional network such as might be expected in young-age creation theory—and as indicative of the triune nature of God—but not in the single, unambiguous pattern expected in evolutionary theory.

Summary

It is claimed and it is true: biological evolution is powerfully evidenced. Similar trees of similarity are derived from a study of adult organisms, organismal development, and biochemistry as if they evolved in the branching pattern suggested by those trees. Organisms can be arranged in a hierarchy of increasingly large groups as if they were all derived from a common ancestor. Organisms develop along trajectories similar to the path of evolution they are thought to have traveled, and the biological world is near perfect. Evolutionary theory provides a simple explanation for each of these major features of biology and as such is powerfully evidenced by these same features.

Young-age creation theory, on the other hand, explains the same features presented by biological evolution and more.

- Creationism explains not just the similarities among trees of similarity and the similarity between phylogeny and ontogeny, but also the *dissimilarities* in these things.
- Creationism explains not just the fact that organisms can be arranged in a hierarchy of increasingly large groups, but also why there are so many characters that seem to contradict that pattern.
- Creationism not only explains the near perfection of the world, but it seems to better explain the relative rarity of imperfection.
- Creationism not only explains the similarities among organisms (used by evolutionists to argue for relatedness), but it also explains the commonness of evidence for *unrelatedness*.
- Creationism provides explanation for the incredible beauty of biology, the complexity and integration of complexity that so strongly characterizes the earth's organisms as well as the language structure of DNA.
- Creationism explains the commonness of interspecific hybridization, what seems to be a low mutational load in organisms, as well as the sudden appearance of organisms and communities of organisms in the fossil record.

Even though young-age creation biology is in its infancy, there is reason to believe that it is at least comparable—and even now may be superior—to evolutionary biology in its explanatory power.

As expected of a God Who desires to be known by all humans through all time, it appears that He created the biological world in such a way that it provides compelling evidence of its Creator for as long as it persists—even thousands of years after its creation. It also seems that He created the world in such a way that it functions as a polemic against every creation myth humans would devise to replace the truth—even against biological evolution, which would not be conceived until some six thousand years had elapsed after the creation.

What's Next?

And now, the penultimate creation—the origin of man.

CHAPTER 9

MAN

As we have already noted in chapter 6, humans were created central to God's creation in order to glorify God in a special way. Man was given dominion over the animals and the earth. Plants were created to serve as his food. The sun, moon, and stars were created as markers of time for him. Humans were the last of the creations of God and the only things created with the *image* of God. Man's sin not only brought death to man and a curse upon the world, but it also caused God to send His only Son to die in order to offer salvation—to humans alone. God even created the universe with evidence that He truly is the Creator so man could come to know God. Man is the focus of God's creation—and the focus of this chapter.

The Image of God

Man is the only creation of God that is said to possess the "image of God" (Gen. 1:26, 27; 5:1; 9:6; 1 Cor. 11:7; James 3:9). But what exactly is this "image of God"? On the most basic level, the use of the words *image* (Gen. 1:26–27; 9:6; 1 Cor. 11:7) and *likeness* (Gen. 5:1; James 3:9) suggest that man has some similarities to God—similarities that are reflective and representative of God. The Bible says that God created man "in the likeness of God" (Gen. 5:1) and that Adam "begat a son in his own likeness, after his image" (Gen. 5:3). Since sons often carry characteristics of

140

their fathers that identify them with their fathers and distinguish them from other father-son pairs, it may be that humans possess characteristics of God that likewise identify them with God and distinguish them from any other creation of God. Yet what characteristics are included in the image of God?

Although humans often are preoccupied with the physical, it is unlikely that the image of God includes physical characteristics for several reasons.

- Most of the physical attributes of humans (even artistic ability and intelligence) are found, at least in small measure, in various organisms.
- If physical attributes were part of the image of God, then the image of God would be something humans would grow into as they developed and might be able to lose as they became ill, old, or brain-damaged.
- It could be argued that some people had more of the image of God than others. But it would seem that humanness (including possession of the image of God) is something possessed in complete form from conception to death.

What appears to be confirmation of this is found in an obscure Mosaic law. In Genesis 9:6 we see that capital punishment was introduced as a response to murder because humans have the "image of God." Specific applications of this principle in the Mosaic Law can be seen in Exodus 21:12–25. One of those applications is especially interesting (vv. 22–25). According to this passage, if men were fighting and accidentally injured a pregnant woman, thereby causing injury to the unborn child, these men were to be punished "life for life, eye for eye, tooth for tooth, hand for hand, foot for foot, burning for burning, wound for wound, stripe for stripe."

Since neither the stage of pregnancy nor the gender of the child is specified, it appears that an unborn child—male or female—is being equated part for part with an adult. This in turn suggests that the image of God is possessed by both men and women and is possessed by a child from the beginning of the mother's pregnancy—from the moment of conception!

So perhaps the "image of God" has more of a spiritual orientation—for several reasons.

• Although man was created with the image of God, man is not supposed to create any physical images of God (the second of the Ten Commandments, Exod. 20:4). This suggests that the image of God that appears in humans is more spiritual in nature.

• In the New Testament, the church is called the body of Christ (Rom. 12:5; 1 Cor. 12:27), yet it is not the *physical* bodies of believers that make up the church; the spiritual natures of the redeemed make up the spiritual body of Christ.

• Since God is spirit (John 4:24), it stands to reason that a proper picture of Him would not be physical but spiritual.

Yet the angels are spirits (Heb. 1:13–14), and nowhere are angels said to have the image of God. So if the image of God is spiritual, what spiritual attributes do humans have that are so representative of God that even angels do not have them?

A Special Creation

Genesis 2:7 says, "The LORD God [*elohîm*] formed man [*âdâm*] of the dust of the ground, and breathed into his nostrils the breath of life; and man [*âdâm*] became a living soul." *Elohîm* is a plural word translated "gods" when it has a plural verb associated with it, but it is a name for the one Creator God when it has a *singular* verb associated with it (as is the case in Gen. 2:7). Implicit in this name of God is His trinity—God the Father, Son, and Holy Spirit—plural as well as singular. In Genesis 2:7 this triune God first fashioned the dust of the earth to form man—perhaps man's physical nature. He then breathed life into the physical form, and man was enlivened.

This verse suggests that man is both physical and non-physical. Man's multipart nature—being physically and spiritually representative of the triune nature of God—may be part of what distinguishes man from the rest of the creation. Although the Bible records instances where angels appear in human form, a physical form may be something they can assume but that is not inherently essential to their nature. Humans, in contrast, possess a body; they are given physical bodies even after they die (Job 19:26).

In Genesis 1:26 an even stronger association between the Trinity and the creation of man is made. God said, "Let us make man in our image, after our likeness." The Jews, who have traditionally rejected a triune God, have long interpreted Genesis 1:26 in an interesting manner.[1] They suggest this is a sort of covenant made with Adam and Eve (and potentially every husband and wife) to generate offspring together. This suggests that the generation of a human child requires something far more than the biological union of a sperm and an egg followed by natural biological processes of development. Rather, God must also take an active part in this process—probably in all aspects of development, but perhaps *especially* in the creation of the non-physical part of human nature.

This understanding is even more impressive when we consider a triune God as Creator. In the generation of another human being, the union of three—a man, a woman, and God—is a picture of His nature. The offspring would be fashioned in the image of the physical and emotional attributes of the parents *and* in the image of the spiritual attributes of God. Furthermore, since God has many attributes, it is likely that the image of God in man involves a combination of many attributes. Thus, not only would the physical/emotional/spiritual makeup of humans be a picture of the triune God, but so would the multifaceted emotional or spiritual natures of man.

As a creationist would understand it, every human is a special creation of God. Each person on earth—male or female, young or old, unborn or on life support, disabled or not—possesses in full the image of God. As such, every human is to be respected, not hated (Lev. 19:17; 1 John 3:15)—not even sworn at (Exod. 21:17; Eccles. 10:20; Luke 6:28; Rom. 12:14; James 3:9)! The image of God given to man by the Creator becomes the foundation for proper treatment of others. It is the proper rationale for developing a Christian ethic in issues as diverse as capital punishment, abortion, and euthanasia. Without this foundation, a Christian ethic will never be fully developed.

The Dominion Mandate

According to Scripture, even before man was created God intended for him to have dominion over His creation (Gen. 1:26). In what is often called the "dominion mandate," man was commanded to exercise dominion over the living things in the sea, the land, and the air, as well as the earth itself (Gen. 1:26, 28; 9:2; Ps. 8:6–8). In the hands of fallen humans, the privileges and responsibilities inherent in the dominion mandate have been abused over and over again. So what is the proper understanding of the dominion mandate?

The dominion mandate was first given to Adam and Eve in the Garden of Eden. This initial situation should be understood as normative; it should reveal how the dominion mandate ought to have been exercised. In a young-age creationist understanding of earth history, the pre-Fall world (see chap. 11 on the Fall) was without death, disease, and suffering. It was before the eating of animals for food, before the animals' fear of man. It was before the formation of most of the world's coal and oil, and it was probably in a world supplied with all the resources needed by man. When first issued, the dominion mandate was not justification for such things as eating animals, drilling for fossil fuels, or experimenting on animals to heal human diseases. Since the needs of His creation were probably supplied by God, it was not man's responsibility to provide things essential for creation's survival.

It was man's responsibility to care for and nurture the creation beyond what the creation needed to persist. This is because God is a God of abundance. He did not just offer life; He offered a more abundant life. The original function of the dominion mandate was to enhance what the creation was already doing—to bring more glory to God.

Since the dominion mandate was delivered to the first created humans and is nowhere rescinded in Scripture, the dominion mandate is an obligation of all humans across all time. It remains an obligation for us today. The Fall of man introduced a number of new applications for the dominion mandate that were unknown in the pre-Fall world. But all applications—both before and after the Fall—fulfill the same purpose. Our obligation to the creation is to enhance the glory it brings to God. It is certainly not to abuse the creation or to consume it because it is there and we are capable of ruining it.

Modern environmentalism is based primarily upon non-theistic worldviews. But a young-age creationist understanding of earth history provides a unique foundation for a Christian ethic in environmentalism. It differs substantially even from old-age creationist views of earth history, because they would claim that there was no period in human history when there was no eating of meat, disease, death, or fossil fuels. There is a need for believers to build a proper environmental ethic and to strive to fulfill the dominion mandate that we have neglected for so long.

Mature Language and Culture

Since God created humans so they could glorify God at the moment of their creation, man was created in mature form with intelligence, language capacity, and language itself. God spoke to Adam on the day man was created (Gen. 1:28–29; 2:16–17). On the same day Adam named the animals, the birds, and the woman created from him (Gen. 2:20, 23). Within a few generations, humans were living as shepherds (Gen. 4:2), farmers (Gen. 4:2), and cattle herders (Gen. 4:20). Some people lived in cities (Gen. 4:17); others lived as nomads (Gen. 4:20). Some people were constructing and playing musical instruments; others were smelting and forming brass and iron (Gen. 4:21–22). Within ten generations, a huge ship or ark was constructed and successfully navigated through the worst storm in earth history. High culture, complex language, and high intelligence seem to have been present with man from his beginning.

In a young-age creation model of earth history, the *diversity* of languages and cultures would develop *after* the creation (see chap. 15).

Language and culture were given to man *at* his creation, not developed later. Evidence supporting this has even been recognized by unbelievers.[2] Human language, for example, requires many complex characteristics.

• The brain must be wired in such a way that abstractions can be made, language can be learned, and information can be abstracted into the proper code and linguistic structure.

• The human sensory apparatus must be capable of receiving communication and translating it into a form understandable to the brain.

• Information in the brain must somehow be communicated so it can be understood.

• In the case of humans, communication is done through speech, which requires a further set of complex features.

Noam Chomsky has argued that such a multipart complexity could not have evolved step-by-step. Human speech had to arise suddenly—in complete form—just as young-age creationists claim.

Summary

Man was created with the image of God, was given dominion over His creation, and began his existence with the ability to speak, learn, and contribute to the culture. He is the special creation of God, the object of God's mercy and provision. God made him and "crowned him with glory and honour" (Ps. 8:5).

What's Next?

As creation's time clock chimed the sixth day to a close, God's creation was complete, and God labeled it "very good" (Gen. 1:31). After a day of divine rest, the creation entered a unique epoch of time—different from Creation Week that preceded it and from all of creation's history that followed. This period of time in the Garden of Eden was more or less what things were supposed to be like. The next chapter summarizes what little we know about this intriguing period of history.

PART 4

From the Garden to the Grave

CHAPTER 10

THE EDENIAN EPOCH

"Thus the heavens and the earth were finished, and all the host of them. And on the seventh day God ended his work which he had made" (Gen. 2:1–2a). Once completed, the physical world was in a perfect form. But how long did this first order last? How long were Adam and Eve in the Garden of Eden? What was it like—this period that might be called the Edenian Epoch?

How Long?

The Bible does not tell us how long this period lasted, but it does put some limits on its length. In Genesis 5:3 we are told that Adam had been in existence for 130 years at the birth of his son Seth. Since at his conception Eve considered Seth a replacement for Abel (Gen. 4:25), we know that Seth was conceived after the death of Abel. Since both Abel and his murderer Cain were born after Adam and Eve were cast out of the garden (Gen. 4:1–2), the expulsion from the garden was at least the age of Cain at the slaying of his brother subtracted from 130 years. Since maturation rates seem to be a bit longer before the Flood (see chap. 11), Cain may have been at least 30 to 60 years old at the time of the murder, putting the upper limit of Adam and Eve's stay in the Garden of Eden at 70 to 100 years.

The lack of children before the Fall poses no restrictions on time. When people live forever, the centuries that pass before or between children would mean nothing at all, and it is God's decision when children are born anyway. No biblical clues other than these are given on how long the universe remained in this perfect state. Hebrew mythology suggests that the period was seven years. This is perhaps as good a guess as any. But the number seven may have been proposed because of the significance of the number, not as a measure of actual time.

The Earth Before the Fall

What was the world like before the Fall? In many ways, it was probably similar to the present world. The sky was full of stars; the moon and the sun shone in all their glory. The galaxies we see now were in the sky over Adam's head, as were the planets. Comets were probably in place, as were rings and moons about the planets. The earth had a core, mantle, and crust. The earth had a protective magnetic field and an ozone layer. It had an atmosphere with nitrogen, oxygen, and carbon dioxide needed for its organisms. It had dry land and oceans and streams and probably great variety in all. The land and the sea were created with nutrients, with fully developed soils and sediments needed for organisms to live. Water and nutrient cycles were in motion, continually supplying the things needed for the earth's organisms.

The heavens and the earth declared the glory of God in this epoch. They showed His invisible attributes and His character; they provided compelling evidence of their Creator. The creation showed symmetry and beauty, complexity and order, unity and variety, language and mathematical precision, completeness and abundance, persistence and adaptability, provision and the centrality of man. Let's look at a few specifics:

Climactic Conditions. In Creation Week, "waters" were created above the "firmament" (Gen. 1:6–7).[1] The "firmament" was then called "heaven" (Gen. 1:8). Since the birds flew in the "firmament of heaven" (Gen. 1:20) and the sun, moon, and stars were placed in the "firmament of the heaven" (Gen. 1:14–17), it appears that whatever the waters above the firmament were, they were placed beyond the farthest stars.[2] Since "waters above the heavens" were still in existence during the time of David (Ps. 148:4), it seems that neither the Fall nor the Flood destroyed them. So whatever the "waters above" are and whatever their function may be, it appears that they serve the same function to this day, and this was no different during the Edenian Epoch.

Although some young-age creationists have suggested that the world before the Flood lacked rain and climatic seasons, evidence suggests otherwise.[3] Rain is not mentioned in the biblical text before the Flood, but this is probably because rain was too common of a phenomenon to mention in such an abbreviated description of earth history.[4] Genesis 1:14 and 8:21–22 suggest that the post-creation, pre-Flood world did experience seasons, including the climatic changes associated with seasons. Furthermore, trees preserved in what seem to be Flood sediments indicate that at least some areas of the earth's surface experienced temperate conditions before the Flood.[5] Although there is some evidence in those same trees that the earth might have been a bit warmer than it is today, there is also evidence of wet seasons and dry seasons, even early and late frosts.

Land Formations. As mentioned in chapter 7, the configuration of the continents at their creation is unknown because the Flood changed their positions substantially (see chap. 13). They may have been distributed in the form of the theoretical supercontinent Rodinia. Reconstructions of Rodinia depict the large continents we are familiar with today broken up into pieces and rearranged in orientation and relationship. Most of the continental pieces seem to have been somewhat close together, but they may or may not have been in actual contact or combined into a single land mass. We don't have enough information to determine what the configuration was. Our best guess at the time of this writing is that the continental pieces made up a group of large islands with extensive, shallow seas between them, cumulatively making up a large region of the tropical to temperate portion of one half of the southern hemisphere. The remainder of the earth's surface was probably a single huge ocean.

The Oceans. The salinity of the pre-Flood oceans is unknown. Perhaps they were created as fresh water, and the Flood later caused them to become salty. The identification and study of ocean sediments from the antediluvian world has only begun.[6] Although salt crystals have been found in some of these sediments, it is not impossible that the salinity was high only in the region where those specific sediments were deposited.[7] Much more study must be done to determine how extensive the evidence for salt in the pre-Flood oceans really is.

Since organisms that can only live in salt water today are very common in Flood sediments, some people may think the pre-Flood oceans must have been salty as well. But organisms have been created with great potential for change (see especially chap. 14), plus there are species of freshwater organisms that are closely related to species of saltwater organisms—probably part of the same baramin. Furthermore, some organisms can live in both fresh- and saltwater, and some can even migrate between the two. Therefore, it is not impossible that fresh-water organisms before the Flood may have been able to adapt to salt water after the Flood.

Although the evidence from geology and biology is inconclusive, this author is inclined to think that it is most likely the oceans of the Edenian Epoch were salty. This would be consistent with salt evidences in the sediments that we have found, and it would require less biological transformation after the Flood. The sudden mixture of fresh lake waters with salty ocean waters during the Flood may explain the origin of the extensive salt deposits we see among the Flood sediments.

Underground Springs. Another uncertainty in the Edenian world is the role of springs. Genesis 2:5–6 describes events that occurred on Day 6 of Creation Week—specifically before the creation of man. We are told that by the time of the creation of man, no rain had fallen upon the dry earth (Gen. 2:5). So a "mist" came up from the surface of the earth and watered the face of the earth (Gen. 2:6). From this watered ground, God fashioned man (Gen. 2:7), then planted a garden (Gen. 2:8a) where He would place the man He had created (Gen. 2:8b). No further reference to this "mist" is made in Scripture. Whether it was a flowing spring (as suggested by the use of the word in languages similar to Hebrew), whether it was heavy ground fog that dropped a dew, or whether it was something else altogether, the "mist" of Genesis 2:6 may have occurred only once in earth history. As a child growing up in an agricultural community, I always thought of this mist as a beautiful picture of how God prepared the soil just before creating man and planting a garden.

If on the other hand the "mist" of Genesis 2:6 persisted beyond Day 6 of Creation Week, it may have been the source of the river that ran out of the Garden of Eden. Since the river ran out of Eden and split into four rivers that ran into four different countries (Gen. 2:10–14), it seems probable that Eden was higher than the four lands around it. So the garden's source of water had to come from within the garden itself. Since Eden's river was created "to water the garden" (Gen. 2:10), it is possible that most of the garden did not receive watering from above in the form of rain or mist. This could mean it was fed by a spring—perhaps one of the "fountains of the great deep" mentioned in Genesis 7:11.[8]

Since the Hebrew word translated "mist" in Genesis 2:6 is similar to words in other languages that mean "spring" or "flow," it can be argued that the mist may have persisted after its initial function to become the source spring for Eden's river.[9] No river today divides into four other rivers (as does the river of Eden). This suggests that the topography or the water cycle in the Edenian Epoch may have been different than it is today. Perhaps many more rivers sprang from springs during this period than is the case today. We do not know. Considering the extent of the destruction of the Flood (see chap. 13), we may never know much more about the pre-Flood rivers than we are told in Genesis 2.

The Heavens. There were other characteristics of the pre-Fall world that probably differed from our present world but that we simply don't know much about. We don't know whether or not stars exploded into supernovae during this period. Also, since many of the craters on the moon and planets may date from the Flood (see chap. 13), we don't know how many craters there were before the Fall. We don't know if asteroids were in existence, or if they are the result of a catastrophe at the time of the Flood.

But the greatest difference in the Edenian earth may have been the absence of natural geological evil. The world's current earthquakes and volcanoes, for example, seem to be residual effects from the Flood—God's judgment on the sin of man (see chap. 13). There may have been no earthquakes or volcanoes before the Fall.

Life in the Garden

In some ways the organisms on earth during the Edenian Epoch were very much like today. Upon its surface and in its waters and skies, the earth contained a complex array of distinct organismal groups—from bacteria to protists, algae to fungi, plants to animals. Adam and Eve were highly intelligent, cultured, and communicative. Like every other created thing, the plants, the animals, and man declared the glory of God. They showed His invisible attributes and His character; they provided compelling evidence of their Creator. The organisms showed beauty and symmetry, order and complexity, variety and unity, mathematical precision and language, abundance and completeness, adaptability and persistence, mosaic similarity and provision.

But in other ways, the organisms of the Edenian Epoch were very different than those on earth today. Incredible changes occurred in the baramins following the Flood (see chap. 14). The baramins of the present would certainly have existed at the time of Adam and Eve, but many of the particular species with which we are familiar today probably were not. Although elephants were probably named by Adam, neither the Indian nor the African elephant species of today were probably known to him. Although one or more members of the camel baramin were probably known to Adam, it is unlikely that the dromedary, the bactrian, or the llama of today would have been. The same was probably true of cats and dogs, finches and doves, fruit trees and grasses. Although the animals were similar in general ways, they probably differed from modern species.

The Edenic world differed the most from the modern world in its lack of natural biological evil. Natural biological evil was introduced at the Fall—a consequence of the sin of man (see chap. 11). This fact alone made the Edenic world unlike our own experience. For example, God created plants to serve as food for both animals and man (Gen. 1:29–30). Thus, animals were not eaten by other animals or by man in the Edenian Epoch. The eating of meat entered the world with the Fall.

We know from Scripture that the new creation takes away the curse (Rev. 22:3), that "there shall be no more death, neither sorrow, nor crying, neither shall there be any more pain" (Rev. 21:4). Death, disease, and suffering entered the world with the Fall and will end with the creation of a new heaven and a new earth. But how could our world exist without some measure of death? Doesn't eating a carrot kill the carrot plant? Doesn't eating fruit kill the cells in the fruit? The answer to that seems to be what Scripture defines as living and dying.

In the Bible, life seems to be an attribute only of animals, man, and God. Plants are never described as living or dying.[10] "Every living thing of all flesh" and "all flesh, wherein is the breath of life" were to be taken on the ark (Gen. 6:17, 19–20). Then Noah was to take food (Gen. 6:21). The plants he took on board as food were not included among the living things. Also, by the end of the Flood "every living substance was destroyed which was upon the face of the ground" (Gen. 7:23). Yet after the Flood, the dove sent out from the ark flew back with an olive leaf in its beak (Gen. 8:10–11). Again, the green olive plant is not included among living things. Additionally, the physical characteristics often connected with "life" in Biblical passages[11] seem to be associated only with man and higher animals—not plants, fungi, protists, algae, or bacteria.

It appears then that "life"—at least as the Bible defines it—is not possessed by individual cells in our bodies, or by plants, fungi, algae, protists, or bacteria.[12] And if they are not (biblically) alive, such things cannot (biblically) die. It appears, then, that the entrance of death into the world introduced death for the first time to animals and man. Therefore, the Edenian Epoch not only lacked the natural evils of the eating of flesh, disease, and physical suffering; it also lacked the natural evils of human and animal death. It is likely that pre-Fall animals and humans somehow maintained a state of dynamic equilibrium. When a cell in their bodies ceased to operate, it was promptly replaced through the division of an adjacent cell, thereby maintaining the state of the whole organism indefinitely.

What's Next?

The Edenian Epoch was the way things should have been—or at least *could* have been. But a single act of disobedience by man fractured the structure of this idyllic creation at every level of organization, from subatomic particles to galaxies. What follows is a brief discussion of this tragic event and its effect on God's creation.

CHAPTER 11

THE FALL

The transition between the Edenian world and the antediluvian world that followed was substantial. No other change in the history of the physical universe has been so dramatic. In fact, it's likely that the sum of all the changes that have occurred since this monumental event does not begin to approach the magnitude of the drastic change recorded in Genesis 3. The world as Adam and Eve knew it took on a darker feel as the Edenian Epoch was transformed from the here-and-now into earth history.

Why?

What brought about this change in the created order? Sin. But not just anyone's sin. For example, it wasn't the sin of the angels that hastened the Fall. This is inferred from a close examination of the curse pronounced on the serpent in Genesis 3:14–15. The curse begins as if it is a curse on the reptile itself: "Because thou hast done this, thou art cursed above all cattle, and above every beast of the field; upon thy belly shalt thou go, and dust shalt thou eat all the days of thy life." It ends with a curse that seems to go *beyond* the serpent, to a being that will persist thousands of years into the future to at least the time of Christ: "And I will put enmity between thee and the woman, and between thy seed and her seed; it shall bruise thy head, and thou shalt bruise his heel." Who *was* this cursed being?

Something similar occurred in a woe pronounced upon the king of Tyre in Ezekiel 28, where the declaration was at first applied to the actual human king but then seemed to transcend him to a being that lived in the Garden of Eden thousands of years before. From these passages and others, we infer that Satan was the one who influenced both the serpent in Genesis 3 and the king of Tyre in the Ezekiel passage. Satan was cursed along with the beings he was influencing. So even before the interaction between Eve and the serpent recorded in Genesis 3:1–5, Satan himself had already sinned. Presumably, by this time the fallen angels also had followed him into sin. Yet the sin of these spirit beings did not seem to affect the physical universe, nor did God curse the physical world in response to their sin. This may be because the angels were not the focus of His creation but rather were servants of God and of the beings that possessed the image of God.

The curse was specifically a response to the sin of man. And notice that it was a response to their sin, not a direct result of it. After Adam and Eve had sinned, their perception was immediately changed, but it does not seem that the world around them changed at the same instant. After their sin, humans could apparently still live forever (by eating of the tree of life: Gen. 3:22–24). It was not the *sin* of man that caused the world to change; it was God's *response* to the sin of man—in the form of the curse.

The changes that occurred at the time of the Fall can be understood to be providential—not just in the obvious sense that they were done by God (also known as providence) but because they optimized the conditions of the fallen world. Once man had sinned, his sin would separate him from God. Unless some intervention took place, he would forever lack the ability to restore perfect fellowship with God. But God's love for man would constrain Him to sacrifice Himself for the sin of man to restore man's tainted spiritual nature. The devastation would not be as hopeless as it could have been.

But sin would not taint only the *spiritual* nature of man; it also would cause him to abuse the physical creation—everything he was given dominion over. But God was prepared even for this. The physical creation, though initially designed to last forever, was also designed by its Creator to be adjusted (cursed) in such a way that it would die. But just as redeemed man has the hope of resurrection, creation itself will one day be transformed by God into a new heaven and new earth. The curse was fatal, but not final.

The Law of the Fall

Scripture suggests that this curse was applied to the entire universe. Just like humans, for example (Isa. 50:9), the heavens and the earth "wax old like a garment" (Ps. 102:26; Isa. 51:6; Heb. 1:10–11). Just like humans (Rom. 8:23), the entire creation is under the "bondage of corruption," and it "groaneth and travaileth in pain" (Rom. 8:21–22). But we are told that it was not initially created that way. Some time after the creation it "was made subject to vanity" (Rom. 8:20). It was cursed and subjected to corruption, suffering, and aging. Yet this was done "by reason of him who hath subjected the same in hope" (Rom. 8:20). It was done so the "aged garments" of man (Rom. 8:23) and the entire universe (Rom. 8:19) could be changed (Ps. 102:26; Heb. 1:12). God did something in response to the Fall of man to cause the entire universe to age, to deteriorate, to fall agonizingly short of the perfect reflection of God it was created to achieve, though He did it for His own higher, redemptive reasons.

Perhaps this change was accomplished by the suspension of one law from the original creation—a law that restored heat energy *from* the universe to energy generators *in* the universe. With such a law (or one similar to it) still in effect, the energy of the universe would be constantly cycled and never run out. Without such a law, heat energy would be unusable and would accumulate in the universe. This is due to another natural law we know today as the Second Law of Thermodynamics (see chap. 6). The Second Law maintains that the energy of the universe tends to move toward a state of entropy or disorder. Energy tends to move from a carefully packaged form (such as in stars and molecules) to a spread-out, unpackaged form (like dissipated heat energy). A consequence of the Second Law is that complex systems tend to break down. Systems—even the universe as a whole—tend to age, deteriorate, and depart steadily further from their initial design.

The largest-scale features of the curse seem to be generated by the Second Law of Thermodynamics. Yet the Second Law predated the curse, because this same principle that deteriorates large-scale complexity also causes oxygen to pass into the blood from the air, and it causes carbon dioxide to enter the air from the blood. It also causes digestive juices to spread through the food in the intestine and provides for necessary food molecules to be taken into the blood and then into body cells. It drives waste products from the blood, and it drives life-enhancing water into the tissues.

So it appears that what caused the large-scale effects of the curse was not the introduction of a *new* law (the Second Law of Thermodynamics) but the suspension of some other law. It is interesting that something designed for good (the Second Law) in the original creation could—with as "small" a change as the suspension of another law—cause what is generally perceived as huge negative effects. This is consistent with the idea that the original creation was created by God in such a way that it could exist (at least temporarily) in a fallen state.

There is at least one more interesting side effect from the post-Fall status of the Second Law. According to this law, there is a tendency for complex systems (including the universe) to change downward (or devolve) in complexity, rather than to change upward (or evolve) in complexity. Although this is consistent with the biblical image of a creation that is "waxing old," it seems at odds with traditional evolutionary theory. For the universe—or for life—to increase in complexity since its origin, the Second Law has to be overcome somehow.

If our experience is correct (as reviewed in chap. 6), the Second Law cannot be overcome without three things: (1) an external energy source, (2) an energy converter, and (3) some sort of plan for organizing the energy. If God does not exist, all three of these things are missing from the evolution of the universe. If God does exist but does not intervene in the evolution of life, all but the energy source is missing. Although the Second Law fits into a creationist understanding of the universe's history, it seems to stand as a significant theoretical barrier to non-theistic histories.

The Death of Eternal Life

According to Genesis 2:16–17 and Romans 5:12–21, death entered the world as a result of the sin of man—as a result of the Fall. This was not just spiritual death but physical death as well, as shown in Genesis 3:22–23 where Adam and Eve were banished from the garden; otherwise, they could have lived forever by enjoying access to the tree of life. That this death—physical death—was shockingly new to the economy of the creation seems clear in the repetition of the haunting phrase "and he died" in the genealogy of Genesis 5 (found in no other genealogy of Scripture).

In chapter 10 it was argued that aside from God, only animals and man seem to have life in the biblical sense. It is likely, then, that death in the biblical sense is possible only for animals and man. Young-age creation theory suggests that the physical death that came as a result of man's sin was imposed upon both man and animals as part of the "bondage of corruption" of Romans 8, as it applied to the biological creation. That this is possible is evident in the fact that all living things (all humans and animals) ate only plants before the Fall (Gen. 1:29–30). This means that before the Fall, animals did not kill other animals for food. And since young-age creationism proposes that there was no disease before the Fall, animals would not have died from disease, either.

The inclusion of animals in the death sentence on human sin also clarifies the strong association between human sin and animal sacrifices. Since death was the penalty for sin, sin could be addressed only by death. Since plants do not have life as the Bible defines it, plant sacrifices would have been unacceptable. There were to be offerings of crops and plants in man's worship of God, but not as sacrifices for sin. With animal death being a consequence of the sin of man, the death of any animal stands as a strong reminder of the significance of man's sin. Even the death of a pet tends to be traumatic, and there is good reason for this. More than emotional trauma is associated with the death of an animal; there is also spiritual trauma as the animal's death reminds us of our own depravity. In other theistic origins models, animal death preceded man's sin and is thus part of God's mode of creation. The young-age creation model for the origin of death is more consistent with a good and merciful God.

The Cost of the Curse

With the onset of the curse and its resultant death and deterioration, many of the expectations and experiences that were known and enjoyed during the pre-Fall world were radically changed, leaving us with many problems.

Mutations and Disease. One effect of the Fall was the lessening of efficiency in biological systems. Before the Fall, genetic information was apparently copied without error—or at the very least, all copying errors were corrected. The mechanism by which this occurred is unknown, but for biological systems to persist indefinitely, errorless copying seems to be essential. Beginning after the Fall, genetic copying errors (such as mutations) entered the world and began to accumulate in the DNA of organisms. Some mutations compromised the design of the organism, leading to failed or impaired function. This led to diseases such as diabetes and sickle-cell anemia.

Some mutations caused entire populations of organisms to change their behavior and begin to hurt other organisms, taking more away from them than they gave back—even to the point of death. Examples are parasites and pathological bacteria. In the young-age creationist model, these diseases are the result of small imperfections in otherwise magnificently designed systems. This would explain how two similar strains of Ebola could impact humans in such radically different ways: one not harmful at all, the other one of the deadliest disease organisms known to man. Young-age creationism suggests that mutations are a

Bio-Evolutionary Evidence:

Mutation

Mutation: an error made when cells copy DNA—usually the loss, insertion, or change of a nucleotide in a DNA molecule.

In bio-evolutionary theory, mutation is thought to have been a part of life from its very beginning—for more than four billion years. Mutation is thought to be the major source of the genetic change needed for organisms to evolve their way through the "tree of life."

In young-age creation theory, mutation is thought to have begun only after man's Fall, some six thousand years ago. Given that organisms were created optimally, mutation is thought to have gradually degenerated the perfect genetic information God created in organisms during the Creation Week. Mutation is probably responsible for much of the pathology (disease) of the world.

Of carefully studied mutations, most have been found to be harmful to organisms, and most of the remainder seem to have neither positive nor negative effect. Mutations that are actually beneficial are extraordinarily rare and involve insignificant changes. Mutations seem to be much more degenerative than constructive, just as young-age creation theory would suggest. Additionally, the number of mutations in organisms seems closer to the number that might be generated in thousands rather than billions of years of life history.

recent rather than an old feature of life. The low mutational load of organisms (see chap. 8) seems to confirm this expectation of young-age creation theory.

Overproduction. Before the time of the Fall, organisms were supposed to reproduce until they filled the earth. It is likely that once this happened, the generation of young would cease. This in turn suggests that God fashioned organisms with efficient reproductive mechanisms that produced only as many offspring as needed, expecting all of them to survive. Unless this changed at the Fall, disease and death would gradually (or perhaps quickly) wipe out organisms on the earth. To counter this, God apparently introduced overproduction into the biological world. Since many organisms would die before they reproduced, more offspring had to be produced than would survive. This explains the extra work that man had to do after the Fall (Gen. 3:18–19)—to get rid of certain plants (weeds) that were overproducing and competing with the desired food crops.

Natural Selection. God created organisms to survive not just before the Fall but through changes in the earth that He knew would follow after the Fall. This shows that He created a great capacity in organisms to change and to pass those changes on to the next generation. This hereditary variation combined with overproduction to become what is commonly known as "natural selection." Organisms were forced to struggle against other organisms for limited resources. Those that were able to adapt to changes in those resources or to specialize on different resources tended to survive. Natural selection in young-age creation theory is a process created by God to maintain His creatures through changes on the earth that followed the Fall.

Thorns. With the introduction of disease and the overgrazing that came as a result of overproduction, the plants became prone to extinction unless they were protected. God apparently provided thorns and tannins to accomplish this task. This explains why thistles and thorns came after the Fall (Gen. 3:18).

Carnivory. Animals were also at risk of being wiped out by disease unless some mechanism was introduced to protect them. The eating of flesh, or carnivory, seems to fulfill that function. Since carnivores tend to eat the slower prey, diseased and young organisms are the ones most often eaten. This increases the fitness of the entire population. As awful as animals eating other animals seems to be, it is providential in a world where disease reigns.

Exactly when all these changes occurred is not clear. Whether organisms were transformed immediately or whether they produced these

Bio-Evolutionary Evidence:

Natural Selection

Natural selection: the preferential survival of those individuals
with heritable characters that give advantage to them in the
environment in which they find themselves. Charles Darwin
introduced this theory in 1859.

In bio-evolutionary theory, natural selection is thought to have been a
part of life from its very beginning—more than four billion years ago.
Natural selection is thought to be how advantageous changes are chosen over other changes and thus ultimately how organisms have
changed through time.

In young-age creation theory, natural selection was a process God
introduced following man's Fall about six thousand years ago. Natural
selection is a natural consequence of two things—heritable variety and
overpopulation. In the Creation Week God established heritable variety
in organisms to perpetuate the variety that reflects His nature. With the
Fall of man, the entrance of mutation, death, and disease would have
destroyed that variety unless something was introduced to maintain it.
God apparently did this at the Fall by introducing "overproduction"
(organisms producing more offspring than would survive long enough
to create offspring of their own). The resulting natural selection functions to *preserve* the variety of organisms in the face of mechanisms that
tend to destroy it.

In carefully studied cases (*e.g.,* the famous peppered moth) natural
selection (1) involves rather small changes, (2) usually dampens change (*e.g.,*
the increase in numbers of dark peppered moths during the second half of
the nineteenth century was reversed during the first half of the twentieth
century), and (3) works most effectively in taking out harmful mutations.
Natural selection seems to act more to prevent organisms from changing (as
suggested in young-age creation theory) rather than facilitating their change
(as suggested in evolutionary theory).

changes in the years, decades, or centuries after the Fall is not clarified in Scripture. Based upon fossils found in what we interpret to be Flood sediments, we infer that carnivory and disease had become widespread by the time of Noah's Flood. We thus know only that the transformations occurred somewhere within the nearly two thousand years that separated the creation from the Flood.

The young-age creation model suggests that these biological evils of death, disease, struggle for survival, poisons, thorns, and carnivory were all a consequence of man's sin. Other theistic models of origins are forced by their time lines to claim that all these things preceded man's sin and are part of the world the way God created it. Since this seems to strain the conventional understanding of goodness and mercy, the young-age creation model for the origin of biological natural evil is more consistent with the nature of God as revealed in Scripture.

The Human Impact

The curse's impact upon the universe and biological life was deep and far-ranging. But humans felt this impact more strongly, since many aspects of the curse were focused on man alone—primarily because of his greater responsibility.

Toil and Labor. Man had been given a dominion mandate, to care for and nurture God's creation. The sin of man brought a curse on this creation. Rather than the joyful experience it had been before, caring for the creation became a daunting task—simply to survive! Before the Fall, the tasks man had were probably rewarded with enjoyment similar to the refreshment we receive in participating in our favorite hobbies. Some people invest a lot of time in their hobbies yet never tire because they seem to be uplifted at least as much as they labor. It was probably the same before the Fall with everything man did. After the Fall, though, it was a different matter. It would take great effort from then on to carve out a living (Gen. 3:17–19).

Insurmountable Problems. Before the Fall, man did not have to care for the physical needs of the creation. But there were times after the Fall when the survival of portions of the creation would be at risk. Man would be beset with the challenge of deciding how to deal with this, being responsible for the outcome no matter what he chose to do.

Man Vs. Animals. Before the Fall, animals did not die. After the Fall, animals would not only die, but man would be forced to kill them in order to atone for his sin. After the Flood (Gen. 9:2–3), the animals would be given an innate fear of man, and man could kill them for food. The ravages of disease, the failures in the struggle for survival, the attacks of animals upon man, and the animals being eaten by other animals would be agonizing, continual reminders of the consequences of human sin and the inadequacy of man to fulfill the dominion mandate.

Human Suffering. Much more pain would be involved in the activities of life, like child-bearing (Gen. 3:16)—a kind of pain exceeding that which is necessary to alert us to danger, such as when pain tells us to take our hand off the stove to keep from being burned. This new level of pain and suffering—death, disease, human abuse—would cause emotional, physical, and spiritual suffering that never existed before the Fall.

Shame. According to Scripture, Adam and Eve were naked before the Fall (Gen. 2:25), with nothing to hide and nothing to be ashamed of. But as soon as they sinned, they became ashamed of their nakedness, apparently because it represented their sinful condition. They made clothes from fig leaves (Gen. 3:7) and hid themselves from God (Gen. 3:8). After God pronounced the curse, He killed an animal to make clothes for Adam and Eve (Gen. 3:21).

In this death—perhaps the first biblical death ever to occur on earth—God graphically showed man the consequences of his sin. Imagine the horror that Adam and Eve must have felt at seeing the death of an innocent animal, impressing upon them the magnitude of their sin. It was a first glimpse of what they had done—and of what would have to be done to redeem them. Fig leaves were not to be a proper covering, since blood would have to be shed for their sin. It would require the death of a living being.

This means that at its deepest level, the primary function of clothing is to be a covering for sin—a reminder of human depravity. To be unclothed before another person suggests that there is nothing to be ashamed of before that person—that there is no sin between them. This is appropriate between husband and wife as they become one and transparent with each other. But it is inappropriate in any other situation. In fact, to flaunt nudity is akin to claiming sinlessness, wanting no accountability to anyone for any sin. Since all other purposes for clothing (such as protection, warmth, and comfort) are secondary, the sin-covering function of clothing provides a foundation for a proper Christian ethic on apparel.

A final consideration concerns medicine. In the young-age creation model, all human suffering—physical, emotional, and spiritual—comes after the Fall. Suffering was not part of the original creation, was not the norm, and is ultimately a consequence of human sin. According to Scripture, we are commanded to relieve the suffering of others. We are to give the gospel to those who are spiritually suffering—those heading for hell. We are to confront those who are sinning, encourage the weary, and comfort the hurting. We are to give bread to the hungry and drink to the thirsty.

In each of these cases, we are to address departures from the norm. Before the Fall, people were not heading for hell. They were not sinning, weary, or hurting. They were not starving or suffering from dehydration. We have a responsibility, then, to address the suffering that has come as a result of human sin. This applies to medicine and the healing of disease. There is apparently no clear biblical mandate to heal others in any way other than by prayer in faith. Young-age creationism provides a biblical justification for medicine that is not provided by any other perspective. In no other perspective (including any other Christian perspective) is there a normative condition better than what we currently experience—a time when things were better than they are now. In fact, consistently applying a Darwinian perspective might suggest that the stronger should eliminate the weak, rather than try to keep them alive.

What's Next?

Now cursed, the creation entered a new era. Henceforth at every level of organization, the creation "groaneth and travaileth in pain" (Rom. 8:21–22). In that sense, the creation was more similar to what we have today than it was to the Edenian Epoch that preceded it. On the other hand, the great reworking accomplished by the Flood had not yet occurred. In many ways, this pre-Flood world still had vestiges of the creation that would seem quite unfamiliar to us today. Some highlights of this second major epoch of earth history will be summarized in the next chapter.

CHAPTER 12

The Antediluvian World

The world that existed between the Fall and the Flood—also known as the antediluvian world—was quite different from the worlds before and after. The Bible tells us very little about it, but it does speak of humans living between these two events for nine centuries! For most of the information we have about the antediluvian world, we must lean on inferences from the evidence that remains—largely the evidence left in the fossil record of the Flood, which we have just begun to unravel in such a way that we can picture the world destroyed in the days of Noah more clearly.

Because there is so much to learn and so little has been done, this will be one of the most exciting areas of young-age creation research in the years to come. It is also likely that the ideas expressed below will be modified greatly in the course of time. If the conclusions of science are to be taken tentatively, this is certainly the place for it. Yet the nature of the antediluvian world remains a most interesting, intriguing quest.

The Floating Forest

The God Who loves diversity because of His triune nature seems to have created organisms in a fascinating array of unique communities—communities that were destroyed in the Flood. After the Flood, land animals and much of their food had to disperse from the same location. This means that the different communities we know today developed from similar stock. So the differences among present communities are probably much less than the differences originally created in antediluvian communities.

For example, more than 88 percent of the plant species in the present world are classified in one division (or phylum) of plants—the *Anthophyta,* or flowering plants. If we are properly identifying the rocks that were formed in post-Flood times, it seems that flowering plants have been the dominant plant on earth since the Flood. But that may not have been the case *before* the Flood—at least not everywhere on earth.

The lowest great division of Flood rocks was originally called the Primary.[1] Although the Primary rocks contain many plant fossils (most of the world's coal, for example), they contain no anthophytes at all. Instead, the plants are from divisions that are either extinct or are represented in today's world by relatively few species. Actually, most of the fossils of the Primary—including sediments closely associated with those containing plants—were not plants at all but sea creatures. Even most of the world's coal (which is formed from a dense accumulation of plant material) is surrounded and even invaded by sediments containing fossils of sea creatures. It is almost as if the plants of the Primary were somehow associated with the animals of the ocean.

Based upon this, it has been proposed[2] that the Primary plants actually formed the basis of a large floating forest biome. Based upon how much organic material made up the coals of the Primary, this floating forest may have been subcontinent-sized or even continent-sized. The basic structure was probably broadly similar to the "quaking bogs" found on a number of lakes in the upper midwestern United States. Quaking bogs are floating vegetation mats whose outer edges are made up of aquatic plants.

These aquatic plants expand the edge of the mat by means of root-like extensions known as *rhizomes*. Farther in from the edge of the mat, where plants have been growing for some time, the intertwined rhizomes are dense enough to capture a bit of soil in which small land plants can grow. Even farther in, where the mat is thicker and has been there longer, enough soil accumulates for larger plants to grow. This increase in soil quality continues as the distance from the open water increases, until a soil layer thick enough to support full-sized trees and all the understory plants of an entire forest is developed. These floating plants also provide a home for animals. This makes the quaking bog an entire complex ecosystem with everything from bacteria, to protists, to algae, to fungi, to plants, to animals.

A similar ecosystem is proposed for the floating forest biome of the antediluvian world. Since the choppy seas of the Flood probably destroyed the floating forest from the outside in, the plants on the edge of the floating forest were probably the lowermost plants of the Primary. The plants just inside the edge of the floating forest were probably buried next, and so on. This hypothesis provides an explanation for a number of features of the fossil record of the Primary.

First, the floating forest biome is not likely to have been able to re-form in the choppy seas following the Flood. This would explain why most of the "land" plants and "land" animals of the Primary are extinct today.

Second, the plants from the edge to the center of such a floating forest would progress from plants that loved water and needed it to survive to plants that needed less water. The series of divisions of plants in the Primary shows just such a progression—from those plants that require standing water for reproduction to those that need less and less standing water.

Third, the plants in the Primary from the bottom up show a progression from short to tall—just as is true in quaking bogs today.

Fourth, most of the plants in the Primary do not have true roots. They have rhizomes instead—root-like structures that seem to be incapable of penetrating true soils. But they would be capable of intertwining with rhizomes of other plants to create a floating forest.

Fifth, many of the plants of the Primary—especially the large ones—are hollow. Very often their rhizomes, their branches, and even their main trunks contain large cavities as if the entire plant was designed to weigh less for the purpose of floating.

Sixth, the most common rhizome in the coal plants, *Stigmaria,* is hollow, circular in cross-section, and large in diameter. Departing at right angles to the surface of this rhizome in every direction around it are small, hollow rootlets. Neither the rhizomes nor the rootlets seem to be designed to penetrate soils, but they are similar to the smaller-scale root-like structures of several plants that float in water.

Seventh, among the animals preserved in the Primary sediments are large amphibians that seem to be morphological intermediates between fish and land animals. Such animals would seem to be designed to live in the pools of water that might be scattered along the floor of such a floating forest—in the ecologically intermediate position between sea and land that such pools would afford. The floating forest biome must have been beautiful and (from our perspective in the present) bizarre.

The Dinosaur and More

But what most people want to know when it comes to the fossil record is where the dinosaurs fit into the biblical picture. Since dinosaurs are known to us from sediments we believe to have been deposited in the Flood, they must have lived in the pre-Flood world. Since the dinosaurs are land animals,[3] they must have been created on Day 6 of the Creation Week and lived on the earth at the same time as man in the pre-Flood world.

Now before one starts thinking of scenes from the film *Jurassic Park* or the like, the fossil record gives us more information of value. In the same layers with the dinosaurs, we tend to find animals and plants that we either don't see at all on the earth today or see only infrequently. There are animals found with dinosaurs that are classified as mammals (based upon their teeth) but are strange mammals. With the possible exception of the opossum, no modern mammal group is found with the dinosaurs.

As for plants, flowering plants tend to be found only rarely with the dinosaurs. Instead, the dinosaurs are generally found with gymnospermous plants—the "naked seed" plants that do not have flowers. In the present world, the naked seed plants (like cycads and ginkgos) appear to be rarer than they were in association with the dinosaurs. This suggests that the dinosaurs probably ate gymnosperms rather than flowering plants. Since they ate different foods, it is likely that dinosaurs lived in a separate location from humans. In fact, the gymnosperms probably formed the foundation of a separate biome than the one in which humans lived. Perhaps one or more island continents housed the gymnosperm-dinosaur biome, while other island continents housed the angiosperm-mammal-man biome.

It is also likely that the gymnosperm-dinosaur biome was located at a lower altitude or closer to the shore of the antediluvian world. This would explain why members of the gymnosperm-dinosaur biome are consistently buried beneath members of the other biome. This is also consistent with the biblical claim—inferred from Eden's river—that the Garden of Eden was a high point geographically.

Stromatolite Forests

A continent-ringing hydrothermal biome may be yet another unique biome of the antediluvian world.[4] Dome-shaped structures (known as *stromatolites*) are made of layers upon layers of organic material alternating with some sort of sediment such as sand. The organic layers of modern stromatolites are made from communities of bacteria and are rare and relatively small in the present world. They tend to grow in extreme environments such as hot springs or salty bays. These bacterial communities provide desirable food for a variety of animals. This may explain why they tend to be small and grow only in places where browsing animals are not likely to live.

In the fossil record, however, stromatolites tend to be relatively common, at least in what seem to be antediluvian sediments. Sites examined by the author tend to have a lot of evidence of hot spring activity and seem to be located near the margins of pre-Flood continents. It may be that offshore, around some of the antediluvian continents, God created a long, wide zone of hot springs that generated ideal living conditions for algae and bacteria to produce extensive stromatolite reefs. These hot springs may have been more of these "fountains of the great deep" that were broken up at the beginning of the Flood.

Perhaps this catastrophic breakup is why such stromatolite reefs no longer exist in the present.

It is also possible the strange organisms that currently inhabit scattered hot springs on the land and vents in the ocean ultimately were derived from these extensive antediluvian communities. Like coral reefs of today, the offshore stromatolite reefs may have protected a lagoon between the reefs and the shoreline from severe storms. In these lagoons—perhaps especially in the warm waters closer to the reefs—the strange animals that get preserved in the lowermost Flood strata may have lived.

Human Longevity

Perhaps no other issue about the antediluvian world has generated more discussion than the long life spans of humans as recorded in Scripture. Genesis 5 lists one lineage of ten generations between the creation and the Flood, with the average human life span listed there exceeding nine hundred years. In Genesis 11, another lineage of ten generations is given, this one between the Flood and Abraham. In this genealogy, the generation time drops from the 950 years that Noah lived to the 205 years that the father of Abraham lived. Although it has been suggested by many that the change in life spans was due to environment, it is more likely that the change was genetic. Several observations lead to this conclusion.

First, experimentation on animals has been unable to increase the maximum death age of organisms by changing their environment. Organisms can be killed early by the environment (for example, you can roll a rock over them!), and organisms can be protected by the environment in such a way that they live a greater percentage of their maximum life span.[5] However, the maximum life span seems unaffected by external factors.

Second, the change in human life span documented in Scripture occurred over a long period of time. In fact, Moses' generation was still living consistently for 120 years[6] approximately one thousand years after the Flood. Although temperature and rainfall changed during this period (see chap. 14), none of the changes that we think might have occurred seem capable of changing human longevity.

A third consideration is that the change in life span after the Flood seems to be smoothest when the life spans are graphed against generation time rather than actual time of birth or mid-life. It seems that the life span of humans was changed by a set percentage each generation. Such a change sounds like a genetic change over the generations.

A final consideration is that although aging is not fully understood, it appears that it is genetically controlled. Early in development, cells in our bodies divide to take the place of adjacent cells that die. If this function were never turned off, it is likely that human organs could be maintained much longer than they are. Based upon the longevity of antediluvians, our bodies would probably last for nine hundred years! But most cell types in the body quit replacing adjacent cells at some point. After this, tissue degenerates. In different tissues there is a different moment when replacement actually stops, and the body ages as more and more tissues deteriorate in this manner. The life span of the human body, then, is programmed in the genetics of the cells.

It is likely that a different programming existed in the antediluvian world. At this point we do not know what that initial programming involved or how that programming changed.[7] This is probably the kind of thing that researchers into the aging process will identify in the years to come.

What's Next?

The idyllic Edenian Epoch was terminated abruptly because of God's response to the disobedience of man. His reaction to man's disobedience also led to the sudden end of the antediluvian world that followed, mirroring the universe-changing catastrophe of the Fall with the world-changing catastrophe of the Flood in the days of Noah. Because the Flood is closer to us in time, much more is known of its physical events than of those before it. But the magnitude of the catastrophe will probably always elude our comprehension. The next chapter touches on what we think happened during this incredible divine judgment.

PART 5

FROM NOAH TO THE NEW EARTH

CHAPTER 13

THE FLOOD

According to 2 Peter 3:3–8, in the last days of earth history, people will scoff at the idea that Jesus Christ will come again. Desiring to follow their lusts, they will choose to believe they will never be judged for their sins. The passage further states that among their reasons for doubting a coming judgment is their denial of two facts from earth history: the Creation (because it would mean there was an authority over them with the right to judge) and the Flood (because it would mean that mankind had been judged at some point in the past). We have already discussed some of the evidence that must be ignored in order to reject a creation. We will now consider some of the evidence that must be ignored in order to reject the Flood.

Local or Global?

Scripture makes it clear that the Flood in the days of Noah was global in extent—that is, it covered the whole face of the planet earth.[1] Both the Genesis account and other biblical mentions of Noah and the Flood leave little doubt of this:

The purpose of the Flood was the destruction of all humans, all land animals and birds, and even the earth itself (Gen. 6:5–7, 11–13, 17; 7:4). A global flood was the only way to fulfill this purpose, given the world-wide distribution of humans and animals.

The ark would not have been necessary if the Flood had been local, because man and animals could simply have moved to another region. Even with only hours of warning, for example, Lot was given a chance to escape from Sodom. In the case of the Flood, Noah may have been given 120 years warning.[2] He at least preached righteousness for some time leading up to the Flood (2 Pet. 2:5).

The description of the Flood utilizes inclusive terms. "The same day were *all* the fountains of the great deep broken up" (Gen. 7:11, emphasis added). "*All* the high hills, that were under the *whole* heaven, were covered" (Gen. 7:19, emphasis added). "And *all* flesh died that moved upon the earth, both of fowl, and of cattle, and of beast, and of *every* creeping thing that creepeth upon the earth, and *every* man: *all* in whose nostrils was the breath of life, of *all* that was in the dry land, died. And *every* living substance was destroyed which was upon the face of the ground, both man, and cattle, and the creeping things, and the fowl of heaven; and they were destroyed from the earth: and Noah *only* remained alive, and they that were with him in the ark" (Gen. 7:21–23, emphasis added). "The waters were on the face of the *whole* earth" (Gen. 8:9, emphasis added).

The depth of the Flood waters necessitates a global Flood. "All the high hills, that were under the whole heaven, were covered" (Gen. 7:19), "the mountains were covered" (Gen. 7:20), and only after the water had come *down* for a while "were the tops of the mountains seen" (Gen. 8:5). Long before the water was high enough to cover the mountains, the entire earth would have been covered.

The biblical terminology is descriptive of a one-time global Flood. The Hebrew word translated "flood" in the following passages is *mabbul* (Gen. 6:17; 7:6–7, 10, 17; 9:11, 15, 28; 10:1, 32; 11:10). Whereas other Hebrew words are used to describe a variety of floods, this particular word is used only for the Flood in the days of Noah.

The promise of God evidenced by the rainbow declared that the Flood would never occur again (Gen. 9:8–17). If the Flood of Noah's time had been local or even regional, each of the millions of local and regional floods that have occurred since the time of Noah would have broken that promise.

The rivers described in Genesis 2 exist today in a much different arrangement. Something must have radically changed the topography of the Middle East in order to destroy the river system that originally flowed from the Garden of Eden to water surrounding regions. Local and regional floods are incapable of producing that much change.

The length of the Flood was too long for a local or regional flood (one year and ten days: compare Gen. 7:11 and Gen. 8:13).

The Flood disrupted the summer/winter cycle of the earth. This is consistent with the length of the Flood and is strongly implied in Genesis 8:22, where God promised that "while the earth remaineth, seedtime and harvest, and cold and heat, and summer and winter, and day and night shall not cease." This is more than would be expected of local or regional floods.

The Bible equates the Flood with other global events. In 2 Peter 3:3–7, three events are listed as among the most significant in earth history: the Creation, the Flood, and the judgment to come. The worldwide (even *universe*-wide) nature of the first and third events suggests that the second—the Flood—was global in extent. Jesus Christ drew a similar comparison when He said that His return would be "as it was in the days of Noah" (Matt. 24:37 NIV). The global impact of Christ's return suggests the global impact of the Flood of Noah.

A recent global Flood also provides a good explanation for the widespread nature of Flood traditions in the different cultures of the world. Scores of cultures have Flood traditions, and most of them cannot be explained by these cultures having had contact with missionaries or others bringing the Scriptures to them. Non-creationist theories of human history have difficulty explaining the similarity among such diverse traditions (see also chap. 15).

Under the Surface

But how did this global Flood come about? And what lasting changes did it leave behind in its cataclysmic wake? Let's begin with Genesis 7:11, which refers to "fountains of the great deep" existing on the pre-Flood earth. These fountains were probably springs scattered across the earth's surface, both on continents and in the oceans.[3] In what seems to be the major geologic event in earth history[4]—the Flood—the Bible claims that all these fountains were broken up on a single day (Gen. 7:11). Perhaps their breaking up resulted in the shattering of the earth's crust at numerous locations. We know that the current ocean crust is broken into a number of different pieces or plates. Perhaps it was early in this Flood that the earth's crust was broken into its present plates. The present and past motion of these plates is described in a theory called *plate tectonics*. This activity takes some doing to explain, but it yields some simple expectations.

Any rock has a melting point—a temperature above which the entire rock is liquefied. But if we heat a solid rock toward its melting point, some of the minerals in the rock that have lower melting points begin to melt and separate from the original rock before the melting point of the entire rock is reached. Because this partial melt does not contain all the minerals of the original rock, it winds up with a different composition.

When the rocks that we infer to exist in the earth's mantle are partially melted like this in the laboratory, the partial melt cools to form basalt. When basalt is partially melted, the partial melt cools to form andesite. According to *sea-floor spreading theory* (which is part of *plate tectonics theory*), the partial melt from mantle rocks rises between spreading plates and is then plastered to each plate along the separation line (A in fig. 13.1), so that the farther one gets away from the separation line, the older the ocean crust is. Based upon laboratory melting studies, this molten rock should cool as basalt. Since all the ocean crust is thought to have been formed in this manner, basalt should then be found beneath ocean sediments across all oceans (fig. 13.1). Just as volcanoes have to be fed by molten rock, and therefore ocean floor volcanoes have to be fed by molten *mantle* rocks, ocean floor volcanoes should also be made of basalt (fig. 13.1).

Because cooler rock shrinks, the ocean floor is expected to stand highest at this separation line and to become gradually lower away from it—as the rock cools. This means the separation line should stand up as a linear

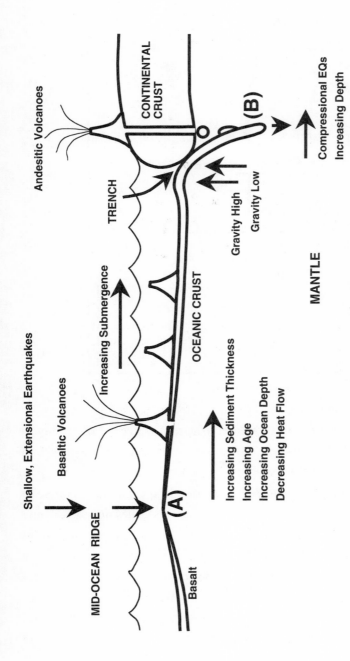

Figure 13.1: Simplified Cartoon of Sea-Floor Spreading Theory and Its Predictions. The ocean crust sinks into the mantle at the trenches (B) and is created at the mid-ocean ridges (A). The age of the ocean floor features should get older away from ridge, so ocean depth and sediment thickness should increase and heat flow should decrease away from the mid-ocean ridge. Sinking crust will cause trenches and low gravity anomalies in them, as well as high gravity anomalies seaward. Earthquakes will be shallow along the mid-ocean ridge and show extension. Most of the rest of the ocean floor earthquakes are compressional and are found at the trenches and hardwired at progressively greater depths. Volcanoes on the ocean floor should be basalt. There should be andesitic volcanoes just landward of the trenches.

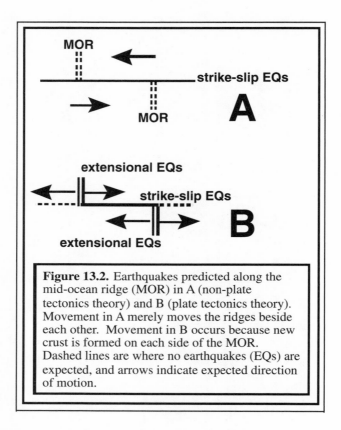

Figure 13.2. Earthquakes predicted along the mid-ocean ridge (MOR) in A (non-plate tectonics theory) and B (plate tectonics theory). Movement in A merely moves the ridges beside each other. Movement in B occurs because new crust is formed on each side of the MOR. Dashed lines are where no earthquakes (EQs) are expected, and arrows indicate expected direction of motion.

ridge or mountain range on the ocean bottom. And since it produces new basalt on either side of the ridge at about the same rate, the ridge should be found near the center of most of the ocean basins. This would explain the mid-ocean ridge (MOR) system on the ocean floors (A in fig. 13.1).

In addition to these, we can add a few more expectations. Since solid rocks in the mid-ocean ridge system are not very old, they are cooled only to a shallow depth. Earthquakes, then, that are formed by masses of solid rock rapidly moving past one another, should be restricted to shallow depths. These earthquakes should be extensional along an active spreading line, reflecting the separation of the plates (A in fig. 13.1). In places where fractures have displaced pieces of an active spreading line, earthquakes should be restricted to the portion of the fracture zone found *between* the spreading lines, and they should show side-by-side motion that seems to bring the spreading lines together (fig. 13.2). This is quite different from what it *looks* like—namely, a fracture in the spreading line itself. If that were the case, the earthquakes would be spread along the entire length of the fracture and would show side-by-side motion that seemed to *separate* rather than bring together the spreading lines.

The cooling of rocks in areas away from the mid-ocean ridges should also change a variety of other ocean features (fig. 13.1). Following are some reasons why.

Extinct volcanoes that once poked out of the ocean should eventually sink beneath the ocean surface as the ocean crust beneath them cools and shrinks to produce *guyots* (submarine mountains).

Since the cooled layer of rock at the ocean bottom should thicken with time, and since cooled rock acts as an insulator, less and less heat should leak from the ocean floor as one moves farther away from the MOR.

Total sediment thickness and the age of the deepest sediment should increase away from the ridge system.

Since cooling basalt preserves evidence of the direction of the earth's magnetic field, and since the field direction has switched numerous times in earth history, a series of parallel bands of alternating magnetic orientation should be found paralleling the mid-ocean ridge.

And perhaps most drastic of all: since cooled basalt is actually more dense than the mantle rock from which it is derived, the ocean crust should eventually cool enough to be pulled into the earth's mantle, thus sinking it below the continental surface (B in fig. 13.1). As it is forced under the lower edge of the adjacent piece of crust, the ocean should be much deeper at that point. This explains the linear ocean trenches of the world. As this cold ocean crust is pulled into the mantle (being difficult to bend), it is forced to bow upward on the seaward side of the trench. That's why less rock is found under the trenches—and more rock is found under the bow that is seaward of it—than is found on the remainder of the ocean floor. This should show up as a stronger gravitational force over the bow and a weaker gravitational force over the trench (fig. 13.1).

During the time when the crust is being pulled into the mantle, the top surface of the sinking slab should generate earthquakes that increase in depth as one moves landward of the trench. These earthquakes should show that the ocean crust slab is sliding under the adjacent crust. If the plate is being pulled into the mantle, then earthquakes in the center of the plate should show extensional motion—as if it were being stretched. In locations where the slab has been in the mantle long enough to get heated up, partial melting of the basalt should produce magma that punches through the edge of the adjacent slab to produce chains of volcanoes of andesite that parallel the ocean trench on the side opposite the ocean basin (fig. 13.1).

Does That Explain Everything?

All of these simple expectations from plate tectonics theory are indeed found in the geology of the earth's oceans.[5]

Basalt. Hundreds of drill holes made into the ocean floor have verified that the entire ocean floor is underlain by basalt.

Volcanoes. These oceanic volcanoes are of two types. First, there are andesitic volcanoes that parallel the trenches on the side opposite the open ocean. An example of these are the volcanoes of the Andes Mountains, which gave their name to the rock type that is found paralleling the trench on the western margin of South America. The second type are basaltic volcanoes, which are found everywhere else.

Guyots. The older of the ocean's basaltic volcanoes are guyots (such as the Marshall Islands and guyots, compared to the younger Hawaiian Islands in the same chain), which deepen beneath the ocean surface with their age.

Magnetic Fields. The strength of the earth's magnetic field over the ocean floor varies in alternating strong and weak bands paralleling the mid-ocean ridge, as if the rocks underneath have alternating magnetic orientations.

Consistent Characteristics. Total sediment thickness and deepest sediment age increases away from the ridges.

Differences in Gravity. Bands of higher gravity parallel the ridges on the ocean basin side, and the trenches themselves show lower gravity.

Earthquakes. As expected, earthquakes are found in the ocean trenches as well as in the mid-ocean fracture lines between and along the spreading lines. These earthquakes are *compressional* along the trenches on top of the plates, deepening away from the trench. They are *extensional* along the spreading lines and in the center of the plates beneath the trenches. And they are *side-by-side* along fracture lines between offset spreading lines, falsely suggesting that separated spreading lines are approaching each other.

So plate tectonics theories are rather simple; they are also extremely successful. No other theories have been able to better explain such a huge number of diverse geologic features. It appears that the earth is broken into a series of plates, and that the plates in the world's oceans are extending in some places and sinking in others as suggested in plate tectonics.

It also appears that plate tectonic activity is not only active now but has been active in the earth's past. This is indicated on the ocean floor by rocks of increasing age being found away from the mid-ocean ridge. It is indicated by even more evidence on the continents. Think of it this way: if one end of a slab of ocean crust was sinking into the mantle while the other end was attached to a continent, the continent would be pulled along behind the ocean crust, the rocks under the continents being generally much too light to be pulled into the mantle. However, as ocean crust between two continents was sinking into the mantle, the continents might even be brought into contact or collision. And there is much evidence on the continents themselves that they have indeed moved—both with respect to one another and with respect to the earth itself.

The continents on either side of the Atlantic Ocean have complementary shapes, as if they broke and moved apart from a single continent at some time in the past.

Many geologic features can be matched with continents on either side of the Atlantic Ocean, yet they are not found in the ocean between (such as geologic layers, fossils, directions of sediment transport, directions of

Permian rock grooves, Appalachian/Scandinavian mountain fold belts, mineral deposits, and rock chemistry).

Similar matchings are found between Antarctica and Australia, and between Antarctica and India. In each case there are mid-ocean ridges between these continental pairs with ocean sediments increasing in age away from the ridges but younger than the geologic features that are matched across the oceans. This is exactly what would be expected if the continental pairs were once in contact but became separated by the creation of new ocean crust along spreading lines between them.

Environments and sediments that are formed only in particular latitudes indicate that continents have moved through those latitudes.

The direction of magnetism preserved in rocks indicates that the continents have moved with respect to the earth's magnetic pole. These relative motions are called *polar wander curves* because they were originally interpreted as movements of the earth's magnetic pole with respect to continents. If the continents are assumed to be motionless, the polar wander curves from different continents are in conflict with one another. But if the continents are moved as the geologic evidence seems to indicate, the polar wander curves coincide (as they should). The evidence that continents have moved in the past and that plate tectonics is responsible for most of that motion seems strongly evidenced in the geologic record.

Catastrophic Plate Tectonics

But is the reliability of plate tectonics enough to explain what happened in the Flood? Many of the events that occurred at that time may have been events we are familiar with today, just operating at bigger and faster scales. If the beginning of the Flood broke up the earth's crust, perhaps subsequent events in the Flood moved the plates around, but at a much faster rate than is observed in the present. It is interesting that with all its success at explaining geologic features, there are indications that simply projecting present plate motion into the past cannot explain all the geologic evidence. For example, direct satellite measurements of plate motion are somewhat conflicting. Sediments in some trenches show extension rather than compression, and the interiors of some ocean slabs in the mantle show compression rather than extension. Although these evidences are often presented as reasons to reject plate tectonics completely, they may indicate simply that plate tectonics operated differently during the Flood than it does now.

A few years ago some young-age creation scientists presented a variation on plate tectonics theory to explain plate motion during the Flood.[6] This theory is called *catastrophic plate tectonics* (CPT). Ultimately, the reason for the slow movement of the usual plate tectonics theory and the rapid movement of CPT theory results from the temperature of the pre-Flood ocean crust. Most of the present ocean crust is hot or warm; only a small amount of it is cold. Most plate tectonics theories suggest that the ocean crust has always had this mixture of hot and cold temperatures. In contrast, CPT theory proposes that just before the Flood began, the vast majority (and possibly all) of the oceanic crust was cold, making it denser than the mantle beneath it. Without warm crust resisting the pull into the mantle, plates moved at much faster rates than they move in the present.

On the day the Flood began, the earth was balanced critically on the edge of catastrophe. More than 70 percent of the earth's surface[7] was about to be destroyed by being pulled into the heat of the earth's interior.[8] According to the numerical modeling done by John Baumgardner,[9] if all the ocean crust on the present earth was cold, a global Flood like that described in the days of Noah would probably result. Follow along with Baumgardner's thinking:

A sinking slab of ocean crust heats up the surrounding mantle by deforming it and rubbing against it. This heating causes the mantle to become less viscous, less resistant to movement. This in turn makes it easier for the slab to sink. So it falls faster, causing even more heating, which causes the slab to sink even faster still. The slab accelerates until it is sinking at several miles per hour, pulling along ocean crust and continents at the same rate—*billions* of times faster than is observed in the present. These slabs of oceanic crust eventually sink all the way to the bottom of the mantle, causing material to circulate throughout the entire mantle. Rapid separation of the plates at the spreading lines causes a rapid pressure drop, which causes rapid partial melting. The hot magma comes in contact with ocean water and flash-boils it, propelling it into the earth's atmosphere. This produces a linear geyser for tens of thousands of miles around the earth's surface—interpreted in CPT theory as the broken up "fountains of the great deep" of Genesis 7:11. Some of the steam in this geyser was probably tossed out of the earth's gravitational field. The remainder spreads out in the earth's upper atmosphere, cools by radiation into space, and comes down as intense global rain—interpreted in CPT theory as the "windows of heaven" of Genesis 7:11.

That is catastrophic plate tectonics. It explains all the evidence answered by slow plate tectonics and more, producing directions and relative rates of motion that no other plate tectonics modeling has been successful in doing. Let's look at the progression of evidence in more detail and in contrast to traditional plate tectonics theory:

Speed. Baumgardner's modeling arrives at these results only if the initial ocean crust is entirely cold and it generates only very rapid motion. Therefore, the plate tectonic motion that is conventionally thought to occur over hundreds of millions of years occurs within a *single* year, thus fitting into the biblical chronology of Noah's Flood.

Depth. Present ocean slabs whose edges reach deep into the mantle under the trenches are under compression. This suggests that the slabs have hit some sort of barrier that prevents their passing through. Because of this, plate tectonics models before 1990 suggested that mantle motions have always been restricted to the uppermost mantle. In the 1980s, Baumgardner's modeling suggested that if the entire ocean floor was cold, the ocean slabs would be able to penetrate that barrier. Furthermore, the plates would be able to sink quickly enough to make it all the way to the bottom of the mantle without melting. Since it should take millions of years for plates of this thickness to melt and be incorporated into the mantle, they should still be there if their sinking occurred during the Flood of Noah only thousands of years ago.

In contrast, conventional plate tectonics theory says that even if the plates were somehow able to penetrate the mantle barrier, they would be falling so slowly that they should be incorporated into the mantle long before they would make it to the bottom. This is why the seismic tomography studies in the early 1990s came as a surprise to geophysicists.[10] These studies indicate that there are zones of cooler material reaching from the ocean trenches down to the bottom of the mantle. The evidence suggests that mantle motions occurred through the entire mantle, just as Baumgardner's modeling predicted. It also suggests that there is cold material at the bottom of the mantle, confirming Baumgardner's predictions and contradicting the expectations of old-age plate tectonics models.

Mantle Circulation and Magnetic Field Reversals. In Baumgardner's modeling, as soon as ocean crust begins to sink, mantle circulation begins throughout the mantle. Under the sinking slab, mantle material sinks. This immediately brings shallower, cooler material to lower positions, including to the bottom of the mantle—even before the ocean crust makes it there—creating different temperatures at the base of the mantle.

D. Russell Humphreys[11] has suggested that these temperature contrasts create circulation in the outer core. Located directly underneath the mantle, the outer core is liquid with a runniness similar to liquid water. If distributed in the right way, temperature differences in various places at the bottom of the mantle would cause the core material to circulate—just as warm water begins to circulate when ice cubes are dropped into it, and just as cold water begins to circulate when placed upon the burner of a stove.

According to Humphreys's modeling, this circulation causes the earth's magnetic field to reverse regularly in much the same way as the sun's internal circulation causes the sun's magnetic field to reverse every eleven years. The kind of temperature contrasts in the earth's core suggested by Baumgardner's modeling could produce reversals even more frequently—perhaps every couple of weeks or so—rapidly enough to create most of the known reversals during a year-long flood. Although non-creationist theories have been created to explain reversals of the earth's magnetic field, many years—in fact, *hundreds* of years—are always required for the reversals to occur.

In 1986 Humphreys predicted the kind of evidence that would demonstrate that magnetic reversals occur in days rather than centuries. It works like this: magnetic particles in molten rock are free to orient themselves like compasses in the earth's magnetic field. As the rock cools, the magnetic particles are set in place, indicating the direction of the earth's magnetic field when the rock was still molten. If the earth's field changes after the outer surfaces of a lava flow cool but before the inside of the flow cools, one direction of the earth's field will be preserved on the outside, and another direction will be preserved inside. Since we know how long it should take a lava flow to cool, we can determine how long it took for the reversal to occur. To explain all the magnetic reversals in the course of a year-long Flood, reversals would have to occur every couple weeks. Humphreys predicted that such reversals should be observed within a basalt flow some 1.5 to 3 feet thick. And sure enough, basalt flows with such evidence have been found[12]—evidence explained by young-age creation theory, but contrary to old-age theories of earth history.

The Wide Expanse of Magnetic Field Reversals. Humphreys's theory of rapid reversals also explains a feature of the sea floor that cannot be explained by old-age theories of earth history. Old-age theories require something on the order of one thousand years to effect a reversal of the earth's magnetic field. Following this time line—with plates spreading apart an inch or so every year—something on the order of one hundred to three hundred feet of new ocean plate should be produced during a reversal. With the magnetic field changing and the rock requiring some time to cool, a mixture of magnetic directions might end up being preserved in rocks formed during the reversal period. Since an average of millions of radiometric years separate these reversals, tens of miles of new ocean plate should be produced between reversals—where no evidence of mixed-up magnetic directions should be found. If this were true, far less than 1 percent of the ocean floor should display mixed-up magnetic field directions.

If, however, both Baumgardner and Humphreys are right, new ocean floor was being created during the Flood at *miles per hour* with reversals occurring every couple of weeks. And it's likely that there were always pockets of the ocean floor that stayed hot well into the next reversal period. The young-age creationist would then predict that the *entire ocean floor* should be magnetically mottled, with adjacent pockets throughout the basalt having opposite magnetic orientations. Such mottling does seem to exist in *every one* of the hundreds of cores made in the basalts of the ocean floor. This is consistent with young-age creation theory and contrary to alternative theories.

Magnetic Field Strength. Also according to Humphreys's model, while the magnetic field was reversing, the strength of the field measured at the earth's surface should have been weaker than it was before the reversing episode. Then immediately after the reversal period, the field should have risen to a higher strength before it began a free decay again (described in chap. 5). The magnetic field evidence from rocks confirms that while Flood rocks were being deposited, the field was both reversing *and* weaker than the field is today. Magnetization of human artifacts suggests that more recently than that the field was stronger than even the present magnetic field. In fact, direct measurement of the magnetic field strength shows a substantial decrease in the last one and one-half centuries or so. Although alternate theories can explain a fluctuating magnetic field strength, the consistently low field strength suggested from the earth's rocks is somewhat difficult to explain.

A variety of evidences suggest that Humphreys's magnetic field model—and not any other model—is correct. Humphreys based his magnetic field model upon Horace Lamb's model of free decay (see chap. 5). If Humphreys's model is correct, Lamb's may also be. This would suggest that the earth's magnetic field is only thousands of years old. In fact, it would almost have to be less than ten thousand years old. And since the rocks thought to have been formed in the Flood show evidence of having been formed with a magnetic field in place, this suggests that the Flood occurred less than ten thousand years ago. A young-age creation model of earth history provides the best explanation for magnetic field evidence—

its strength through time, its rapid reversals, and the mottled nature of reversal patterns on the sea floor.

Rapid Eruptions. CPT theory claims that during the Flood the mantle moved much more rapidly than it does at the present and in other plate tectonics models. This rapid motion provides an explanation for kimberlites and flood basalts that the conventional model does not provide. Kimberlites are a kind of rock that often contain diamonds. They originate deep in the mantle, since that is the only place where pressures are high enough to produce diamonds. However, if the kimberlite rocks are not quickly cooled (by, say, raising them rapidly to the earth's surface), diamonds will not form—only graphite. This requires extremely rapid vertical motions—perhaps scores or hundreds of miles per hour. A *flood basalt* very thick pile of basalt lava flows. Studies of flood basalts all over the earth's surface suggest very rapid eruption times (days to weeks). This in turn suggests that the mantle is somehow able to supply the magma and remove the magma it supplies. This suggests that mantle motions were much faster than is true in the present—just as CPT theory suggests.

Rapid Collisions. The very rapid continental motions of CPT theory result in rapid collisions. The momentum of CPT-driven continents is tens of times greater than is proposed in conventional plate tectonics. When continents collide in the CPT model, they do so with energies billions of billions of times the energies of continents colliding in alternate models. This probably provides the energy necessary to raise mountains collision point that alternate theories cannot provide. This energy is to provide a better explanation for the large number of high-energy geologic events evidenced in the earth's rock record.

For example, there is evidence of earthquakes strong enough to collapse the continental margins[13] and earthquakes strong enough to pick up tens of thousands of feet of sediment and shove it over the top of other continents.[14] Rapid collisions also have the potential of producing sufficient pressure to create high-pressure minerals. If this is true, even minerals produced by high pressures deep beneath the earth's surface could be excavated and revealed on the surface in very short periods. Unlike old-age models, this provides too little time for the rock to reach the temperature of surrounding rocks. This means that minerals formed at both high pressure and low temperature would be expected in CPT theory. Alternate (old-age) theories would expect minerals to have needed time to heat up to the temperature of the surrounding rock, creating high-pressure minerals that were also high in temperature. The existence of high-pressure/low-temperature minerals is explained by CPT theory and not alternative theories.

It all seems to add up. The replacement of cold ocean crust with more expanded hot ocean crust raised the ocean bottom. The strong pull of the ocean crust into the mantle dragged that portion of the earth crust down as the rising mantle material swelled the spreading lines. The rising ocean bottom displaced water on the continents, raising sea level perhaps more than a mile over antediluvian levels. This produced the Flood itself. These waters raised the ark upon their surface and ultimately passed it over the tops of the highest antediluvian mountains.

Global Catastrophism

Any theory of the Flood—CPT or not—has to postulate much, much higher rates of erosion and deposition than alternate theories of geology do. The Flood was a geologic catastrophe and should have left its evidence everywhere. The degree to which this expectation is borne out is apparent from a brief history of geology in the last two centuries.

In the 1830s, Charles Lyell championed *anti-catastrophism*. This became the dominant bias of geologists for more than one hundred years. But beginning in the 1970s and continuing to the present day, the atmosphere of geology has changed quite a bit.[15] *Neocatastrophism* (which admitted that small, local catastrophes occur on the earth from time to time) became rather popular in the 1970s. With the suggestion in 1980 that the dinosaurs may have been killed off by an asteroid hitting the earth, there was a rise in the acceptance of a few global catastrophes in earth history. This trend has continued to the present. It has taken some time, but the fact that geologists have come to accept so much geologic catastrophe in a climate of anti-catastrophism suggests that the evidence for it must be strong.

A global Flood should involve much larger scales for geologic processes. Events would be expected to impact much larger areas, involve much more material, and move items much farther from their source than is generally accepted in old-age theories of earth history. Consequently, Flood geology seems better prepared to explain why Primary and Secondary (also known as Paleozoic and Mesozoic) sediments are often deposited in great thicknesses, with remarkably uniform compositions, spread over very large areas, and many times displaced hundreds of miles from their source area.[16] On the present earth, sediments are being carried toward and within the ocean in all directions. Anything that indicates the direction of currents (such as ripple marks, dune structures, or drag marks) should show a random pattern on every continent. But evidence amassed by Arthur Chadwick[17] suggests otherwise. It is as if during the deposition of Primary and Secondary rocks, the currents on the earth were consistently in one direction—more or less east to west.

The rapid deposition of Primary and Secondary sediments should also produce a very different fossil record than that expected by alternate models of earth history.[18] If the earth's sediments were deposited while organisms were evolving (as many alternate theories suggest), then a vertical sequence of fossils should document that transition. Organisms should be found in the order they evolved. Intermediates should be found in layers between their ancestors and descendants. And species should be seen changing up through the record. Just as a branching tree can become broad only after it has produced many branches, so also evolving life can only generate markedly different biological forms after it has produced many species.

In Flood theory, however, the organisms that lived on the earth at a particular point in time were rapidly buried, community by community. Therefore, organisms should not be found in the order evolution predicts. Intermediates should not be found in layers between proposed ancestors and descendants. Organisms should not change up through the fossil col-

Bio-Evolutionary Evidences:

Fossil Order

Fossil order: the sequence of fossils that changes regularly with
depth. Fossils found in the earth's layered rocks are thought to be
remains of organisms that lived in the past. Since it's difficult to slip
a new rock layer under one that already exists, lower rock layers at
a given place are considered older than higher layers in that place.
Vertically adjacent rock layers often have very similar fossils. Generally,
the more different the vertical position of the rock layer, the more
different the fossils are. The sequence of changing fossils with depth
is reflected with consistent regularity from place to place, suggesting
a global change in organisms through the fossil record.

In bio-evolution, organisms change through time. While they did, the
rock record was continuously forming. Fossils, then, would be expected to
show the consistent global change seen in rock column.

In young-age creation theory, the fossil record can be divided into
three parts: a portion formed before the Flood, a portion forming during the Flood, and a portion forming after the Flood. Given the
destructive nature of the earliest Flood, almost all pre-Flood rocks and
fossils were probably destroyed. Most fossils in Flood sediments were
probably of pre-Flood organisms transported long distances by the
waters of a global Flood. Fossils were buried in an order reflecting the
spectrum of pre-Flood environments. In the post-Flood world, sediments were burying organisms at the same time that they were diversi-
fying. Young-age creationists, then, would be expected to show the
consistent global change seen in the rock column. Because of the more
rapid burial, fossils should be more common and better preserved in
young-age creation theory. Young-age creation would also expect few
fossils in the right place to be evolutionary transitional forms and more
diversity among fossils from the very beginning. The fossil record
seems more consistent with these expectations than with the corresponding expectations of evolutionary theory.

Bio-Evolutionary Evidence:

Transitional Forms

Transitional forms: organisms developed during the transformation
from one group of organisms to another. Formed during a transition,
they begin after the first appearance of the ancestral group and
before the first appearance of the descendant group. They would be
expected to have a body form intermediate between the body form
of the ancestral and descendant groups. When preserved as fossils, transitional forms should show up as "stratomorphic intermediates"—fossils
intermediate in body type and rock position between
ancestral and descendant groups.

In bio-evolutionary theory, all organisms are thought to have evolved from
other organisms. Transitional forms should have been produced during the
origin of every type of organism. According to the same theory, the fossil
record has been preserving organisms during virtually all of earth history.
Consequently, stratomorphic intermediates should not only be common,
but should be found in nearly every rock layer and associated with nearly
every type of organism—especially easily preserved groups.

In young-age creation theory, change occurs within the created
kinds (baramins). Because God designed most of the body forms into the
system at the beginning, many species may have originated without
transitional forms. Few transitional forms between species may have ever

umn, and markedly different organisms should be evidenced from the
very beginning of the record. In fact, it is rare that organisms are found in
the order predicted by evolutionary theory. Intermediates are only very
rarely found between proposed ancestors and descendants. Organisms
usually show stasis up through the fossil record. And high disparity of
organismal form appears at the very beginning of the fossil record—usually *before* the number of species rises.

existed. Furthermore, in the young-age creation model, the fossils in Flood sediments preserve a snapshot of the organisms living on the earth the day the Flood waters reached them. Because of this, transitional forms would be extraordinarily unlikely in Flood sediments. On the other hand, rising Flood waters may well have preserved organisms in the order they were encountered. So, if adjacent pre-Flood communities had intermediates between them (*e.g.*, mammal-like reptiles living in a zone between a mammal-dominated community on one side and a reptile-dominated community on the other), then stratomorphic intermediates might be expected between these two communities. Stratomorphic intermediates, then, should be rare in Flood deposits (Primary and Secondary?), but when they are found they should be ecological intermediates between adjacent communities. Post-Flood sediments (Tertiary? and Quaternary) were deposited during the period of highest intrabaraminic diversification. In these sediments one might find stratomorphic series of fossils documenting intrabaraminic diversification and reflecting the cooling and drying climate of the post-Flood world (see chap. 14).

In point of fact, stratomorphic intermediate fossils are rare and apparently not found at all among the groups with the best fossil record (shallow marine invertebrates like mollusks and brachiopods)—many fewer than expected in evolutionary theory. The few examples claimed in Primary and Secondary sediments (*e.g.*, *Seymouria*, mammal-like reptiles, *Archaeopteryx*) may well be ecological intermediates. Those in Tertiary sediments (*e.g.*, horses, elephants, camels, and whales) may well be stratomorphic series documenting intrabaraminic diversification.

All other things being equal, a lower deposition rate should preserve fewer fossils.[19] Under these conditions, much more time is available for organisms to destroy the layers of sediment; therefore, fine sedimentary layering should be rarer. Yet the fossil record has an abundance of both well-preserved fossils and finely-layered sediments over the whole earth. Also, if the fossil record is a documentation of hundreds of millions of years of time, then the approximately 250,000 fossil species documented to date would have to be an extremely low percentage of all the species that have ever lived. In contrast, the rapid deposition rate of the Flood would probably result in a very large percentage of fossil species being preserved. Our observation is that a very large percentage of modern species have a fossil record. This suggests that the fossil record is as good as young-age creationism suggests and not as poor as alternate theories might suggest.

In addition to the evidence of the fossil record and the wide distribution of earth sediments, the short time scale of Flood geology provides explanation for other geological observations, as well. Consider the following.

Sediments deposited at different points in the course of the year-long Flood can be separated by millions of radiometric years. Simultaneous tight folding of different sediment layers is easier to explain if the sediments did not turn to rock before the folding. Their not turning to rock is easier to explain if the sediments were deposited only months apart rather than millions of years apart.[20]

Periods of non-deposition between sedimentary layers is also easier to explain if the sediments were deposited only weeks apart rather than millions of years apart. There has been a trend over the last several decades to reinterpret individual sedimentary layers as being more quickly deposited than originally thought. As this is done, less and less of earth history is represented directly by the rocks of the earth. If the earth is billions of years old, a very small percentage of earth history is evidenced at all,[21] *and* the fossil record should be nowhere near as complete as it appears to be. The time gaps in the rock record are easier to explain by young-age creation theory.

Another time issue has to do with the geologic activity associated with mountains. If the earth is very old, the earth's eroded fold-belt mountains are very old. The Appalachians, for example, would be hundreds of millions of years old. The only geologic changes that should be occurring would be erosion slowly taking off the top of the mountains and the minor rebounding of the mountains in response to this loss of mass. But if the Appalachians were formed by continental collision early in the

Flood, they were formed only thousands of years ago and the top of the mountains was eroded off soon thereafter—only thousands of years ago. Since it should take the earth's surface some twenty-five thousand years to respond fully to quick vertical changes, the mountains that were formed and shaved off during the Flood should still be recovering. This would explain the large number of earthquakes associated with the Appalachians. Young-age creation theory leaves more room for this than alternative models.

Finally, the energy released in the Flood was many times more powerful than the geologic activity of the present, yet the geologic activity of the Flood period itself was probably not uniform. The breakup of the "fountains of the great deep" that started the Flood (Gen. 7:11) may have involved the greatest destructive energy of any event of the entire Flood. The earthquake (or multiple quakes) associated with this event may have collapsed continental margins,[22] preserving the first Flood deposits—the bacteria and stromatolites of the antediluvian hydrothermal environments. As the Flood waters overwhelmed successive environments of the antediluvian world, the Primary and Secondary sediments of the world would be laid down on top of these first deposits.

Questions and Challenges

But while young-age creation geology is superior to alternate models in a number of areas, it is admittedly weak in a variety of others. Much research is needed to provide adequate young-age creationist reinterpretations of these issues.

It is common for Flood critics to argue, for example, that there are *in situ* communities in the fossil record—fossil assortments thought to represent communities of organisms that must have grown at the place they are found as fossils. Since such communities require more time to develop than is available during the Flood, these communities argue against a Flood interpretation of the containing sediments.

Since trees do not move, claims of *in situ* fossil forests are often used against Flood theory. Coals and apparently rooted trees that are often associated with them are many times used against a Flood interpretation of Carboniferous sediments. In the laboratory, however, plant debris sprinkled with any of various clays can be formed into any grade of coal in a matter of days to weeks.[23] There is even evidence that plant material on the Colorado Plateau was made into coal in something less than a single year.[24] Furthermore, all coals contain clay. So coal formation *can* occur in the short time period required of Flood geology.

But can the huge amount of plant material required to make coal be accumulated during a single Flood? Most of the world's coals are made of the large trees of the antediluvian floating forest described in chapter 12. This provided the sheer mass of plant material necessary to produce most of the earth's coals. As the Flood destroyed the outer perimeter of the floating forest, the plants became waterlogged and sank to the ocean bottom to be deposited with sea creatures. Once the central forest of large trees was all that remained, the abrasive action of Flood waves probably ripped up most of the plant material, allowing it also to become waterlogged and sink to the ocean bottom below the dwindling forest mat.

This is a variation of Steven Austin's *floating log mat model.*[25] That model provided an excellent explanation for a particular coal seam in western Kentucky. The log mat floating on the surface of Mt. Saint Helens after the 1980 eruption also produced a layer of bark on the bottom of Spirit Lake just as Austin's log mat model predicted it might.[26] This may provide a good explanation for coals in general, but it has only been applied to one coal seam in Kentucky. It needs to be systematically applied across a variety of Flood coals.

The sinking of vertical logs from the Spirit Lake log mat provides a reasonable model for the origin of the logs associated with coals.[27] The vertical logs in coal sediments probably represent whole logs ripped from the antediluvian floating forest. Unlike the trees floating atop Spirit Lake, the trees of the antediluvian forest were made of bark and hollow. They probably became waterlogged in a matter of hours to days—not long after the ripped-up bark fragments sank to the bottom to form coal. This would explain why the logs are often sitting directly on top of coal seams and would better explain why they seem to penetrate a number of soil layers.[28] These logs need to be restudied by young-age creationists.

In the marine fossil record there are numerous claims of *in situ* fossil communities, although there are fewer marine hard rock communities than one would expect if the earth is very old. These and many other claims need to be examined carefully by young-age creation paleontologists. The best-known type of intact marine community is the reef. Modern reefs grow very slowly. Fossil reefs, then—and there are some huge ones—are also thought to require long periods to form. A number of the fossil "reefs" seem to actually be more a pile of corals and sea creatures than a growing reef structure.[29] The core of one of these, which is exposed in Thornton Quarry south of Chicago, may even be upside-down, as if it were transported from its growth location to its present burial position.[30] It might be that early Flood erosion broke up antediluvian reefs and redeposited large pieces at distant locations. These large blocks may have acted as a baffle, slowing down Flood waters and causing heavy organisms like corals and other sea creatures to fall out of the moving Flood waters around the large blocks. Once again, however, fossil reefs have not been adequately restudied by young-age creationists.

Trace fossils represent another area needing further exploration. These are marks left in sediments by organisms. If the sediments are moved around after the traces have been made, the traces will, of course, be destroyed. Therefore, trace fossils are evidence of organism activity that occurred at the particular location they are found. Some traces in the present world (like organismal burrows) require considerable time to be produced. Trace fossils are often used to argue against a Flood interpretation of sediments. A young-age creation reinterpretation of trace fossils has not been done.

Some traces interpreted as living burrows may be pathways through which buried organisms tried to escape. Other traces interpreted as feeding paths and otherwise normal biological activity may merely be instinctive movements that organisms make even when captured in life-threatening situations. Abundant surface traces, which are often found on sediment surfaces, may represent frenzied biologic activity that occurs in catastrophic situations. Some traces may be misinterpreted because they were made by organisms now extinct. Since burrowing organisms tend to destroy the fine layering of sediments, the common association of trace fossils and thinly-bedded sediments may be evidence of the rapid deposition expected in Flood theory. Trace fossils are often found below the oldest body fossils.[31] This is consistent with the idea that the traces were made by organisms trying to escape catastrophic conditions—conditions that would eventually kill most of them.

Chalks and other microfossil accumulations are often presented as challenges to Flood theory. The fossil record contains layers that would take great amounts of time to accumulate in the present—much more time than is available in the Flood. A number of young-age creationists have argued back and forth about the origin of chalks and chalk-like deposits, but none of these areas has been studied as it ought to be. It is likely that chalks are the result of algal blooms that occurred during the Flood. With all the organisms killed in the Flood, there was probably a lot of food available in Flood waters. Magma interacting with ocean water at the spreading lines heated up the world's oceans during the Flood. The warm, nutrient-rich waters of the Late Flood would have created ideal conditions for algal blooms. Occurring in global oceans with virtually unlimited nutrient supplies, algal blooms during the Flood were probably vastly different from those in the present, which are likely poor models of their Flood-era counterparts.[32]

Claims of exposure are further challenges to Flood theory. In the simplest understanding of a global Flood, all sediments are formed under water. Desert sand dunes would not be expected to be formed, nor would tidal flats and mud cracks. Soils and caves would not be expected either, since these things require more time to develop than is available in the Flood. Each of these things, however—desert dunes, tidal flats, mud cracks, soils, and caves—are claimed to exist in rocks that young-age creationists consider to be Flood sediments. As is the case with *in situ* claims, exposure claims need to be reexamined carefully by young-age creationists. Sandstones that are thought to be desert sands may actually be antediluvian desert or coastal sands redeposited in huge underwater dunes during the Flood.

This, for example, seems to be the best interpretation of the Grand Canyon's Cocconino Sandstone.[33] The frosting of individual sand grains suggests that they were originally deposited on land by wind. But the size range of those sand grains, the steepness of the dune faces, and the quality of the trace fossils suggest that the sands were ultimately deposited in huge underwater dunes and sand waves. The Cocconino dunes and sand waves are much larger than any underwater structures of the present, so they seem to be better explained by the Flood than by alternate theories. Similar desert dune claims have been made around the world in similar-aged sediments. Global reburial of desert sands at a particular stage in the Flood may (upon careful study) turn out to be a better explanation for these Permo-Triassic sandstones than any alternate hypothesis.

As another evidence of exposure, shrinkage cracks are often interpreted to be mud cracks. But the lack of curled edges on the cracks and the fact that some cracks penetrate both up and down suggest that shrinkage may have occurred after burial.[34]

Most rocks claimed to be fossil soils lack every chemical evidence found in soils, but so do many individual soils in the present. Most structures claimed to be fossil caves lack characteristics of modern caves, but neither fossil soils nor fossil caves have been systematically restudied by young-age creationists.

Finally, red shales in the rock record are often interpreted as muds oxidized red by the air—for example, on tidal flats. Restudy may conclude that they are actually muds oxidized red after burial by hot waters passing through the Flood sediments from below. Red beds in the rock record tend to be found over much larger areas and tend to be much more uniform than any muds exposed to the air on the present earth. This suggests that restudy will likely conclude that Flood geology provides a better explanation for red beds than any other hypothesis.

Bigger than Global?

Perhaps many of the things discussed so far in this chapter on the Flood are familiar to you—issues you have been exposed to at various degrees and with various interpretations. But this one might be new to you: there is some evidence that the Flood in the days of Noah was even *bigger* than the earth. As mentioned before, 2 Peter 3:3–7 classifies the Flood with the creation and the judgment to come. Since the Creation and final judgment affect the entire universe, this passage infers in some small way that the Flood may have done the same. And believe it or not, physical evidence for this does seem to exist.

First, there are scores of large craters on the earth's surface that are cut into and buried by Flood sediments. These are commonly interpreted to have been created by large meteorites or asteroids impacting the earth's surface.[35] If this turns out to be a correct interpretation for more than one of these structures, then meteorite/asteroid bombardment was much higher during the Flood than has been true for the last few thousand years of earth history. This in turn would suggest that the Flood involved objects that, at least originally, were located outside the earth.

Physical evidence of catastrophism also seems to exist on the moon.[36] The large, dark, circular areas that can be seen in the upper left quarter of the moon are called *maria* (meaning "seas," since they looked a bit like oceans to the ancients). The generally circular shape of the maria suggests that they are actually huge impact craters. Rocks brought back from the moon's maria by Apollo astronauts were found to be basaltic lavas. It is thought that the impacts that created the maria cracked the moon's surface and caused magma from the moon's interior to flow out and fill the crater. By the time the magma filled the large craters, a number of smaller craters had already been formed within them. These partially buried craters in the maria are called *ghost craters*. Not much time could have elapsed between the large impacts and the outflowing of lava. This suggests that while the huge impactors were hitting the moon to create the maria, smaller impactors were hitting the moon at a rate millions of times greater than is seen in the present.

Additionally, the maria themselves appear to be curiously distributed on the moon's surface. Eleven of the twelve maria are found in a single quadrant of the moon. Although we know the moon keeps the same face toward the earth at all times, it shows a different face to objects elsewhere in our solar system as the earth moves through space and the moon continually revolves around it. It seems highly unlikely that maria-creating objects hitting the moon at very different times could possibly have hit that close to the same bull's-eye eleven out of twelve times. The proximity of the maria suggests that the objects that made them came in as a group at approximately the same moment. It would seem that at least eleven huge impactors—and probably millions of smaller impactors—pelted the moon during just a few days. And since the maria are on the side of the moon always facing the earth, the impactor swarm probably skimmed right past the earth.

It is likely, then, that the earth was also pelted during this time. Dating of moon rocks by magnetic field strength[37] suggests that at least some of the impacts may have occurred during the Flood, and it may be that Flood craters on the earth occurred as the result of the same bombardment. Catastrophism may have impacted the moon at the same time as catastrophism impacted the earth.

Outside the earth-moon system, the surface of Venus is known to have many fewer craters than other objects in the solar system. In fact, it even appears that Venus has been completely resurfaced at some time in the past.[38] Could the Flood possibly be responsible? We calculate that about 70 percent of the earth's surface sank into the earth's interior during the Flood, while approximately 30 percent of the earth's surface remained as continents. On Venus it seems that *all* the crust sank into the planet's interior. Based upon the number of craters on Venus's surface and old-age estimates of crater accumulation, the resurfacing of Venus occurred three hundred to six hundred million years ago. These dates correspond to radiometric dates for Flood rocks on the earth. Therefore, the resurfacing of Venus may have occurred at the same time as the Flood. Even on the surface of Mars there is some evidence of failed resurfacing of an unknown age. Perhaps the catastrophism on Mars also occurred at the same time as the Flood.

It is not impossible that the Flood may have occurred as a result of God's changing some physical constant or constants of the universe. The sudden changes in radiometric decay rates suggested by some[39] is consistent with this claim. If true, then the catastrophism in the days of Noah may have actually impacted not just the earth but perhaps the entire solar system—even the entire universe. Could the dust of the solar system be the result of this catastrophe? How about the asteroids? And what of exploding stars? There is opportunity for much young-age creationist research and reinterpretation.

The Flood Ends

When all the antediluvian ocean crust had disappeared into the mantle, the ocean crust that replaced it was still warm. Being warm, it was less dense than the mantle, so gravity did not pull it into the mantle below, and horizontal plate motions on the surface ground to a halt. Without the plates separating quickly at the spreading lines, molten mantle material was no longer contacting sea water, and the earth-ringing "fountains of the great deep" ceased to spout; they were "stopped" (Gen. 8:2). Without the mid-ocean fountains supplying water, the "windows of heaven" ceased (Gen. 8:2), making it possible for the earth to return to a normal water cycle of evaporating water and condensing water vapor from clouds.

It took a few weeks for the last of the pre-Flood crust to drop to the bottom of the mantle. Once this had happened, the mantle motions ceased. Since it has been only 4,500 years or so since the Flood, temperature differences in the mantle still show up with seismic tomography. At the surface the spreading centers eased back down, and the sinking zones eased back up. From the moment it was first introduced at spreading lines, the ocean crust cooled and shrank as it did so. The settling of mid-ocean ridges and the shrinking of basalt allowed the Flood waters to return gradually to the ocean basins. As the water subsided, the ark was set upon the "mountains of Ararat" (Gen. 8:4). Eventually the water would recede completely from the continents.

Once mantle circulation ceased, no more cold crust was brought to the bottom of the mantle. The great difference in temperature between pre-Flood mantle bottom and ocean bottom began to lessen—the cold crust being heated up by the mantle, and the mantle being slightly cooled by the crust.[40] Since these temperature differences drove the core's circulation, this circulation gradually slowed after the Flood. Eventually the circulation became too slow to cause reversals, and the field settled into a constant orientation—its present orientation—though measurements of the present magnetic field suggest that the core is still circulating. Young-age creationism provides the only known explanation for the temperature differences that still exist at the bottom of the mantle and thus the circulation still occurring in the outer core.

What's Next?

As Noah and his family stepped off the ark, they entered a completely new world—the third radically new world in creation history. Imagine it! No plant, animal, mineral, spring, river, mountain, or even continent was where it had been before. All had been destroyed or displaced. Even the moon looked different. In the years to follow, more changes would occur as organisms repopulated the earth, the seas gradually returned to their basins, the earth sank convulsively or rose to proper levels, and the climate tried aggressively to even out earth temperatures. Undoubtedly, this third age started out the most dynamic and terrifying of all.

Yet this altered world is our own age—the same era on creation's time line in which we now live. In the next two chapters we will survey a few characteristics of the first centuries of our present world—first, the early post-Flood history of the earth and its organisms, then the early post-Flood history of man.

CHAPTER 14

THE POST-FLOOD WORLD

The Bible tells us very little about the centuries immediately following the Flood. But theory and physical evidence suggest that this may have been one of the most dynamic periods in all of earth history. In this chapter, we will consider how the world rebounded from this jolt to its very foundations, evidenced by several dramatic transformations: changes in climate that carved canyons and dried deserts, changes in organisms that developed new species and endangered others, and changes in location that took the remaining creatures to the far reaches of the globe. We will witness a world still laboring to recover—even today—from the awful fallout of the Flood.

Still Feeling the Effects?

After the earth was hit with a global catastrophe, it took considerable time for it to recover. Colliding plates produced mountains in days, and rapidly moving Flood waters eroded them down in weeks. Continents were pressed down by thousands of feet of water and then uncovered only months later. Earthquakes moved rocks up and down by thousands of feet in seconds, minutes, and hours. Mid-ocean ridges rose and sank, while trenches sank and rose in weeks and months. By the end of the Flood, rocks and plates everywhere across the planet were sitting either too high or too low. Just as ice cubes pushed beneath the water or pulled above its surface return to their proper position, so also the earth's rocks following the Flood began rebounding to their appropriate locations.

But the earth's mantle does not allow this to happen in seconds, as is the case with ice cubes in water. It is estimated that rocks would require about twenty-five thousand years to return to their proper position. Although most of this motion would probably occur in the first one thousand years or so after the Flood, some of this vertical motion should be occurring even today. This seems to provide explanation for the active earthquakes in old mountain chains such as the Appalachians and rising mountains such as the Tetons. Neither observation is so easily explained in conventional theory.

During the Flood, when all the cold ocean crust had sunk beneath the earth's surface, horizontal tectonics ceased for a time. In the months, years, and centuries that followed, the ocean crust cooled. In places where it was oldest (farthest from the ridge), the ocean crust cooled until it was denser than the mantle beneath it. Other portions of the ocean crust that are still warm buoy the crust upward, preventing the rapid sinking that occurred during the Flood. However, gravity is even now pulling colder crust slabs downward, explaining the extensional earthquakes currently found in the center of shorter descending plates. The small plate motions that occur as a result of this sinking of colder crust explain the position and depth of most of the world's earthquakes. It may be that the restarting of limited plate motion began occurring even before the Flood was over.

At first this motion—combined with the vertical motion of rocks and slabs that were out of position—may have been rather dramatic. As time went on, this energy should have lessened, explaining the incredible amount of energy that appears to have been unleashed around the San Andreas fault in the past. Mountains were actually broken off their foundations and bounced across the earth's surface for dozens of miles and more[1]—a phenomenon not explained in alternative models of earth history. This model also would explain why the frequency and size of earthquakes has been decreasing since we have been able to measure them.[2]

In addition to this plate movement, rocks that had been quickly buried in the earth's interior began to melt, causing rising magma to punch its way to the surface and generate volcanoes. Since partially melted basalt produces andesite, and andesitic volcanism is explosive, explosive andesitic volcanoes were produced over basaltic sources. Since partially melted andesite produces rhyolite, and rhyolitic volcanism is even more explosive than andesitic volcanism, the most explosive (rhyolitic) volcanism occurred over andesite sources. Many of these sources would have been put in place during the late Flood and others in the centuries to follow. This would explain the huge volumes of volcanic ash in Secondary and Tertiary sediments. This ash also created ideal conditions for fossil burial and preservation (such as for Arizona's Petrified Forest and many of the vertebrate bone beds).

As the Flood-buried rocks and slabs were heated by the mantle, less and less magma was generated, and volcanoes would be expected to decrease in size and frequency through time. Since post-Flood tectonics would not be expected to bury much new andesite, the most explosive volcanoes would gradually disappear. This provides an explanation for the gradual disappearance of rhyolitic volcanoes in the Tertiary and the decrease in size and frequency of volcanoes in general to the present[3]— neither of which is explained by alternate theories of earth history.

In young-age creation geology, the earthquakes and volcanoes of the present are largely residual effects of the Flood, meaning that the earth is still reeling from the effects of the Flood. The natural geologic disasters we hear about from time to time are direct results of this. As a result, the death and suffering associated with geologic disasters is likewise a consequence of the Flood—a consequence of divine judgment on sin. Unlike any old-age view of earth history, young-age creationism connects the natural evil seen in geology with man's sin. Man's sin is ultimately responsible not just for his moral evil and the natural biological evil of disease and death, but for natural geological evil as well. Old-age theories of earth history have natural geological evil preceding man by hundreds of millions of years.

The Post-Flood Climate

Of all the features on the earth's surface, the oceans had to bear the major part of cooling the hot ocean crust produced during the Flood. Although much of the heat was probably passed into space,[4] some of the heat had to be taken up directly by ocean water. It is likely that by the end of the Flood the ocean was rather warm—much warmer than either before the Flood or even today. A warm ocean, in turn, would have caused a lot of water to evaporate into the atmosphere. Since continents cool more quickly at night than oceans do, cool air from the continents would tend to move over the oceans to take the place of the warm air rising from their surface. The warm, moisture-laden air would then move over the continents to replace the air moving off to sea. This moist air would be cooled, causing condensation and precipitation—*lots* of precipitation.[5] But over time the evaporation of water from the oceans gradually caused them to cool, causing less precipitation to be generated. In the centuries following the Flood, the entire earth would gradually dry in this way.

Such high precipitation would naturally cause accelerations in both erosion and sedimentation. If the water came down fast enough, it would not channel itself into streams but rather flow in sheets over the earth's surface. In some areas this would erode sediments and rocks in a planar fashion. This might provide an explanation for the widespread planing off of rocks evidenced in Tertiary sediments. In other areas the water would slow down enough to begin dropping out the sediments it was carrying. This sheet deposition may provide an explanation for the extensive, nearly-flat wedges found in Tertiary sediments.[6] Neither the planar erosion nor the widespread deposits is adequately explained by alternate theories. As the precipitation lessened, the deposition and erosion would occur over smaller areas, possibly explaining the large fans of river material that cannot be produced in present precipitation conditions, such as the famous sediment fans of Death Valley that sit on top of huge ramps of earlier sediment.

The high precipitation would also produce lakes—perhaps providing an explanation for many of the lakes evidenced in Tertiary sediments. Fossil Lake, which preserved the famous fossil fish of Fossil Butte National Monument, would be one example of this—as would Lake Manly (which used to be found in Death Valley) and Lake Bonneville (of which the Great Salt Lake is a small, evaporated remnant). Our experience tells us that when lakes fill up and overflow, they tend to cut catastrophically through whatever dam holds them in place, whether natural or man-made. The same precipitation that generated the post-Flood lakes may have overfilled many of them. This water would have quickly cut through the dams, rapidly drained the lakes, and left behind spectacular canyons. Even the Grand Canyon could have been produced by the actions of this simple model.[7]

Since modern rivers tend to cut primarily into their banks rather than the river bottoms, it may turn out that all the world's canyons were cut during catastrophic floods that occurred within the first one thousand years following the great Flood. It may also turn out that most of the world's caves were carved out during this dynamic period of earth history. Most of the current rivers of the earth may actually be flowing through remnant canyons cut during the post-Flood period of earth history. Once the river canyons had been cut in place, the high precipitation rates would provide explanation for the rapid origin of the world's great deltas, including the huge deltas on the deep ocean floor.

As precipitation rates dropped, the earth dried. And with drying came a change in vegetation. In Abraham and Lot's day, living only a few centuries after the Flood, higher precipitation rates may explain why the Dead Sea region was "well watered every where . . . as the garden of the LORD" and thus attractive to Lot (Gen. 13:10–11). It might also provide explanation why some four hundred years later, the now-desert land of Canaan was an incredibly fertile land that "floweth with milk and honey" (Num. 13:23–27). But the drying of the earth caused woodlands to dwindle worldwide, being gradually replaced by extensive grasslands.[8]

Eventually, the drying generated the world's current deserts, explaining why the Sahara Desert has evidence of rivers and forests beneath its wind-blown sands.[9] The creation of the Sahara Desert in this way also provides a possible explanation for why the Sphinx of Egypt shows signs of being eroded by water, when younger Egyptian edifices (like the pyramids) only have evidence of wind erosion.[10]

The evaporation of water from the oceans finally cooled the oceans after the Flood. For most of this period, the continents would have been substantially cooler than the oceans. Although this contrast is still observed in the present, it would have been much greater in the centuries immediately following the Flood. Traveling from the ocean inland, the temperature would have dropped farther—and faster. As a result of this temperature structure, there were probably different communities closer to the ocean than inland. And since the temperature changed quickly as one went inland, the communities were probably geographically narrow and overlapped with adjacent communities. This may explain why fossils of Tertiary plant communities found near the continental margins tend to have such a mixture of plants with different climactic tolerances.[11]

The young-age creationist Flood model suggests that the oceans heated up during the Flood and cooled down in the centuries following. This claim is evidenced in the shells of single-celled marine organisms. There seems to be an increase in ocean temperatures through the Primary and Secondary, and a decrease during the Tertiary.[12] Once again, this has no explanation in alternate models of earth history.

The Ice Advance

Eventually, the world's oceans cooled sufficiently for precipitation to come down at high altitudes and latitudes as snow. Since it came down so quickly, summer warmth in many places was not able to melt all the snow that had fallen the previous winter. As a result, snow built up and was compacted in some places into ice, which in turn accumulated into huge ice sheets. Eventually, the ice became so thick that it flowed under its own weight, surging over areas where there was no ice. Starting with warm oceans, early results from numerical modeling studies[13] suggest that the ice accumulated in the places we know it actually did, and that this happened in the matter of a few centuries. When the ice had accumulated sufficiently, it surged out in a couple of decades and then melted in another couple of decades. Because of its brevity, this rapid buildup and surging of ice is more appropriately called an *Ice Advance* rather than an *Ice Age*.

This numerical modeling (which fits into the young-age creation time scale) seems to be the only modeling that successfully produces ice sheets where we know they were. The ice accumulation and melting of these models is too rapid for alternate theories, which also cannot explain how the ocean became warm in the first place.

The Ice Advance model has a lot of advantages, because it explains the same evidence explained by conventional Ice Age theory but goes well beyond that. For example, Ice Advance theory suggests that there was only *one* ice advance (with multiple surges). It also claims that the ice was much thinner and did not remain as long as conventional theory believes. Therefore, it more easily explains how there could be ice-free regions, such as around Appleton, Wisconsin—places that glaciers completely surrounded but that were never covered in glacial ice.

Also, if thick ice had remained on the continent for a long time, it would have bowed the continent down under its own weight. Since it takes the earth some twenty-five thousand years to recover completely from being depressed in this fashion, it should still be rebounding. However, most of Ohio, Indiana, and Illinois show very little to no rebound—as if the ice was either very thin or it was not there very long.

Changes in Organisms

When God created the organisms of the world, He did so with the desire that they would persist through time. He designed them to survive not only in the pre-Fall world but also in the fallen, cursed world to follow. He also designed them in such a way that they could adapt to changing world conditions, such as those that followed the Flood. Creation biologists are only beginning to investigate these mechanisms, so there is much more to learn. But among those being studied are *altruistic genetic elements* (abbreviated AGEs).[14] These are pieces of DNA (genetic elements) that are designed to multiply and move around, both within and between organisms. Many of these genetic elements function something like switches for genes that are already there. A given genetic element might affect one or more genes. It might act on genes that are already in use—speeding them up, slowing them down, or turning them off. It might act on genes that have not been active, turning them on.

Switching on genes—especially genes that affect a cascade of other genes—can change organisms a lot . . . and quickly! Since these genetic elements were created by God to benefit the organisms, they reproduce themselves and are spread around for the benefit of the earth's organisms. Thus the reason for their name: altruistic genetic elements.

AGEs may provide an explanation for several interesting features in the DNA of organisms not explained well by other theories. Past activity of AGEs might show up as numerous copies of certain DNA segments (the AGEs themselves)—both within the genetic material of one organism and between the genetic material of different organisms. This may be the origin of some of the repetitive DNA in individual organisms. It may also be the origin of DNA shared among different organisms, which is thought to arise due to *lateral gene transfer.* Since we can now examine DNA in minute detail, we may be able to recognize genes that either no longer function because they have been turned off by AGEs or have never (yet) been turned on by AGEs.

This may also explain some of the pseudogenes that have been identified so far. More research is needed to test the validity of AGE theory— and more mechanisms of organismal change will have to be discovered by young-age creationists. In the meantime, the prospects for AGE theory look good.

The effect of these and other, as yet undiscovered built-in mechanisms of change is that organisms changed quickly and dramatically in the centuries following the Flood. The Bible describes some modern species existing within one thousand years of the Flood (camels, for instance, in Gen. 12:16; lions in Job 4:10–11; horses in Gen. 12:16). The fossil record suggests that almost all modern species were in place soon after the Ice Advance, which likely occurred within a thousand years after the Flood. The archaeological record has modern species of plants and animals represented in human art and preserved in archaeological sites early in the development of post-Babel cultures. This would suggest that new species must have arisen at a stunningly high rate in the centuries immediately following the Flood.

In perhaps as few as three centuries, scores of new species arose within most mammal baramins, and thousands of species arose within many of the insect and plant baramins. Many of these animals would be extinguished by the catastrophic and changing environments after the Flood, but many others would survive for a time—long enough, at least, to produce new generations of different organisms. This rapid increase in diversity occurred entirely within baramins, so it can be called *intra-baraminic diversification.*

It is possible that the sediments of the Tertiary and Quaternary actually document the events of this wild and changing world following the Flood. It might be that the increasing frequency of modern species in Tertiary sediments (starting at zero percent in the lowermost Tertiary rocks) is explained by this intrabaraminic diversification. During this period the world was also cooling. Bulkier animals, of course, are better able to survive in cooler environments. Thus the tendency for mammal species to increase in size through the Tertiary and into Quaternary (known as Cope's Law) may be explained as a biological response to the post-Flood cooling trend.

The drying of the earth after the Flood also had an effect. Grasslands spread at the expense of woodlands. Baramins that seem to exclusively browse on trees and shrubs low in the Tertiary, come to be represented in the higher Tertiary by organisms that prefer grass (grazers). Simultaneously, in several mammal baramins (horses, camels, rabbits, and elephants, to name a few), species with a unique arrangement of teeth arose. Their teeth stood higher above the gumline and were flatter and

---

Bio-Evolutionary Evidence:

Vestigial Structures

Vestigial structure: a structure of an organism that has a reduced function from the same structure in similar organisms or fossils.

In bio-evolutionary theory, organisms are continually changing—evolving new structures and phasing out old structures. Vestigial structures are evidence of this evolution—at least of the phasing out of old structures—and should be common features of life.

In young-age creation theory, many intrabaraminic changes have occurred—including the loss or partial loss of structures. Furthermore, with the Fall, imperfections began entering the system, causing some structures to lose all or partial function. Young-age creationism suggests that these changes occurred within the last few thousand years. This means that in most cases change has not eliminated all the information to build those structures. Thus, the occasional genetic throwback (*e.g.,* the rare occurrence of a multitoed horse) and the ability to produce all or part of a long-lost structure (*e.g.,* the development and resorption in *some* unborn sperm whales of bones for a rear leg and hip) is easier to explain in young-age creationism than in evolutionary theory.

---

larger—all useful in chewing grass. This may explain several of the fossil series found in the fossil record.

Some of the changes that have occurred among organisms seem to be evidenced in vestigial structures (features that had a strong function in the past but now seem to have reduced function or no function at all) and *genetic throwbacks* (past structures that appear spontaneously in a small percentage of offspring in the present). Hip and leg bones that appear in some foetal sperm whales, for example, are vestigial structures. They suggest that modern whales might be descendants of whales in the past that had hind limbs. In a rare number of births, a horse is born with multiple toes. This is a genetic throwback, suggesting modern horses might be descendants of horses in the past that had more than the single toe that modern horses have.

The same vestigial organisms and genetic throwbacks also suggest that the transformations were not made long ago. Complex structures that provide no advantage to the organisms tend to get eliminated by natural selection, and the genetic information needed to build them tends to get destroyed rapidly by mutation. The existence of vestigial structures and genetic throwbacks is more easily explained by young-age creationist claims that it occurred only thousands of years ago, rather than conventional claims that it occurred tens of millions of years ago.

Since intrabaraminic diversification is recent, it also explains why *interspecific hybridization* is common. It is much easier to explain successful hybridization after only thousands of years of separation than it is to explain compatibility after millions or tens of millions of years (see discussion in chap. 8). In the same way, it provides an explanation for species complexes (groups of similar, hybridizable species that live in a particular area) and ring species (a circular string of populations, all of which can interbreed with adjacent species except two at one point on the ring). And since it involves change without using the process of natural selection, intrabaraminic diversification may better explain cryptic species—populations that look identical but differ enough in their DNA to suggest that they do not actually interbreed.

A New Place to Live

Biogeography is the science of where organisms live and how they came to live there. The biogeography of the antediluvian world (chap. 12) was largely determined by God's activity in Creation Week. However, the Flood destroyed many of these pre-Flood communities, and the oceans of the catastrophe-ridden post-Flood world were probably far too choppy to allow for the redevelopment of the floating forest. This accounts for the extinction or near-extinction of all the plants and animals of this environ-

Bio-Evolutionary Evidence:

Speciation / Ring Species

Ring species: a set of populations arranged geographically in a closed loop (*e.g.,* frog populations along the shore of a lake or fruit fly populations around the base of a mountain) where all but one pair of populations can interbreed with adjacent species.

In bio-evolutionary theory, organisms are continually changing. Thus, separated populations (*e.g.,* frog populations that spread in opposite directions along a lake shore or fly populations that spread in opposite directions around the base of a mountain) can each change enough to become unable to cross when they meet again on the other side of the obstruction. Ring species comprise one type of evidence for speciation—the origin of species by natural process. Other evidences include populations that show different degrees of interbreedability, lab populations that become incapable of crossing with the original population, and polyploidy—where the young cannot interbreed with the original population because they have a different number of chromosomes.

Young-age creation theory accepts considerable intrabaraminic change—including the loss of interbreedability. Ring species and other evidences of genetic incompatibility are thus fully accepted by young-age creation theory. Because speciation is more recent in young-age creation theory, however, widespread and common hybridization between different species is easier to explain in young-age creation theory than in evolutionary theory.

ment. The reformed continents seem to have lacked the hydrothermal margins of the pre-Flood world, forcing hydrothermal organisms to survive in small, isolated places in the post-Flood world (such as mid-ocean ridges and geysers). The slower reproductive rate of gymnospermous plants (as opposed to flowering plants) probably led to their being crowded out by competition. This in turn probably led to the rarity of

Bio-Evolutionary Evidence:

Biogeography

Biogeography is the study of where organisms live
and how they got there.

According to bio-evolutionary theory, new species arise from preexisting species. This means that they start out living in the same place. This means that more closely related species (in other words, those that are more similar) will tend to live close together. Also, if descendant species don't go very far (*e.g.,* because they are land organisms caught on an island or aquatic organisms caught in a land-locked lake), then the entire group and all their fossils will be restricted to this region. Finally, since evolution results in organisms being fit for the place where they lived, it's possible for organisms found in one place to be more fit than organisms on, for example, another continent. As evolution expects, similar species are found near each other, and Australian marsupials and their fossils are only known (in the wild) in Australia. Also as evolution expects, newly introduced species often spread rather rapidly (*e.g.,* rabbits and dingoes in Australia; Kudzu, Dutch elm disease, and starlings in North America).

In young-age creation theory, intrabaraminic diversification after the Flood produced many new species from preexisting species. This should result in many of the same expectations as evolutionary theory—similar species being found near each other, more similar groups of species (and their fossils) being restricted to one region, and introduced species from one area out-competing the species in another area. However, young-age creation theory also suggests that these changes occurred both rapidly and recently (only thousands of years ago). The widespread hybridization possible between many species is consistent with such a recent diversification and difficult to explain in conventional evolutionary theory.

post-Flood dinosaurs, making them prone to extinction (perhaps ultimately at the hand of humans).

The survivors of the Flood (water-loving organisms outside the ark as well as land-dwelling organisms inside the ark) had the responsibility of repopulating the earth, and they soon began spreading over the face of the planet. This probably happened in several ways.

Warm, post-flood oceans created a wet tropical climate along the shorelines of the entire world, while cool, dry continents generated parallel zones of subtropical, warm temperate, and cool temperate climates inside the tropical bands. These occurrences allowed organisms to migrate along shorelines in their climates of choice.[15]

As the earth cooled and precipitation began accumulating in continental glaciers, the sea level dropped, opening up land bridges across shallow seas, such as the Bering Strait between Asia and North America, the English Channel between England and France, and much of the ocean between Indonesian islands.

Since some of the plants of the present world can float for decades (like the Douglas Fir on Spirit Lake near Mt. St. Helens), plant rafts may have floated about on the world's oceans for many years following the Flood. These rafts may have provided transport for many organisms across the oceans in the post-Flood world. Faster-moving organisms (such as marsupials, which don't have to stop as long to care for young) may have been the first to ride these rafts over and colonize island continents (like Australia and Antarctica—even South America, which has only recently joined North America). By the time slower organisms made it to key locations, the plant rafts may have been destroyed. Although much work needs to be done in this area, young-age creationism has a good chance of developing a strong, testable theory of biogeography.

What's Next?

While the earth was recovering from the Flood and organisms were repopulating the earth, man was not recovering quite so well—or obeying quite so completely. Perhaps man didn't believe God's promise that He would not destroy the earth by water again. Perhaps man didn't believe God could comfort him when he was alone. Or perhaps man was just being defiant. Whatever the reasons, man's disobedience led to another catastrophe—this one affecting man's culture. The effects of this catastrophe and the dispersal that resulted are considered in the next chapter.

CHAPTER 15

THE BABEL DISPERSION

Most Christians associate the word *Babel* with a tower and with confusion of language. In the young-age creation model, however, Babel's place in history may be much more significant than that. In this chapter, we will discuss how this pivotal event in earth history explains the differences between the language and culture of the people of the world and the origins of the various races of mankind. We also will look briefly at the best-known fossils of early man and the reasons why some widely held conclusions about them are inconsistent with the biblical record.

When Did It Happen?

Adam and Eve were created to bond together as one, picturing the love that binds the members of the Godhead. Since such bonding includes communication, it is reasonable to assume that Adam and Eve were created with the ability to speak . . . and to speak the same language. So for a time at least, there was only one language on the earth. Since Adam's son was still living during the early years of Noah's lifetime, it is reasonable to assume that the same language was spoken from the creation to the Flood. Since Noah, his wife, his three sons, and their wives were the only humans to survive the Flood, probably only a single language was spoken in the immediate period that followed. And since Noah lived for 350 years after the Flood (Gen. 9:28), it is also reasonable to assume that unless something happened to change it, a single language persisted for centuries after the Flood. This seems confirmed by Genesis 11:1: "The whole earth was of one language, and of one speech."

But something did happen to disrupt this—an event known as Babel.

When did Babel occur? A review of the early biblical genealogies helps us make a fairly accurate guess. It is rather typical in the Bible to introduce a narrative with a genealogy. The Flood in Genesis 6–9, for example, is introduced by the genealogy in Genesis 5. Abraham's life story beginning in Genesis 12 is introduced by the genealogy in Genesis 11. In the same way, the Babel narrative of Genesis 11:1–9 is preceded by the genealogy of Genesis 10. Here, after the genealogy of each son of Noah (vv. 5, 20, and 31)—and in the summary verse of the entire chapter (v. 32)—we are told that the people of the post-Flood world eventually became "divided" according to language, family, and nation. The verses that follow (Genesis 11:1–9) describe specifically how it happened. It seems, then, that the purpose of the genealogy in Genesis 10 is to reveal the generations that led up to Babel.

Two generations of descendants are listed for Japheth, three generations for Ham, and five generations for Shem. In Shem's genealogy from Genesis 10 (v. 25), the son of Eber was named Peleg, "for in his days was the earth divided."[1] In Shem's genealogy from Genesis 11, we see that Peleg was born 101 years after the Flood (by adding the figures in vv. 10, 12, 14, and 16) and died 340 years after the Flood (by adding the figures in vv. 18–19). We also learn from Genesis 10:25–29 that the division of languages apparently occurred after Peleg's thirteen nephews became heads of families.[2] Since the average generation time in Genesis 11 is a bit more than thirty years, Peleg was probably more than eighty years old[3] when Babel occurred. This means that Babel occurred some time between the second half of the second century and the first half of the fourth century after the Flood.

New Languages

But what exactly happened at—and after—the tower of Babel? And what were the historic repercussions of this monumental event?

It was not uncommon in ancient times to make clear distinctions in language that would be considered subtle to us today. For example, we might call a particular water course a river or stream, regardless of whether it has water in it. The ancients, in contrast, would tend to consider the water of the river as being distinct from the river channel itself. The ancients also thought of language as requiring two different abilities. First, people had to be physically capable of creating the sounds and inflections needed to communicate. Second, people had to be able to choose and control which sounds and inflections to form and in what order—much in the same way as the river channel constrains the water of the river. The first point related to the language itself; the second point related more to the mental perspective or viewpoint of the person who used the language.

Literally translated, Genesis 11:1 states, "The whole earth was of one lip, and of one and the same words." The terms *lip* and *word* probably refer to these two concepts. "Words" are the sounds of language; they represent the physical ability necessary to make them. The "lip" represents the constraining of these sounds—the person's perspective—the river channel. This understanding of Genesis 11:1 suggests that toward the end of the second century after the Flood, there was not only a single language (in the sense of a uniform set of words and linguistic rules) but also a single mental perspective or viewpoint. That all people were thinking similarly is certainly suggested by the fact that all the people banded together to build a single tower (Gen. 11:2–4), probably under a single ruler, Nimrod (Gen. 10:10).

The fact that the Babel account begins with a comment about the unity of language and perspective suggests that at least one of the two were to be changed as a result of the Babel event. That a single language was divided into multiple languages is obviously stated (Gen. 10:5, 20, 31; 11:9), and the fact that more than just the words and terms of language was involved can certainly be implied. God's reasoning behind the Babel event (Gen. 11:6) was that as long as all humans were unified, there was no limit to what they could do—including any *evil* they desired to do.

His response was to divide the language. If that involved only the creation of a new set of words, however, it would have been relatively easy to translate from one language to another. Each word would simply have to be translated into the word of another person's language. But God desired to make communication among humans so impossible that they would scatter from one another over the entire earth (Gen. 11:9). Dividing not just the *languages* but also the *perspectives* would be the best way to accomplish this task.

At the end of the Babel event, then, it is likely that each family on earth had both a distinct language *and* a distinct perspective of the world. This is certainly consistent with the fact that—even today—learning a new language usually involves not only learning a new list of words but also a different way of thinking. Therefore, it is likely that the distinct cultures of the world arose as a direct result of the distinct languages and perspectives introduced to man at Babel.

New Cultures

The culture and technology developed before the Flood was probably preserved *through* the Flood in near-complete form. The progression is not hard to follow. Noah had lived in the pre-Flood culture for six hundred years (Gen. 7:11), and his sons had lived in it for approximately one hundred years each (Gen. 5:32; 11:10). This makes for something on the order of nine centuries of familiarity with antediluvian culture. The ability to build a wooden ship the size of the ark would likely have required the use of whatever technology had been developed in pre-Flood times. We also know from Scripture that Noah (Gen. 9:28), Shem (Gen. 11:11), and probably the other sons of Noah lived for centuries after the Flood—well after the Babel incident, which involved the building of a city and a heaven-reaching tower that reveals a sophisticated culture that had survived the Flood.

But in the Babel event, God created new languages—and new perspectives. As was the case when He made things during Creation Week, God probably created these languages as already fully developed and these perspectives as fully mature. This would result in the instantaneous appearance of languages and the rapid origin of fully developed cultures. Different perspectives led people to create different expressions of culture. This is why different Babel families probably produced distinct forms of music, fine art, literature, and architecture. So the Babel account provides ample explanation for many of the differences we see throughout history and in our present world.

Language. There seem to be something on the order of a couple of hundred distinct language groups on earth—and no easy way to explain how these languages were derived from fewer earlier languages. This may point to the creation of languages at the tower of Babel. Among those languages, some of them developed written forms of communication. These written languages are so different from one another (from cuneiform to hieroglyphics to Chinese characters) that they also seem to confirm the sudden creation of language diversity at Babel. Furthermore, the age of the oldest evidences of those languages seems to decrease as we move away from the tower of Babel—apparently evidence of human dispersion away from that region.

Culture. Cultures seem to show the same pattern. They appear on the scene rather fully developed and do not seem easily derivable from one another. Different language groups seem to have distinct musical forms and art perspectives not derivable from one another. The oldest evidences of human culture also seem to get younger away from the Middle East, which yields further evidence of human dispersion away from Babel. The extraordinary technologies evidenced in ancient cultures, such as the building of pyramids, sophisticated irrigation systems, huge statues and temples seem to reflect the high culture that man was created with—a range of knowledge and skill that survived the Flood.

Worldviews and Ways of Thinking. The Babel dispersion also provides a potential foundation for comparative ethnology, musicology, and the study of comparative religions. As a preliminary example, Western culture is dominated by the Indo-European language group. This branch developed a musical scale that is mathematically scaled off actual sound waves in the physical world. It is also the culture that developed modern science—a mathematics-based study of the physical world. It also developed the religion of naturalism—the belief that the physical world is all that exists. These similarities may be due to some sort of physical world perspective being given to the Babel ancestors.

Religion. Noah and Shem (and probably the other sons of Noah) survived the Flood and lived at the time of Babel; they also believed God and knew the truth about Him. Noah, for example, had firsthand knowledge of more than one-third of earth history up to that point. He also lived for 42 years before the death of Adam's third son, Seth, who would have had firsthand knowledge of all but the first 130 years of the remainder of earth history before the Flood. Thus, Noah had firsthand knowledge of one-third of earth history, possibly secondhand knowledge of most of the remaining two-thirds, and thirdhand knowledge of the very first decades of earth history.

It is likely, then, that everyone living at the time of Babel knew the true history of the world—about the one true God, the Creator of all things. And that same knowledge was carried away from Babel by all the peoples of the world, though understood in different languages and interpreted from different perspectives. According to Romans 1:21–32, most people who once knew God have rejected Him and created their own religion. And these false religions were probably developed from the perspectives they were given at Babel. This may ultimately permit young-age creationists to explain why different cultures produced the particular kinds of music, art, architecture, and even religion that they developed.

Traditions. The common knowledge possessed by all those who dispersed from Babel also explains similar traditions found in multiple cultures. Although each family group will likely distort the true stories over time—both in details and in chronology—similarities may be expected to persist. This would provide a good explanation for why more than 120 different cultures have Flood traditions[4] and why so many of them have Creation and Fall traditions. Many cultures speak of a golden age of man—often before a world-destroying flood—when humans lived for a long time. The common knowledge at Babel would also explain the evidence in the oldest characters of the Chinese language that the earliest Chinese were monotheistic and believed the Creation and Fall accounts of Scripture.[5]

Red and Yellow, Black and White

Only one family survived the Flood. It is likely, then, that even if there was more than one race before the Flood (and there is no hint in Scripture of this), only one race survived it.[6] It is also likely that even by the time of Babel, there was still only one race. But the population may well have had a range of characteristics reflective of different races. And when the Babel event divided the human population into different languages and perspectives, it divided them according to their respective families.

Because of the breakdown in communication, these families spread across the earth—each apparently going to a distinct place and separated from all other groups. Each family group became the start of a new people, which for many generations did not cross with any other family or people. Any physical differences that might have existed in the pre-Babel population were probably divided up among the different family groups—each one slightly different than the others.

In each family group following the great dispersion, a phenomenon called *genetic drift* began to take over. Genetic drift occurs in small inbreeding populations, such as the families who were dispersed from Babel. It is really just a luck-of-the-draw problem. Take as an example the survival of surnames. Since women usually take on the surname of their spouse, surnames are generally passed down through the sons across the generations. Daughters eventually marry or die, thereby marking the end of the surname they carry. In large families with common names (such as

Bio-Evolutionary Evidence:

Paleoanthropology / Human Fossils / Cavemen / Lucy

Paleoanthropology is the study of human and human-like fossils. Such fossils range (from older to younger) from generally scrappy (but occasionally good) specimens of African apes called australopithecines (including "Lucy"), to excellent and fairly common specimens of *Homo erectus* (including "Java Man" and "Peking Man"), to common specimens of Neanderthals and beautiful and common specimens of modern *Homo sapiens.*

In bio-evolutionary theory, humans are thought to have evolved from some single-celled ancestor through a long series of forms before evolving from some ape-like ancestor in the fairly recent past. In this theory, apes should not appear as fossils until well up into the fossil record and should appear before human fossils. Furthermore, human traits should show up in a stepwise fashion through the fossil sequence. The fossil record seems to confirm these expectations, with apes not found as fossils until well up in the rock column, apes with human-like characteristics (*e.g.,* australopithecines, which walk upright) above the first ape

Miller or Smith), it is unlikely that the family name will ever disappear. For this to happen, thousands of married couples would have to give birth to girls only. In small families (like the Gallot family—the maiden name of the author's mother-in-law, where there has been a grand total of fifty-two people bearing the name since immigration in the mid-eighteenth century) the chances are much greater that the family name could disappear because it would take just a few married couples bearing girls only.

In a similar way, genetic drift can take a given character trait that is not really more advantageous than any other and make it the only char-

fossils, and human-like fossils (*e.g.*, *Homo habilis* and *H. erectus*) occurring even farther up section. Furthermore, whereas the first tools were chipped rocks, subsequent tools were stone arrowheads. Evidence of hunting and gathering fruits and nuts occurs before evidence of agriculture, and evidence of cave-dwelling predates the building of cities. The fossil record shows evidence of the cultural evolution expected in evolutionary theory.

In young-age creation theory, man was created human and with the intelligence and manipulative ability necessary for high culture. When man stepped off the ark, however, the world was reeling with residual catastrophe, and all its resources had been completely rearranged in a wholly unfamiliar manner. Though intellectually capable of culture, the priorities of survival would delay its development. Agriculture would have to wait until permanent residence could be secured, and cities would have to wait until resources could be secured to build them. Also, since man refused to disperse immediately, as he was supposed to, he would arrive at distant locales long after organisms already had. This explains why humans are found above ape fossils and why it takes awhile for humans to acquire full evidences of culture. The young-age creationists' claim that humans were intellectually advanced from the very beginning provides a better explanation for the beauty and sophistication of early cave paintings, the sophistication of the possessions of the "Ice Man," and the amazing capabilities of the earliest civilizations (*e.g.*, the canalization of Mesopotamia, the pyramids of Egypt).

acter trait in the population. Different skin colors, for example, do not cause a huge difference in human survival. Yet in small populations, genetic drift can eliminate the genetic information for all skin colors but one. In the generations following Babel, different families probably developed unique combinations of physical characteristics. Some of these combinations were distinct enough to define what we have come to call the human races.

Once particular traits were fixed into a particular family group, those traits may well have influenced where that family chose to live.

Dominantly tall and thin families would find cold environments very uncomfortable. Light-skinned families would probably tend to avoid the tropics because of the sensitivity to sunburn. Very dark-skinned families would tend to avoid high latitudes where there was not enough sunlight to penetrate the skin and allow Vitamin E production. This would explain why many of the human races ended up where they did. The recency and rapidity of these changes is certainly consistent with the very small changes that separate the different races. The differences are literally only skin deep.

The differences in skin color are primarily due to different amounts of melanin in the skin. Some of the skin color differences, as well as the differences in eye shape and lip fullness, are due to the distribution of subcutaneous (or skin) fat. Even hair distribution is due to differences in the skin. There seem to be no measurable differences in any other characteristic.[7]

Genetically, different skin colors can be generated in the course of a single generation. Pure-bred whites and blacks cannot produce anything other than whites and blacks, respectively. Genetic information has apparently been lost in those lineages—probably through genetic drift in the centuries following Babel. Most people know, however, that the marriage of a pure-bred black and a pure-bred white will generate children with a wide range of skin colors between white and black. In fact, it appears theoretically possible for a marriage of people with a particular set of DNA to generate children of just about every skin color in the next generation. The skin color of such a couple would be brown—reasonably enough the dominant skin color on the earth today. Another curious observation is that in descendants of each of the sons of Noah, there is a wide range of skin colors known—something that would be expected in the Babel model of human dispersion.[8]

Cave Men?

What were these people like—those who were scattered by the hand of God from the tower of Babel? Arphaxad, the son of Shem, was born 2 years after the Flood and lived for 438 years (Gen. 11:10–13). He thus lived through not only the tower of Babel incident but most of the incredible changes of the post-Flood earth discussed in chapter 13. The period of time during which Arphaxad lived—and during which the generations following Babel lived—might be called the *Arphaxadian Epoch.*

Aside from things that occurred during the Flood, the Arphaxadian Epoch saw some of the most interesting geological and climatological events in earth history. During the same period some of the most interesting events in human history also occurred. Human longevity was dropping at a steady rate. Humans gathered in Babel to create a great tower and were then dispersed worldwide by a confusion of language. It was also during this period that most of the great races, religions, and cultures of mankind arose.

When Noah and his family stepped off the ark, they entered a far different world than the one they lived in before the Flood. The antediluvian land was faulted, flooded, eroded, and buried with an average of one and one-half miles of sediment. All lakes and rivers, hills and mountains, and even the air and the soil were different. Plants and animals assembled into different communities and then began changing. Whatever animals and plants were sought before the Flood for medicine or food would be changing. Copper and iron would have to be searched for in new locations. Even with the highest cultural and technological ability, humans immediately after the Flood would have to live otherwise. Food would have to be gathered where it could be found, tools would have to be fashioned from crude materials, and shelter would have to be secured in different ways and places.

As conditions stabilized and resources could be found in their new locations, these hunting-gathering, stone-tool-based, cave-dwelling societies would change into agricultural, copper- and then iron-tool-based, city-dwelling societies. These changes, however, would occur in the course of decades to centuries—well within the course of a single human lifetime.

The first such transition must have led to the foundation of Babel's civilization. Once the family groups dispersed from Babel, each one would have found itself in the same situation again—lacking shelter, agriculture, and metals for tools. In each situation, agriculture, metal-working, and cities would have to be developed independently. The rate of culture development would vary considerably from location to location—some never moving out of the hunting-gathering mode at all. Most of the time, however, culture could develop through stages of stone tool development to copper and bronze tool development—and beyond—in the space of a single lifetime.

Then, like ripples from pebbles thrown into a pond, culture would move outward from cultural centers. At any given point in earth history after Babel, different cultures could be found in every different stage of culture development—just as is the case today.

The most ancient cultural evidences of these activities are interpreted very differently in young-age creationism than any alternative model of earth history. A particular quality of stone tool, for example, is tradition-ally interpreted as indicating a particular period of earth history, as if that specific tool was made only at one time in earth history. In young-age cre-ationism, however, the same potential for cultural evolution was pos-sessed by numerous, closely related families at many different places across the earth. It is very likely that the same type of stone tool was devel-oped independently by many different Babel families at many different locations on earth. At each location it was probably developed at a differ-ent time and was produced for a much briefer period than is thought in other theories.

The oldest cave paintings of the earth, then, are understood to be rather sophisticated paintings of a culturally capable people forced to sur-vive in caves, forced for a time to eat what they could hunt and gather. The relatively low frequency of such cave sites, ancient burial sites, and even stone tools is better explained by rapid multiregional cultural evolu-tion such as is suggested in young-age creation theory. The sophisticated clothing and artifacts found on "Ice Man"[9] and his inferred behavior is understandable in young-age creation theory, but it is rather difficult to explain in any other model.

Fossil Humans

God's interest has always been for man to glorify Him in the entire creation. He commanded the first family to reproduce and multiply and fill the earth (Gen. 1:28). He also commanded the first post-Flood family to reproduce and multiply and fill the earth (Gen. 9:1). But just as the early church disobeyed Jesus' command to go and preach the gospel to everyone throughout the world (Matt. 28:19; Mark 16:15) and was therefore forced to disperse by persecution (Acts 8:1–4), so Noah's immediate descendants also disobeyed their command (Gen. 11:2). And God forced them to disperse by dividing their language (Gen. 11:9).

In the meantime (while humans built a city, a tower, and a government at Babel), God had ordered creation in such a way that the animals and plants acted in accordance with His command and spread to the most distant places on the earth's surface. The humans would arrive later. This explains why animal fossils—including the fossils of apes—are found below the first evidences of humans. Evolutionary theories interpret this as evidence that humans evolved from a lower life form. But young-age creationists interpret this same evidence as another example of man's stubborn refusal to live the exalted life that God desires him to live.

The humans who lived soon after the Flood lived under unusual circumstances. The changing plants and animals must have generated a changing and perhaps unreliable diet. This problem was made even worse by changes in medicinal plants as well as new diseases that arose through never-before-seen mutations. Remaining healthy was probably a great struggle for man just after the Flood. Humans in the Arphaxadian Epoch lived much longer than they do today. Noah lived over nine centuries (Gen. 9:29). It is not known exactly how humans weathered such age. It is possible that with a longer life span, people matured more slowly. The ages of fathers at the birth of their sons average much higher before the Flood when life spans were longer. But ten generations after Noah, Abraham lived less than two centuries (Gen. 25:7).

The decrease in life span may have been partially caused by accelerated development. If so, this might explain why the first temporary teeth in children are coming in at earlier ages and why female menstrual cycles are starting at steadily earlier ages. And it may be the cause of much improper reconstruction of fossil humans.[10] The slower development of post-Flood people may have led to the development of a different stature and bone structure. These differences may account for some of the differences between living and fossil humans. Other differences may turn out to be due to different diet and climate.

Ultimately, fossils dubbed *Homo erectus* and *Homo sapiens* are almost certainly humans who lived in the first couple of centuries after the Babel dispersion. The brain size indicated by these fossils overlaps the range found in modern man. The bones (aside from the skull) can hardly be distinguished from modern humans. One of the oldest known *Homo erectus* skeletons is of what appears to be (at modern maturation rates) a sixteen-year-old boy who stands over six feet tall. The remaining fossils that have been interpreted by some as human or as ancestors of humans are interpreted by young-age creationists to be extinct apes that lived in the Arphaxadian Epoch with man. All these fossils have brain sizes well below that of modern humans and in or near the range of modern apes. Even the non-skull bones are relatively easily distinguished from modern man.

Young-age creationism interprets much of earth history very differently from alternate theories. We have dealt with many of them in this book. And—as we have often stated—much study and research remains to be done to see the truths of Scripture revealed in the evidence we hold in our hands or will uncover in the future. But young-age creationism does not have a totally divergent view of earth history. By about the time of King David, radiocarbon dates seem to correspond to biblical dates. Much of the conventional interpretation of archaeology from about 1000 B.C. and forward are interpreted very much the same as it is in other theories. We differ on many fronts, but we do share some points of agreement.

What's Next?

The first two worlds in creation's time ended with divine judgment. The present third world—our world—will also end in judgment. We are living now in the waning hours of our age, the entire creation anticipating the extraordinary world to come. The next chapter briefly considers the coming judgment . . . and the world to follow.

CHAPTER 16

THE END, THE BEGINNING

The end will end as the beginning began—focusing upon its Creator. God created the universe with characteristics that reflect His very nature. He created us along with the space, matter, and time of this universe for the purpose of bringing glory to Him forever. That purpose is still to be fulfilled, and it will be fulfilled.

In the meantime, however, a short parenthetical note of some six thousand years (so far) has been inserted. Not long after the creation, the image-bearer of God disobeyed the God Who created him. That disobedience placed a wedge of sin between man and God—a wedge too deeply embedded for man to extract. The wedge cracked the perfection of the entire physical creation, impacting instantly even the farthest stars. Man's sin, our sin, my sin, and your sin was—and is—a tragedy. As a result of it God cursed the universe, and the entire creation groans in pain because of it.

But even in the execution of the curse, God displayed mercy and love. He modified the physical creation in such a way that it would survive the Fall of man, the entrance of sin, and the burden of the curse. Better than that, God's providence had already designed the world to survive that event. He designed it also to survive the Flood, the great judgment on man's sin. Even more spectacularly, He decided on a way to bring man back to Himself—a way to pull out the wedge of sin.

When Adam hid from God following his disobedience, God did not go seeking Adam in the garden only to find him and try to figure out what He should do to rescue the man He had created. God sought Adam because a way had already been decided upon. The wedge of sin between God and man could be extracted only by God, but it could be extracted only if God touched that sin. The only way the wedge could be taken away was for sinless God to become sin in man's place. The Lamb of God would have to die in man's place, and this decision was made even before God began to create. It would take abundant love for God to look down at sinful man and decide to die in his place. In fact, it took more love than that. For before God began to create, He realized that if He created man, man would fall. He knew that He would have to die in man's place to rescue man from his own sin. Yet God had enough love for man to create him anyway.

God became flesh and lived among us in the form of Jesus Christ so He could die for your sins and mine. Jesus then conquered death and was raised again to show that He has victory over all effects of sin. Just as centuries before in the wilderness—when men, women, and children by the thousands were dying of snake bites, and Moses placed an image of a snake on a pole and lifted it up so all could see, allowing anyone who looked upon the uplifted snake to be instantly healed—God Himself came in the image of man and was placed upon a cross and lifted up so all could see. All who look upon that cross and trust in the completed work Jesus has done to take care of their sin are bought back from the death of the curse and adopted into the family of God.

If you have not done this, won't you do it today?

God cannot allow His creation to remain under the burden of the curse. He cannot allow the pain and suffering of His creation to continue forever. The marred picture must be erased and redrawn. The people who have been purchased out of the bondage of sin must be taken out of the presence of sin. According to Romans 8:19, even "the earnest expectation of the creature waiteth for the manifestation of the sons of God."

So the story of the creation does not end when our memories begin, or when the dates of radiometry correspond with those of the Bible, or at any particular event of the past. The story of the creation was never supposed to end. The creation was supposed to reflect perfectly forever the perfect nature of God. For the highest purpose of the creation to be continued, the parenthetical note of sin and its consequences must be closed. Sin must be extracted from the creation, the curse must be lifted from it, and the old creation must be destroyed so a new creation can be put in its place.

In 2 Peter 3, we are told of scoffers who in the end times will reject the Creation and the Flood—in order to reject the judgment to come. If a person properly understands the purpose of the original creation and the effects of sin upon it, he expects the end to come. It is a necessary consequence of the beginning. These scoffers reject the truths of the past and the truth of the future in order to continue in their sin. I beg of you, do not let that be you.

"The heavens and the earth, which are now, by the same word [as they were created] are kept in store, reserved unto fire against the day of judgment and perdition of ungodly men" (2 Pet. 3:7). Perhaps you think that such a thing is not likely to happen in your lifetime; after all, people have been standing on mountains waiting for this end of things for centuries, yet it hasn't come. Carefully consider the rest of the passage:

> But beloved, be not ignorant of this one thing, that one day is with the Lord as a thousand years, and a thousand years as one day. The Lord is not slack concerning his promise, as some men count slackness; but is longsuffering to us-ward, not willing that any should perish, but that all should come to repentance. But the day of the Lord will come as thief in the night; in the which the heavens shall pass away with a great noise, and the elements shall melt with a fervent heat, the earth also and the works that are therein shall be burned up. Seeing then that all these things shall be dissolved, what manner of persons ought ye to be in all holy conversation and godliness, looking for and

hasting unto the coming of the day of God, wherein the
heavens being on fire shall be dissolved, and the elements
shall melt with fervent heat? Nevertheless we, according to
his promise, look for new heavens and a new earth,
wherein dwelleth righteousness. Wherefore, beloved, seeing
that ye look for such things, be diligent that ye may be
found of him in peace, without spot, and blameless
(2 Pet. 3:8–14).

Are you blameless, my friend? The same God Who created the universe is coming back to destroy all sin, all sinners, and everything corrupted by sin. Are you ready for that? This passage in 2 Peter was actually written for believers. If you are already a believer, are you living for Him as you ought? If you are not a believer, you can be today. God showed His love toward you in that while you were still a sinner, still rebelling against Him, God incarnate died for your sin (Rom. 5:8). "If thou shalt confess with thy mouth the Lord Jesus, and shalt believe in thine heart that God hath raised him from the dead, thou shalt be saved" (Rom. 10:9).

After the "dead, small and great, stand before God" (Rev. 20:12) and are "judged every man according to their works" (Rev. 20:13), "death and hell [will be] cast into the lake of fire . . . and whosoever was not found written in the book of life [will be] cast into the lake of fire" (Rev. 20:14–15). John the apostle was given a vision of new creation, and he described it as follows:

I saw a new heaven and a new earth: for the first
heaven and the first earth were passed away; and there was
no more sea. And I John saw the holy city, new Jerusalem,
coming down from God out of heaven, prepared as a bride
adorned for her husband. And I heard a great voice out of
heaven saying, Behold, the tabernacle of God is with men,
and he will dwell with them, and they shall be his people,
and God himself shall be with them, and be their God. And

God shall wipe away all tears from their eyes; and there
shall be no more death, neither sorrow, nor crying, neither
shall there be any more pain: for the former things are
passed away. And he that sat upon the throne said, Behold,
I make all things new. And he said unto me, Write: for
these words are true and faithful. And he said unto me, It is
done. I am Alpha and Omega, the beginning and the end
(Rev. 21:1–6).

As John ends his book and as the Holy Spirit ends written revelation,
so also we end this book by declaring: "He which testifieth these things
saith, Surely I come quickly. Amen. Even so, come, Lord Jesus. The grace
of our Lord Jesus Christ be with you all. Amen" (Rev. 22:20–21).

Selected Bibliography

Arct, Michael J. "Dendrochronology in the Yellowstone Fossil Forests." M.A. thesis, Loma Linda University, Loma Linda, California, 1979.

———. "Dendrochronology in the Fossil Forests of the Specimen Creek Area, Yellowstone National Park." Ph.D. dissertation, Loma Linda University, Loma Linda, California, 1991.

Austin, Steven A. "Depositional Environment of the Kentucky No. 12 Coal Bed (Middle Pennsylvanian) of Western Kentucky, with Special Reference to the Origin of Coal Lithotypes." Ph.D. dissertation, Pennsylvania State University, 1979.

———. "Mount St. Helens and Catastrophism." *ICR Impact Article 157* and *Creation Science Movement Pamphlet 252,* 1987.

———. "The Declining Power of Post-Flood Volcanoes." In *ICR Impact 302:i–iv* (1998).

———. (ed.) *Grand Canyon: Monument to Catastrophe.* Santee, Calif.: Institute for Creation Research, 1994.

Austin, Steven A., John R. Baumgardner, D. Russell Humphreys, Andrew A. Snelling, Larry Vardiman, and Kurt P. Wise. "Catastrophic Plate Tectonics: A Global Flood Model of Earth History." In Walsh, *Proceedings of the Third International Conference on Creationism.* Pittsburgh: Creation Science Fellowship, 1994, pp. 609–21.

Austin, Steven A., and D. Russell Humphreys. " The Sea's Missing Salt: A Dilemma for Evolutionists." In Walsh and Brooks, *Proceedings of the Second International Conference on Creationism*. Pittsburgh: Creation Science Fellowship, 1990, pp. 17–33.

Austin, Steven A., and John R. Morris. "Tight Folds and Clastic Dikes as Evidence for Rapid Deposition of Two Very Thick Stratigraphic Sequences." In Walsh, *et al., Proceedings of the First International Conference on Creationism*. Pittsburgh: Creation Science Fellowship, 1987, pp. 3–15.

Austin, Steven A., and Kurt P. Wise. "The Pre-Flood/Flood Boundary: As Defined in Grand Canyon, Arizona and Eastern Mojave Desert, California." In Walsh, *Proceedings of the Third International Conference on Creationism*. Pittsburgh: Creation Science Fellowship, 1994, pp. 37–47.

Baumgardner, John R. "3-D Finite Element Simulation of the Global Tectonics Changes Accompanying Noah's Flood." In Walsh and Brooks, *Proceedings of the Second International Conference on Creationism*. Pittsburgh: Creation Science Fellowship, 1990, pp. 35–45.

———. "Computer Modeling of the Large-Scale Tectonics Associated with the Genesis Flood." In Walsh, *Proceedings of the Third International Conference on Creationism*. Pittsburgh: Creation Science Fellowship, 1994, pp. 49–62.

———. "Runaway Subduction as a Driving Mechanism for the Genesis Flood." In Walsh, *Proceedings of the Third International Conference on Creationism*. Pittsburgh: Creation Science Fellowship, 1994, pp. 63–75.

Brand, Leonard. *Faith, Reason, and Earth History: A Paradigm of Earth and Biological Origins by Intelligent Design*. Berrian Springs, Mich.: Andrews University, 1997.

Coffin, Harold G. "Sonar and Scuba Survey of a Submerged Allochthonous 'Forest' in Spirit Lake, Washington." In *Palaios* (1987), 2:178–180.

Davies, K. "Distribution of Supernovae Remnants in the Galaxy." In Walsh, *Proceedings of the Third International Conference on Creationism*. Pittsburgh: Creation Science Fellowship, 1994, pp.175–184.

Faulkner, Danny R. "The Current State of Creation Astronomy." In Walsh, *Proceedings of the Fourth International Conference on Creationism.* Pittsburgh: Creation Science Fellowship, 1998, pp.201–216.

———. "Comets and the Age of the Solar System." In *Creation Ex Nihilo Technical Journal* (1998) 11:264–273.

Fouts, David M., and Kurt P. Wise. "The Days of Creation" at www.harborlighthouse.com.

———. "Biblical Evidences for an Immediate Creation Event" at www.harborlighthouse.com.

Frair, Wayne. "Baraminology—Classification of Created Organisms." In *Creation Research Society Quarterly* (2000) 37(2):82–91.

Gentry, Robert V., W. H. Christie, D. H. Smith, J. F. Emery, S. A. Reynolds, R. Walker, S. S. Cristy, and P. A. Gentry. "Radiohalos in Coalified Wood: New Evidence Relating to the Time of Uranium Introduction and Coalification." In *Science* (1976) 194:315–8.

Humphreys, D. Russell. "The Creation of Planetary Magnetic Fields." In *Creation Research Society Quarterly* (1984) 21(3):140–149.

———. "Reversals of the Earth's Magnetic Field During the Genesis Flood." In Walsh, *et al., Proceedings of the First International Conference on Creationism.* Pittsburgh: Creation Science Fellowship, 1987, pp. 113–126.

———. "Physical Mechanism for Reversals of the Earth's Magnetic Field During the Flood." In Walsh and Brooks, *Proceedings of the Second International Conference on Creationism.* Pittsburgh: Creation Science Fellowship, 1990, pp. 129–142.

Kang, C. H., and Ethel R. Nelson. *The Discovery of Genesis: How the Truths of Genesis Were Found Hidden in the Chinese Language.* Saint Louis, Mo.: Concordia, 1979.

Nelson, Ethel R., and Richard E. Broadberry. *Genesis and the Mystery Confucius Couldn't Solve.* Saint Louis, Mo.: Concordia, 1984.

Nelson, Ethel R., Richard E. Broadberry, and Ginger Tong Chock. *God's Promise to the Chinese.* Dunlap, Tenn.: Read Books, 1997.

Phillips, W. Gary, and David M. Fouts. "Genesis 1–11 as Historical Narrative." at www.harborlighthouse.com.

ReMine, Walter J. "Discontinuity Systematics: A New Methodology of Biosystematics Relevant to the Creation Model." In Walsh and Brooks, *Proceedings of the Second International Conference on Creationism*. Pittsburgh: Creation Science Fellowship, 1990, pp. 207–213.

Scheven, Joachim. "Floating Forests on Firm Grounds: Advances in Carboniferous Research." In *Journal of the Biblical Creation Society* (1981) 3(9):36–43.

Slusher, Harold S., and Stephen J. Robertson. *The Age of the Solar System: A Study of the Poynting-Robertson Effect and Extinction of Interplanetary Dust,* 2nd Edition. El Cajon, Calif.: Institute for Creation Research, 1982.

Snelling, Andrew A., and John Mackay. "Coal, Volcanism and Noah's Flood." In *Ex Nihilo Technical Journal* (1984) 1:11–29.

Thaxton, C. B., W. L. Bradley, and R. L. Olsen. *Mystery of Life's Origin: Reassessing Current Theories.* New York: Philosophical Library, 1984.

Vardiman, Larry. *Age of the Earth's Atmosphere: A Study of the Helium Flux Through the Atmosphere* [ICR Technical Monograph No. 14], Santee, Calif.: Institute for Creation Research, 1990.

————. *Ice Cores and the Age of the Earth,* El Cajon, Calif.: Institute for Creation Research, 1993.

————. "A Conceptual Transition Model of the Atmospheric Global Circulation Following the Genesis Flood." In Walsh, *Proceedings of the Third International Conference on Creationism*. Pittsburgh: Creation Science Fellowship, 1994, pp. 569–579.

————. "Numerical Simulation of Precipitation Induced by Hot Mid-Ocean Ridges." In Walsh, *Proceedings of the Fourth International Conference on Creationism*. Pittsburgh: Creation Science Fellowship, 1998, pp. 595–605.

Vardiman, L., A. A. Snelling, and E. F. Chaffin (eds.). *Radioisotopes and the Age of the Earth: A Young-Earth Creationist Research Initiative.* El Cajon, Calif.: and St. Joseph, Mo.: Institute for Creation Research and Creation Research Society, 2000.

Walsh, Robert E. (ed.). *Proceedings of the Third International Conference on Creationism*. Pittsburgh: Creation Science Fellowship, 1984.

————. *Proceedings of the Fourth International Conference on Creationism.* Pittsburgh: Creation Science Fellowship, 1998.

Walsh, Robert E., and Christopher L. Brooks (eds.). *Proceedings of the Second International Conference on Creationism, 1990, Volume II: Technical Sessions.* Pittsburgh: Creation Science Fellowship, 1990.

Walsh, R. E., C. L. Brooks, and R. S. Crowell (eds.). *Proceedings of the First International Conference on Creationism.* Pittsburgh: Creation Science Fellowship, 1987.

Wise, Kurt P. "Baraminology: A Young-Earth Creation Biosystematic Method." In Walsh and Brooks, *Proceedings of the Second International Conference on Creationism.* Pittsburgh: Creation Science Fellowship, 1990, pp. 345–358.

————. "The Fossil Record: The Ultimate Test Case for Young-Earth Creationism." In *Opus: A Journal for Interdisciplinary Studies* 1991/1992:17–29.

————. "Were There Really No Seasons? Tree Rings and Climate." In *Creation Ex Nihilo Technical Journal* (1992) 6(2):168–172.

Wise, Kurt P. and Matthew S. Cooper. "A Compelling Creation: A Suggestion for a New Apologetic." In Walsh, *Proceedings of the Fourth International Conference on Creationism.* Pittsburgh: Creation Science Fellowship, 1998, pp. 633–644.

Wood, Todd. "The AGEing Process: Rapid Post-Flood Intrabaraminic Diversification Caused by Altruistic Genetic Elements (AGEs)." *Origins* (in press).

NOTES

Chapter 1

1. Although some people believe the angels were created before any part of the physical universe, the angels themselves were also created. Therefore, there is some beginning point of creation "before" which there was only God.

2. An order of magnitude is a factor of ten. The shortest duration of the creation, according to young-age creationists (approximately six thousand years), and the maximum human lifetime listed in Scripture (Methuselah at 969 years; Gen. 5:27) is a ratio of approximately 6:1. All other estimates of the age of the creation yield a greater ratio.

3. It is interesting that when we observe the sun, the planets, stars, etc., we are observing things in the past (because of the finite speed of light). We thus have potential observational access into some events that may have occurred before humans came to be—depending, of course, on how the travel experience of that light is to be interpreted.

4. Physical time cannot exist "before" its own beginning. Physical entities that seem to be completely dependent upon physical time also cannot exist "before" the beginning of physical time. However, non-physical time and any entities that are not dependent upon physical time (for example, spiritual entities) have the potential of existing before physical time. God is the Creator of all things, so He is the Creator of physical time.

He is thus independent of physical time. This same God exists before the beginning of physical time (Col. 1:17) and exists after the end of physical time (Rev. 10:6). This suggests there is some sort of non-physical time that (in that time) exists before and after the entire existence (in physical time) of physical time. The bearing of fruit "every month" in the new creation (Rev. 22:2) also suggests the existence of some sort of time post-dating (in that non-physical time) the end of physical time.

5. Some people may argue that the entrance of evil or the decisions of organisms with free will would make impossible the prediction of history from a perfect knowledge of God's nature. However, God had foreknowledge of these things, so He at least was capable of such prediction. And, since the only being who has any possibility of a perfect knowledge of God's character is God Himself, perfect knowledge of God's nature *does* result in perfect prediction of history.

6. All of us probably know unbelieving people who act in a more godly, obedient manner than many believers. Not only is this an argument for the "law written on the heart" of humans; it is also evidence of our own depravity.

7. It is likely that only after a person becomes capable of such perception and deduction (the "age of accountability"?) that his sin imputed to him (Rom. 5:13; 7:7–12).

8. Alpha and omega are the first and last letters of the Greek alphabet.

9. Intelligent design, for example, does not begin with God, but infers a designer, who in turn may be identified with God (or any deity or deities). Scientific creationism specifically places the God of the Bible in the conclusion but attempts to get there without making reference to the supernatural. Some people may choose these methods to disguise the hook while fishing for souls in various forms of apologetics for the purpose of winning unbelievers, but this is not the optimal means by which Christians themselves should either increase in truth or teach others truth.

10. Because God is the starting point of any knowledge, the Christian faith is and must be tautological. One must start with faith. To arrive at a conclusion by any other means than faith is not to accept that conclusion on faith. Therefore, Christianity must begin with faith and *then* find

reasonableness in that faith. The tautology can be seen in 1 John 5:13: "These things have I written unto you that believe on the name of the Son of God; that ye may know that ye have eternal life, and that ye may believe on the name of the Son of God."

Chapter 2

1. The fact that Eve's disobedience involved some incorrect reasoning is implied in Genesis 3:1–6. First, Satan used reasoning as he spoke to Eve. Second, Eve seems to have applied some sort of reasoning to arrive at her modification of God's commandment (compare 2:16–17 with 3:2–3). Third, it was only "when the woman saw that the tree was good for food, and that it was pleasant to the eyes, and a tree to be desired to make one wise" (3:6) that she actually ate of the fruit. Eve did quite a bit of reasoning to put these data together and based upon that decided to disobey God's command.

2. Compare Genesis 2:16–17 with Genesis 3:2–3.

3. It is popular to associate proof with science, but in fact, there is no way to test a theory in all situations and at all times. In general, then, in science "you can never know for sure." Although proofs do exist in mathematics, they are proofs of abstract concepts that are only "true" within the artificial reality of mathematics (that is, assuming the truth of the existence of mathematics and all its assumptions).

4. Catastrophism is an example of non-uniform geological rate. Neocatastrophism (small-scale catastrophes) became popular beginning in the 1970s. Since a 1980 suggestion of an asteroid impact, global catastrophism has become increasingly popular.

5. In this understanding, the days of Genesis 1 are sequential twenty-four-hour days, the genealogies of Genesis 5 and 11 and Exodus 6 are accepted without gaps, and the generation times of Genesis 5 and 11 are accepted as written.

6. This is computed by using the numbers in the Masoretic text of Genesis 5:3–29. Proper error analysis (which would understand "Methuselah lived 187 years and begat Lamech" to mean that Lamech was born between Methuselah's 187th and 188th birthdays that is, 187.5 ± 0.5 years after Methuselah's birth) makes Lamech 52.5 ± 4.5 years old at time

of Adam's death (930.5±0.5 - 130.5±0.5 - 105.5±0.5 - 90.5±0.5 - 70.5±0.5 - 65.5±0.5 - 162.5±0.5 - 65.5±0.5 - 187.5±0.5).

7. This is computed by using the numbers in the Masoretic text of Genesis 9:28–29 and 11:10–25 and computing the age of Terah at Abram's birth (130) as follows: (a) Terah was 205 at his death (Gen. 11:32); (b) Abram did not leave Haran for Canaan until his father Terah was dead (Acts 7:2–4); and (c) Abram was 75 when he left Haran for Canaan (Gen. 12:4). Error analysis (which would understand "two years after the flood" to be within one-half a year of 2 years—that is, 2 ± 0.5 years) places Noah's death 5.0 ± 5.5 years before the birth of Abram (350±0.5 - 2±0.5 - 35.5±0.5 - 30.5±0.5 - 34.5±0.5 - 30.5±0.5 - 32.5±0.5 - 30.5±0.5 - 29.5±0.5 - [205.5±0.5 - 75.5±0.5]).

8. This is computed by using the numbers in the Masoretic text of Genesis 21:5; 25:7; and 25:25–26. Error analysis makes Jacob 14.5 ± 1.5 years old at the death of Abraham (175.5±0.5 - 100.5±0.5 - 60.5±0.5).

9. Jacob went to Egypt after Kohath was born (Gen. 46:8, 11), and Jacob lived after that for seventeen years (Gen. 47:28).

10. Since Joseph was 30 years old when he stood before the Pharaoh (Gen. 41:6), 9 years (7 years of plenty [Gen. 41:53–54] plus 2 years into the famine [Gen. 45:6]) before Jacob (at age 130: Gen. 47:9) came to Egypt, it follows that Jacob was 91 years old when Joseph was born. Since Joseph was born some time after the end of the fourteenth year of service to Laban (compare Gen. 29:15–30; 30:25–31; and 31:41) and Levi was the third-born during that 14-year period (Gen. 29:31–34)—that is, at least three, 9-month periods or more than 2 years into it—Jacob was between 79 and 91 years old when Levi was born. This makes Levi somewhere between 56 and 68 years old when Jacob died.

11. Exodus 6:18–20 indicates that Kohath was the grandfather of Moses, making generational overlap very likely. Furthermore, Kohath's son Amram married Kohath's stepsister Jochebed, and Kohath lived to the ripe old age of 133. Also note that the "fourth generation" comment in Genesis 15:16 combined with the 430 years between Abraham's promise and the giving of the law in Galatians 3:17 suggest that the genealogy of Exodus 6 is complete and that the four centuries of Israel's sojourning

before the Exodus includes the sojourning of Abraham, Isaac, and Jacob before Jacob went to Egypt.

12. The human life spans, which exceeded nine centuries before the Flood (Gen. 5), dropped precipitously after the Flood (Gen. 11), still being somewhat high at the time of Moses (Moses-120, Deut. 34:7; Aaron-123, compare Exod. 7:7, Num. 20:1 and 28, Deut. 34:7) and Joshua (110, Josh. 24:29) but assumed modern values of "threescore years and ten" by the time of David (Ps. 90:10).

13. Which in fact is found in many seminaries today.

14. The passage is mistranslated in a number of versions (for example, the NIV). Rather than saying that the eyewitness and earwitness testimony has made Scripture more sure, the Greek actually reads that Scripture is a more sure truth than even eyewitness and earwitness testimony.

15. The author first understood this principle as it was elaborated by W. Gary Phillips, professor of Bible at Bryan College in 1991. Dr. Phillips also introduced the author to the biblical example.

Chapter 4

1. Phillips and Fouts, "Genesis 1–11 as Historical Narrative."

2. Fouts and Wise, "The Days of Creation."

3. Fouts and Wise, "Biblical Evidence for an Immediate Creation Event."

4. Potential exceptions to the universality of instantaneity in God's miracles would include: (1) the miracles done in multiple steps (for example, the two-step healing of the blind man of Bethsaida in Mark 8:22–26) where each step seemed to be instantaneous; (2) the miracles that had to wait for complete obedience (for example, Naaman's seven Jordanian dunks (2 Kings 5:1–14), Zacharias's restoration of speech (Luke 1), and even the maturation of the Christian.

5. The early birth of Haran's son (Gen. 11:31), the early death of Haran (Gen. 11:28), and the fact that Terah's temporary city of refuge was named Haran (probably after Terah's son) are factors that suggest Abram was significantly younger than his brother Haran. This in turn suggests that Terah was probably 70 years old (Gen. 11:26) when his first son was born. Abram was 75 years old when he left Haran (Gen. 12:4) and did not

leave until after his father died (Acts 7:4). Since Terah was 205 years old at his death (Gen. 11:32), this means that Terah was 130 years old at the birth of Abram.

6. These steps can be calculated in sequence from Galatians 3:16–18 (430 years between the promise given to Abraham and the giving of the law to Moses), 1 Kings 6:1 (479 years between the Exodus and the fourth year of Solomon's reign), the king lists found in Kings and Chronicles (410 years between the fourth year of Solomon's reign and the beginning of the captivity), Jeremiah 25:1 (seventy years of captivity), and the seventy-week prophecy of Daniel 9.

7. Exodus 12:41 specifies the time period to the day, and 1 Kings 6:1 (compared with Exod. 12:2 and following) specifies the time period to the month; other passages do not (for example, the genealogies of Gen. 5 and 11).

8. The Septuagint provides the most significant alteration on this calculation. Using the Septuagint numbers, about one thousand years are added to the age of the earth and universe. Various reasons exist, however, for accepting the Masoretic text over the Septuagint in this particular instance (it was the Hebrew text and not the Septuagint that the Hebrews preserved faithfully through time). It is unlikely that the actual numbers differ much from those given in the accepted Hebrew text.

9. In a young-earth scenario, the Flood completely destroyed the Edenic rivers, allowing the biblical description to be possible.

10. Phillips and Fouts, "Genesis 1–11 as Historical Narrative."

Chapter 5

1. R. Scarborough, Cenozoic Erosion and Sedimentation in Arizona, in J. P. Jenney and S. J. Reynolds (eds.), *Geologic Evolution of Arizona* (Arizona Geol. Society, 1989), 515–537.

2. Arct, "Dendochronology in the Yellowstone Fossil Forests," 1979; "Dendochronology in the Fossil Forests of the Specimen Creek Area, Yellowstone National Forest," 1991.

3. Austin and Humphreys, "The Sea's Missing Salt," 1990.

4. Andrew A. Snelling, "Geochemical Processes in the Mantle and Crust," in Vardiman, *et al.*, *Radioisotopes and the Age of the Earth*, 2000, pp. 126–131.

5.   The National Geochronological Database (USGS Digital Data Series DDS-14, 1995) contains thousands of examples of rocks dated with multiple methods. A careful examination of these records shows that the methods rarely yield the same ages.

6.   See Vardiman, *Age of the Earth's Atmosphere,* 1990. Alpha decay of a radioactive element produces a helium nucleus. Once this nucleus diffuses out of rocks in which it formed and collects some electrons, it escapes into the earth's atmosphere as helium gas. Even though helium is light enough to escape from the earth's atmosphere, it escapes more slowly than it is being produced. The total amount of helium in the atmosphere should increase through time according to the actual age of the earth.

7.   Andrew A. Snelling, "Geochemical Processes in the Mantle and Crust," 123–304 in Vardiman, *et al,* 2000 (especially pp. 188–211).

8.   Gerald E. Aardsma, *Radiocarbon and the Genesis Flood* (El Cajor, Calif.: Institute for Creation Research, 1993).

9.   That unfallen humans would have lived forever is strongly implied in Genesis 3:22 and that the earth was created originally to last forever seems to be indicated by Psalm 78:69.

10. The sun is currently about 93 million miles away from the earth. Light, at its current speed, travels 93 million miles in about 8 minutes. The incredible speed of light (186,000 miles per second) allows us to measure great distances in terms of the time it takes light to travel that distance. The sun, then, is 8 light minutes away from earth.

11. Consider, for example, the discussion in, Eugene F. Chaffin, "Theoretical Mechanisms of Accelerated Radioactive Decay," pp. 305–331 and D. Russell Humphreys, "Accelerated Nuclear Decay: A Viable Hypothesis" in Vardiman, *et al.*, 2000, pp. 333–379.

12. Vardiman, *Ice Cores and the Age of the Earth,* 1993.

13. Gerald Aardsma's (1991) C-14 monograph presents an initial attempt at developing a young-age creationist interpretation of C-14 dating. Aardsma used dates for the Flood and the creation that do not fit Scripture. A revision is needed, utilizing a better post-Flood history of the magnetic field (see, for example, Humphreys, 1987) and atmospheric and ocean circulation (see, for example, D. W. Barnette, and J. R. Baumgardner, "Patterns of Ocean Circulation over the Continents During

Noah's Flood," pp. 77–86 in Walsh, 1994; L. Vardiman, "Numerical Simulation of Precipitation Induced by Hot Mid-Ocean Ridges," pp. 595–618 in Walsh, 1998).

14. Davies, "Distribution of Supernova Remnants in the Galaxy," 1994.

15. Faulkner, "Comets and the Age of the Solar System," 1998.

16. Slusher and Robertson, *The Age of the Solar System,* 1982. This publication needs to be revised and tempered in the light of the comments in Faulkner, "The Current State of Creation Astronomy," 1998.

17. Barnes's renewal of Lamb's model is summarized in Thomas G. Barnes, *Origin and Destiny of the Earth's Magnetic Field,* ICR Technical Journal No. 4 (El Cajon, Calif.: Institute for Creation Research, 1983). Humphreys's revision of Lamb's model to include field reversals is in Humphreys, "Reversals of the Earth's Magnetic Field During the Genesis Flood," 1987, and "Physical Mechanism for Reversal of the Earth's Magnetic Field," 1990—the first article of which contains the prediction about the reversal in a lava flow. The fulfillment of the prediction is found in R. S. Coe, and M. Prevot, "Evidence Suggesting Extremely Rapid Field Variation During a Geomagnetic Reversal," *Earth and Planetary Science Letters* 92:292–98. Humphreys's application of the Lamb model to planetary magnetic fields is Humphreys, "The Creation of Planetary Magnetic Fields," 1984.

Chapter 6

1. The heavens and light in the heavens were created on Day 1; the firmament of heaven where the sun, moon, and stars would be placed were created on Day 2; and the sun, moon, and stars were created on Day 4. The earth was created on Day 1; the firmament of heaven where the birds fly (that is, the atmosphere) was created on Day 2; the dry land and ocean basins were created on Day 3. The plants were created on Day 3; the swimming and flying creatures were created on Day 4; the land creatures on Day 6.

2. For a list of Anthropic Principle claims and references, see Wise and Cooper, "A Compelling Creation," 1998. A few of the many sources written by unbelievers include R. Breuer, *The Anthropic Principle: Man as the Focal Point of Nature,* 1998 (a translation of a book published in German in 1981); J. D. Barrow and F. J. Tipler, *The Anthropic Cosmological Principle*

(New York: Oxford University Press, 1986); J. Leslie, *Universes* (New York: Routledge, 1989); and M. A. Corey, *God and the New Cosmology: The Anthropic Design Argument* (Lanham, Md.: Rowman & Littlefield, 1993). Each of the Anthropic Principle evidences discussed in the text can be found (with a large number of others) in these secular sources.

3. In 1937, Paul Dirac ("The Cosmological Constants," *Nature* 139:323) noted that the number 10^{40} crops up several times in the structure of the universe.

4. Wise and Cooper, "A Compelling Creation," 1998.

5. From General Relativity theory a large number of testable predictions have been made about the universe. In test after test, those predictions have come closer to the real world than the predictions made from any other theory. Although some physicists—and several of them young-age creationists—have been busy creating alternative theories to General Relativity, they seem to explain the observations *after* the fact, not make predictions *before* they are made. As a result, General Relativity theory seems to come closer to a description of the universe than any other known theory.

6. Scientists have long assumed that all events have causes (the law of cause and effect). It has been a successful assumption, as it has prompted much productive research and led to the discovery of many unobserved and even unobservable causes. In quantum mechanics (the world of the very small), events seem to occur without causes. Although it is possible to claim that those events occurred without cause (and some quantum mechanics interpretations suggest that), another possibility is that the actual cause or causes are not observable.

7. The universe did not begin the size of a geometric point, but it began at some very large initial size. The current expansion rate of the universe, therefore, does not indicate anything about the age of the universe. Any proposed history of the universe, like the Big Bang theory, that does not accept its creation in mature form is incorrect.

8. The subatomic particles of the universe were probably directly created. If so, they did not arise because of the collision of gamma rays as proposed by the Big Bang theory (the most popular atheistic theory for the origin of the universe). Atoms were probably also created directly. Their

nuclei did not arise over millions or billions of years by means of fusion in the center of stars and the explosions of supernovae as suggested by nucleosynthesis theory (the most popular atheistic theory for the origin of atoms). Current rates of nucleosynthesis, then, tell us nothing about the true age of atomic nuclei.

9. The moon was not formed out of the earth by collision with an asteroid (the most popular atheistic theory for the origin of the moon), and the bodies of the solar system were not formed from a planetary neb-ulae (the most popular atheistic theory for the origin of the solar system). Stars did not condense from stellar nebulae (the most popular atheistic theory for the origin of stars), and galaxies did not condense from galac-tic nebulae (the most popular atheistic theory for the origin of galaxies). Since stars were created in mature form, rates of stellar aging tell us noth-ing about the true age of the stars.

10. Since stars are continually burning their fuel, it is reasonable to suggest that stars actually do change through time. Some sort of stellar evolution does occur. The existence of a variety of stars in various stages of stellar evolution, however, does not necessarily mean that those stars evolved through all their earlier developmental stages. If God created stars in a variety of forms, they did not evolve through those forms.

11. Atheistic theories of the origin of the solar system argue that the entire solar system was derived from a single gas cloud. The great variety of objects in the solar system (for example, Venus, which rotates back-ward; Uranus, which is tilted so much it rolls in orbit; and the moon, which is one-third less dense than the earth) is very difficult to explain if they were formed from a single cloud.

12. R. Breuer, *The Anthropic Principle: Man as the Focal Point of Nature* (Boston: Birkhauser, 1991), 233–37; J. Leslie, *Universes* (New York: Routledge, 1989), p. 59.

13. One of the consequences of the Second Law of Thermodynamics is that things in high concentration tend to spread out into areas of low con-centration. This causes light so highly concentrated in the interior of stars to move to the outside of stars and then outward from there. This also allows oxygen in the atmosphere to make its way across the membranes in the lungs to enter oxygen-poor blood. It also allows carbon dioxide in high

concentration in cells to make its way into the blood and from there into the lungs to be exhaled from the body. The Second Law is foundational to many processes of the creation.

14. For a good summary of the state of creationist astronomy, see Faulkner, "The Current State of Creation Astronomy," 1998.

15. D. Russell Humphreys made one such attempt at a theory (D. R. Humphreys, *Proceedings of the Third International Conference on Creationism* [Pittsburgh: Creation Science Fellowship, 1994]) but has come under considerable fire (see S. R. Conner and D. N. Page, *Creation Ex Nihilo Technical Journal*, 1998, 12(2):174–94). Even if Humphreys's theory is not correct, it is an example of the kind of theory that creationists ought to be developing.

Chapter 7

1. See M. A. Corey, *God and the New Cosmology: The Anthropic Design Argument* (Lanham, Md:, Rowman & Littlefield, 1993); and Wise and Cooper, "A Compelling Creation," 1998.

2. Humphreys, "The Creation of Planetary Magnetic Fields," 1984, and "Reversal of the Earth's Magnetic Field," 1987.

3. Both because of reflectivity and because of the heat that is held by water (see Corey, 1993 and Wise and Cooper, "A Compelling Creation," 1998).

4. Current research reconstructing Rodinia has not resolved whether Rodinia was a single continental mass or whether it was many or few continents in relatively close proximity. Since much of the evidence used to reconstruct Rodinia is collected and interpreted in the light of non-creationist theories, young-age creationists need to reevaluate this data before Rodinia can be included in their models. The gathering of water into "one place" (Gen. 1:9) may have referred to the creation of a single ocean, not necessarily a single continent.

5. By the time of the Flood there were "high hills" (Gen. 7:19), so the earth was probably created with mountains. The earth was created with multialtitude environments. Because a river flowed out of Eden to water the lands around it (Gen. 2:10–14), Eden was probably located on top of one of those hills. Although there is evidence in the coconino sandstone

of the Grand Canyon that it was deposited by water, there is also evidence that the sand grains had been transported by wind. This would be explained if Flood waters overran a wind-deposited sand dune. The earth may have been created with desert environments. Certain algal mound fossils may indicate the earth was also created with hydrothermal regions.

6. See Corey, 1993 and Wise and Cooper, "A Compelling Creation," 1998.

7. Whether the oceans were created salty or not is debated among young-age creationists. Joachim Scheven ("The Geological Record of Biblical Earth History," *Journal of the Biblical Creation Society,* 1990, 3(8):8–13) suggests the oceans were freshwater because he believes they fed the freshwater springs of the land and supported a floating forest. However, pre-Flood springs may not have been fed in the way Scheven suggests. And since the plants of Scheven's floating forest are extinct, we do not know their salt tolerances.

8. See Corey, 1993 and Wise and Cooper, "A Compelling Creation," 1998.

9. That the earth was created with oxygen from the beginning is evident in the oxidized nature of even the oldest sediments of the earth— unlike what is demanded in non-theistic evolutionary models (see Thaxton, Bradley and Olsen, *Mystery of Life's Origin,* 1984.)

10. Wise, "Were There Really No Seasons," 1992.

11. D. M. Fouts, and K. P. Wise, "Blotting Out and Breaking Up: Miscellaneous Hebrew Studies in Geocatastrophism," in Walsh, *Proceedings of the Fourth International Conference of Creationism,* 1994, pp. 217–28.

Chapter 8

1. See Michael J. Behe, *Darwin's Black Box: The Biochemical Challenge to Evolution* (New York: Touchstone, 1996).

2. See William A. Dembski, *Intelligent Design: The Bridge Between Science & Theology* (Downers Grove, Ill.: Intervarsity Press, 1999), 312; William A. Dembski and James M. Kushiner, *Signs of Intelligence: Understanding Intelligent Design* (Grand Rapids: Brazos Press), 224.

3. "Species" is derived from the Latin word that means "kind." The same Latin word was used to translate "kind" in the phrase "after its kind" in the Vulgate (the Latin translation of the Bible). Thus, even though "species" was intended at some point in time to correspond to the biblical kind, by their current definition modern species do not correspond to the biblical kind.

4. Frank Marsh in *Fundamental Biology,* (1941) proposed the term *baramin. Bârâ* is a Hebrew verb meaning "to create." *Mîn* is a Hebrew noun meaning "kind." *Baramin* is a contraction of anglicized words roughly meaning "created kind."

5. Frank Marsh, *Variation and Fixity in Nature* (Mountain View, Calif.: Pacific Press, 1976), 150.

6. Siegfried Scherer (ed.), *Typen des Lebens* (Berlin: Studium Integrale 1993), 257.

7. The database is called the "hybridatabase." Originally the idea of Ashley Robinson in 1996, the hybridatabase is currently being assembled and hosted by the Center for Origins Research and Education at Bryan College in Dayton, Tennessee.

8. For orchids see Sanders, *Sanders' Complete List of Orchid Hybrids* (Royal Orchard Nurseries, St. Alban, England, 1946), plus a number of Sanders's supplements that update the original list. For grasses, see Reinhard Junker, Der Grundtyp der Weizenartigen (Poaceae, Tribus Triticeae), 75–93, in Scherer, 1993. For roses, see Herfried Kutzelnigg, "Verwandtschaflishe Beziedhungen zwischen den Gattungen und Arten der Kernobstgewächse" (Rosacea, Unterfamilie Maloideae, 113–27, in Scherer, 1993). For fuchsias, see Leo B. Boullemier (compiler), *The Checklist of Species, Hybrids and Cultivars of the Genus Fuchsia* (Blandford Press, Poole, Co. Dorset, England), 309. For lilies, see Eunice Fisher, *Named Lily Hybrids and Their Origins* (North American Lily Society, 1978), 60. For cerion land snails, see Stephen Jay Gould and David S. Woodruff, "Natural History of *Cerion* VIII: Little Bahama Bank—A Revision Based upon Genetics, Morphometrics, and Geographic Distribution" (*Bulletin of the Museum of Comparative Zoology 148*:371–415). For anatids, see Siegfried Scherer, "Der Grundtyp der Entenartigen (Anseriformes, Anatidae): Biologische und paläontologische

Streiflichter," 131–58 in Scherer, 1993. For more bird examples, see Annie P. Gray, *Bird Hybrids: A Check-List With Bibliography* (Commonwealth Agricultural Bureaux, Farnham Royal, Bucks, England, 1958). For mammals, see Annie P. Gray, *Mammalian Hybrids: A Check-List With Bibliography,* Second Edition (Commonwealth Agricultural Bureaux, Farnham Royal, Bucks, England, 1972), 262.

9. J. A. Skidmore, M. Billah, M. Binns, R. V. Short, and W. R. Allen, "Hybridizing Old and New World Camelids: *Camelus dromedarius* x *Lama guanicoe*" (*Proc. Royal Society of London B 266*:649–56).

10. If God created each baramins with built-in mechanisms that prevented successful breeding with other baramins, then all baramins are genetically unrelated. Although this is possible, the Hebrew does not seem to necessitate this (see Pete J. Williams, "What Does *Min* Mean?" *Ex Nihilo Technical Journal 11*(3):344–52.). Another possibility is that there are no actual genetic barriers and that genetic unrelatedness exists for historical reasons—that is, not enough time has elapsed for genetic relatedness to spread among all organisms, and incompatibilities have arisen through genetic error after the Fall. Yet another possibility is that breeding barriers created in organisms can actually be overcome in the course of time (for example, by mutation or by humans forcing the crosses). If this is the case, original baramins might actually be crossable. Regardless of which of these is true, the young-age creationist would expect the existence of groups of organisms that are not related in any way to other groups but that contain organisms that are related to organisms within the groups.

11. Since evolutionary theory suggests all organisms are ultimately related to one another and all biologic structure is derived from other biologic structures, evolutionists don't believe there is any such thing as true discontinuity. Evolutionists did not, therefore, develop a tool for identifying discontinuity. Their classification tools are completely blind to it. Even if the world was full of discontinuity (as young-age creationism suggests), evolutionists would not be able to see it. This necessitated the introduction of a tool that can see biological discontinuity. Walter ReMine (1990) introduced discontinuity systematics, and Kurt Wise (1990) introduced baraminology based upon discontinuity systematics. Discontinuity systematics was created to be usable by either creationists or evolutionists

and involves a minimal number of assumptions specific to either model. Baraminology, in contrast, was originally designed as a young-age creationist tool, since it utilizes assumptions and concepts specific to young-age creationism.

12. For a good summary of baraminology, see Frair, "Baraminology—Classification of Created Organisms," 2000.

13. Lynn Margulis and Karlene V. Scwartz, *Five Kingdoms: An Illustrated Guide to the Phyla of Life on Earth* (San Francisco: Freeman, 1998), 448.

14. See, for example, Stephen Jay Gould, *Ontogeny and Phylogeny* (Cambridge, Mass.: Belknap, 1977), 501.

Chapter 9

1. Mary Rose D'Angelo, "The Garden: Once and Not Again: Traditional Interpretation of Genesis 1:26–27 [*sic*] in 1 Corinthians 11:7–12," pp. 1–41 in Gregory Allen Robbins (ed.), *Genesis 1–3 in the History of Exegesis: Intrigue in the Garden* (Lewiston, N.Y., Edwin Mellen), 282.

2. See chapter 15 for evidence that the diversity of language and cultures arose after Babel. See this chapter also for a reinterpretation of evidence that has been used to argue that humans lacked culture early in their history.

Chapter 10

1. Some young-age creationists have suggested that the firmament was something solid (thus the word *firm*ament in the KJV). The following facts make this untenable: (1) the firmament is called "heaven" (Gen. 1:8); (2) the birds fly in the "firmament of the heaven" (Gen. 1:20); (3) the sun, moon, and stars were placed in the "firmament of heaven" (Gen. 1:14–17); and (4) the "waters above the heaven" are placed in ascending sequence after the heavens, the heights, the angels, the sun, moon and stars, and the heavens of heavens in Psalm 148:1–4. The Hebrew noun *râqîa'*, which is translated "firmament," is derived from the Hebrew verb *raqa'*, which is used primarily to describe the beating of metal into a thin layer (see Exod. 39:3; Num. 16:39; Jer. 10:9), and symbolically used to mean smashing (see 2 Sam. 22:43; Ezek. 6:11) or

stamping (see Ezek. 25:6). When the Hebrew word *râqîa'* was translated into Latin, *firmamento* was utilized, focusing on the nature of the substance that was deformed (usually metal). From this Latin translation the KJV word *firmament* is based. However, it is more likely, given the way *râqîa'* is used in Scripture, that the Hebrew noun was referring not to the object being deformed by the Hebrew verb, but the deformation itself. Thus *râqîa'* may actually mean "something beaten out" or "something spread out" or "something stretched out." As a result, many modern translations translate *râqîa'* with "expanse." This is probably closer to the actual meaning of *râqîa'* in Genesis 1:6–8, 14–17, 20.

2. Although it has been popular in young-age creationist circles of the last century to suggest that the "waters above" referred to a water canopy around the earth, the fact that the sun, moon, and stars were placed in the firmament of heaven below them seems to preclude this. Furthermore, in Psalm 148 not only are the "waters that be above the heavens" placed above the sun, moon, and stars in the sequence, but they still exist in the day of David. Therefore, the "waters above" did not fall to earth at the time of the Flood as many canopy theorists claim.

3. One argument against rain in the pre-Flood world concerns the rainbow that was given as a sign to Noah and his family after the Flood (Gen. 9:12–17). It is commonly thought that if Noah and his family had seen a rainbow in the pre-Flood world, it would not have been interpreted as a promise of no flood to come. However, it may be usual for covenantal signs in Scripture to predate their reinterpretation by God. For example: (1) According to modern scholarship, circumcision (the sign of a covenant with Abraham in Gen. 17:1–14) was widely practiced before Abraham; (2) The Sabbath (the sign of a covenant with Israel according to Lev. 24:8) was probably instituted and followed at the creation (Gen. 1:3; Mark 2:27; and Exod. 16:23, which is before the Law); and (3) The drinking of wine and breaking of bread (the sign of the new covenant in Matt. 26:26–29) was a normal activity during and long before the time of Christ.

4. Genesis 1 and 2 describe a single week of time (Creation Week). The following three chapters describe the next 1656 years of earth history—almost as much history as the remaining books of the Bible describe!

5. Wise, "Were There Really No Seasons? Tree Rings and Climate," 1992. Tree rings indicate changes in growth rates. There are characteristic patterns in the tree rings in tropical and temperate trees. There are indications of variable-length seasons as well as late frosts, insect blights, and droughts. Various fossil trees preserved in flood sediments (presumably living in the antediluvian world) evidence all these things.

6. There is still some dispute in young-age creationist circles about exactly where to place the Flood/pre-Flood boundary in the rock record. This author places the boundary at the base of the Vendian (a rock system below the Cambrian that includes the first-buried animal fossils as well as huge diamictites, which this author interprets as avalanche deposits created with the breakup of the fountains of the great deep).

7. Recently, for example, the author argued that the Chuar Group in the Grand Canyon was deposited in an antediluvian world ocean (Kurt P. Wise and Andrew A. Snelling, "A Note on the Pre-Flood/Flood Boundary in the Grand Canyon," *Origins*). There is evidence that these sediments were made in hypersaline conditions (R. J. Horodyski, *et al.,* in J. W. Schopf and C. Klein, *The Proterozoic Biosphere* (New York: Cambridge University Press, 1992), 189. But the author also believes these sediments were part of an antediluvian hydrothermal ecosystem (see discussion later in this chapter), so the salinity may have been associated only with that local area.

8. The Flood was initiated by a catastrophic breakup of the "fountains of the great deep" (Gen. 7:11). If the source of Eden's river was such a spring, the catastrophic breakup of that spring may explain how Eden came to be destroyed completely in the first few moments of the Flood.

9. It has been argued that the water that flowed through the spring to feed the river of Eden somehow came from the earth's oceans. Usually it is argued that the water comes directly from "waters below" the earth's crust (also known as "the great deep"), and these waters are somehow rejuvenated from the oceans. Problems with this claim include: (1) It has not been shown to be physically possible to cycle water from deep in the earth's crust to the surface and back again; (2) The "waters below" refer to oceans on the earth's surface (see earlier discussion in the text), and "the great deep" refers to springs on the *present* earth's surface (D. M.

Fouts and K. P. Wise, in R. E. Walsh, [ed.], *Proceedings of the Fourth International Conference on Creationism,* 217–28), so there is no scriptural reference to subterranean oceans; (3) Such subterranean oceans, even if they collapsed during the Flood, should show up as seismic reflection lines in the earth's crust, and such things do not exist. Thus, it seems that it is theoretically impossible and both scriptural and physical evidence are lacking.

10. The only possible exception is John 12:24 where the wheat seed is said to have to die in order to bear fruit. Since the seed does not actually die biologically when it is buried, this may refer to symbolic death that occurs with the burial of the seed.

11. *Bâsâr,* translated flesh; *dam,* translated "blood" (the "life of the flesh is in the blood", Lev. 17:11); *nephesh,* often translated "soul"; and *rauch,* translated "breath" ("[God] breathed into his nostrils the breath of life and man became a living soul," Gen. 2:7).

12. Biology is the "study of life." Biologists focus the tools of their trade on the study of man, animals, plants, fungi, protists, algae, and bacteria. Yet life as the Bible uses the term seems to be possessed only by man and animals. Are the other organisms living? Very often the first chapter of biology textbooks includes a section dealing with the question of what is life. The wiser authors will admit that no one knows how to define life or what life actually is. Biologists study things they *believe* to be living and determine what characteristics these things have that things they believe to be non-living don't have. Sometimes these attributes of life are given as the definition of life. They do not define life. They only list some of the things that living beings *do.* Careful examination of an organism just before and just after death reveals that "life"—whatever it is—has no mass, cannot be seen, felt, tasted, heard, or smelled. It cannot be detected by our senses. Life itself does not seem to be physical at all. Since humans were created by God, the (non-physical) life God possesses is almost certainly distinct from the (non-physical) life possessed by man. And, given the unique nature of man with respect to the rest of the creation, the (non-physical) life of animals is probably distinct from human life. Given the diversity of non-physical life possessed by God, man, and animals, it is not unreasonable to assume that a very different kind of non-physical life

is possessed by plants. Biblical life would then include human and animal life, but not the type of life possessed by plants.

Chapter 12

1.   Currently the lowermost Flood rocks are referred to as the Paleozoic Erathem, but since the word *Paleozoic* means "old life" (as opposed to, for example, *Mesozoic,* which means "middle [aged] life" and *Cenozoic,* which means "new life") it tends to suggest that the organisms lived at an earlier time than organisms preserved as fossils in overlying rocks. But if young-age creationism is correct, many of these organisms lived at the same time, so it might be preferable to refer to the lowermost Flood rocks as Primary. There is disagreement among young-age creationists about where to put the Flood/post-Flood boundary. This author believes that Tertiary (Cenozoic) rocks were formed in post-Flood times and Primary (Paleozoic) and Secondary (Mesozoic) rocks were formed during the Flood. If this is the case, Paleozoic organisms are actually from the "old world" (before the Flood) and Cenozoic organisms are actually from the "new world" (after the Flood), with the Mesozoic organisms at least *deposited* in between. If so, the Paleozoic/Mesozoic/Cenozoic distinctions may be acceptable enough to young-age creationism to keep. Without the debate fully resolved, however, this author will use Primary/Secondary/Tertiary/Quaternary distinctions.

2.   A floating forest for coal plants has been advocated by Scheven, "Floating Forests on firm Ground," 1981. A floating forest ecosystem that included all the plants of the Primary was proposed in an oral presentation at the International Conference on Creationism in Pittsburgh, Pennsylvania, in 1990. A second presentation will be by Kurt P. Wise at the Fifth International Conference on Creationism in 2003.

3.   As scientists define them, dinosaurs do not include the flying reptiles like the pterodactyls, nor do they include the swimming reptiles like icthyosaurs and plesiosaurs.

4.   Kurt P. Wise, "Evidence of a Pre-Flood Hydrothermal Biome," *Proceedings of the Fifth International Conference on Creationism,* 2003

5.   This seems to be what modern medicine has done with humans. The average life span of humans has increased, but the maximum age that

a person can live seems to be unaffected. Medicine is only allowing us to live out a greater *percentage* of our maximum life span.

6. Moses: 120 (Deut. 34:7) and Aaron: 123 (compare Exod. 7:7 and Deut. 34:7 and Aaron died in the same year as Moses) and Joshua: 110 (Josh. 24:29).

7. Although we don't know *how* the life span was changed, we do have a good idea *why* it was changed. Genesis 6:3 records a time when God said that His patience with the evil of antediluvian humans had run out and that as a result their days would be 120 years. This verse has been translated two different ways for more than two thousand years: (1) that God said this 120 years before the Flood and gave Noah the assignment to build the ark then, or (2) that God was going to reset the life span of humans to 120 years. It is possible that both meanings are true, and that God sought to change the life span of humans to curb potential evil. The evil humans can perpetrate in a maximum life span of 120 years must be much less than the kind of evil they perpetrated when they lived for nine centuries.

Chapter 13

1. John C. Whitcomb Jr. and Henry M. Morris, *The Genesis Flood: The Biblical Record and its Scientific Implications* (Phillipsburgh, N.J.: Presbyterian & Reformed, 1961), 1–35.

2. As indicated earlier, this is one of the two possible understandings of Genesis 6:3, the other being that the life span of humans would be shortened to 120 years. Actually both meanings may be correct.

3. D. M. Fouts and K. P. Wise, "Blotting Out and Breaking Up: Miscellaneous Hebrew Studies in Geocatastrophism," in Walsh, *Proceedings of the Fourth International Conference on Creationism* (Pittsburgh, 1998), 217–28.

4. Some have suggested that a similar or larger geologic event occurred in the days of Peleg (Gen. 10:25), when the "earth was divided," but (1) it seems unlikely that this event so matter-of-factly referred to in two verses in the Bible could have been more significant than the Flood recorded in three chapters of Genesis and purposed to destroy all humans and animals; (2) characteristic of Hebrew narrative, Genesis 10 seems to be the genealogy that introduces the narrative of the tower of

Babel incident recorded in the first part of Genesis 11; and (3) "the earth was divided" seems related to "the earth was of one language, and of one speech" in Genesis 11:1. Peleg's division seems to be referring to the division of languages at the tower of Babel.

5. See Seiya Uyeda, *The New View of the Earth: Moving Continents and Moving Oceans* (San Francisco: Freeman, 1978).

6. Austin, *et al.,* "Catastrophic Plate Tectonics: A Global Flood Model of Earth History," 1994.

7. About 70 percent of the present earth's surface is covered with oceans. A similar amount of the surface was probably covered with oceans in the antediluvian world. Exactly how much is unknown. Some continents were enlarged during the Flood (for example, the California appears to have been added during the Flood; see Austin and Wise, "The Pre-Flood/Flood Boundary," 1994) and some were reduced in size (for example, several hundred kilometers of southernmost Asia seems to have been pushed underneath middle Asia to produce the Tibetan Plateau).

8. Since the earth was created to persist forever, it was not created teetering on the edge of catastrophe. It would seem that the perilous condition it was in immediately before the Flood developed some time between the Fall and the Flood. What brought this condition about is unknown. Perhaps something was initiated at the Fall that would have gradually made the Flood inevitable. Or perhaps God changed something suddenly that led to the Flood. At this point we simply don't know. Furthermore, there had to be something that, in a sense, kicked off the Flood—something that caused the crust of the earth to crack so the ocean crust could break off and sink into the mantle. What introduced this impulse is also not known. Was it the collision of an asteroid or comet? Or was it the direct hand of God? Again, we don't know.

9. See Baumgardner, "Computer Modeling," 1994; "Runaway Subduction," 1994; "3-D Finite Element Situation," 1990.

10. Seismic tomography uses computers to interpret information from a large number of seismometers to infer subtle differences in the nature of the earth's interior. See the cover story of *GSA Today* 7(4) in 1997.

11. Humphreys, "Reversal of the Earth's Magnetic Field," 1987; "Physical Mechanism for Reversal of the Earth's Magnetic Field," 1990.

12. R. S. Coe and M. Prevot, "Evidence Suggesting Extremely Rapid Field Variation During a Geomagnetic Reversal," in *Earth and Planetary Science Letters*, 1989, 92:292–9.

13. Kurt P. Wise and Steven A. Austin, "Gigantic Megaclasts within the Kingston Peak Formation (Upper Precambrian, Pahrump Group), Southeastern California: Evidence for Basin Margin Collapse," *GSA Abstracts With Programs*, 1999, 31:A455–56.

14. As is seen at the Lewis Overthrust in Glacier National Park and surrounding areas.

15. Kurt P. Wise, "The Science Played Again," in Richard M. Cornelius and Tom Davis (eds.), *The Scopes Trial, William Jennings Bryan, and Issues that Keep Revolving* (Dayton, Tenn.: William Jennings Bryan College, 2000).

16. Steven A. Austin, "Interpreting Strata of Grand Canyon," in Austin, *Grand Canyon: Monument to Catastrophe* (Sanrose, Calif.: Institute for Creation Research, 1994).

17. Arthur Chadwick, "Lithologic, Paleogeographic and Paleocurrent Maps of the World," in http://chadwicka.swac.edu.

18. Wise, "The Fossil Record," 1991.

19. Ibid.

20. A couple of examples: The bending of Cambrian tapeats sandstone along a Cretaceous fault in the Grand Canyon (Steven A. Austin, "Geologic Structure of Grand Canyon," in Austin, *Grand Canyon,* 1994, pp. 9–19), and the bending of rocks in the desert of southeastern California (Austin and Morris, "Tight Folds and Clostic Dikes," in Walsh, 1987).

21. One example are the time gaps between sedimentary layers in the Grand Canyon. (Steven A. Austin, "Interpreting Strata of Grand Canyon," in Austin, *Grand Canyon,* 1994), 21–56.

22. Austin and Wise, 1994.

23. R. Hayatsu, R. L. McBeth, R. G. Scott, R. E. Botto, and R. E. Winans, "Artificial Coalification study: Preparation and Characterization of Synthetic Materials," in *Organic Geochemistry,* 1984, 6:463–71.

24. Gentry, "Radiohaloes in Coalified Wood," 1976.

25. Austin, "Depositional Environment of the Kentucky No. 12 Coal Bed," 1979.

26. Austin, "Mount St. Helens and Catastrophism," 1987.

27. Coffin, "Sonar and Scuba Survey," 1987.

28. Snelling and Mackay, "Coal, Volcanism and Noah's Flood," 1984.

29. Stuart E. Nevins, "Is the Capitan Limestone a Fossil Reef?" in *Creation Research Society Quarterly,* 1972, 8(4):231–48.

30. David B. D'Armond, "Thornton Quarry Deposits: A Fossil Coral Reef or a Catastrophic Flood Deposit?: A Preliminary Study," in *Creation Research Society Quarterly,* 1980, 17(2):88–105.

31. The best-known examples are the trilobite traces that are always found below the oldest trilobite. See, for example, Preston Cloud, "Possible Stratotype Sequences for the Basal Paleozoic in North America," in *American Journal of Science,* 1973, 273:193–206.

32. Various features the author has seen in The Chalk of southern England (fossilization of very large animals, thin volcanic ash deposits over large areas, rare trace fossils, and repetitive bedding) seem to be best explained by extremely rapid deposition under or alongside a huge algal bloom.

33. Steven A. Austin, "Interpreting Strata of Grand Canyon," in Austin, *Grand Canyon,* 1994, 21–56.

34. Ibid.

35. Paul Hodge, *Meteorite Craters and Impact Structures of the Earth* (New York: Cambridge University Press, 1994), 124.

36. Faulkner, "The Current State of Creation Astronomy," 1998.

37. Humphreys, "The Creation of Planetary Magnetic Fields," 1984.

38. R. G. Strom, G. G. Schaber, and D. D. Dawson, "The Global Resurfacing of Venus," in *Journal of Geophysical Research,* 1994, 99(E5):10899–10926.

39. Vardiman, Snelling, and Chaffin, *Radioisotopes and the Age of the Earth,* 2000.

40. Only very slightly on the whole, since there is so much more mantle than ocean crust, but a bit more near the plates.

Chapter 14

1.   See Eric G. Frost, Steve C. Suitt, and Mitra Fattahipour, "Emerging Perspectives of the Salton Trough Region with an Emphasis on Extensional

Faulting and Its Implications for Later San Andreas Deformation," in Patrick L. Abbott and David C. Seymour (eds.), *Sturzstroms and Detatchment Faults, Anza-Borrego Desert State Park, California* (Santa Ana, Calif.: South Coast Geological Society, 1996), 81–121.

2. Steven A. Austin and Mark L. Strauss, "Are Earthquakes Signs of the End Times?" in *Christian Research Journal,* 1999, *21*(4):30–39.

3. Austin, "The Declining Power of Post-Flood Volcanoes," 1998.

4. John R. Baumgardner, "The Catastrophic Plate Tectonics Framework for Biblical Earth History," *Creation Research Society Quarterly,* 2001.

5. Vardiman, "A Conceptional Transition Model," 1994; "Numerical Simulation of Precipitation," 1998.

6. Large flat surfaces produced by sheet erosion are called peneplanes. Large wedges of sediment deposited by sheet deposition are called pediments. Pediments are ubiquitous about the mountains in the Mojave Desert of the southwestern United States (where more recent desert conditions have preserved them to the present). An Eocene pediment coming off the Rocky Mountains stretches hundreds of miles to the East (Michael J. Oard, and Peter Klevberg, "A Diluvial Interpretation of the Cypress Hills Formation, Flaxville Gravel, and Related Deposits," in Walsh, *Proceedings of the Fourth International Conference on Creationism,* 1998).

7. Steven A. Austin, "How Was Grand Canyon Eroded?" in Austin, *Grand Canyon,* 1994.

8. This transition is documented by the change in pollen as one passes up through Tertiary sediments (see Thure E. Cerling and James R. Ehleringer, "Welcome to the C_4 World," in Robert A. Gastaldo and William A. DiMichele (conveners), *Phanerozoic Terrestrial Ecosystems,* The Paleontological Society, USA, 2000), 273–86.

9. J. F. McCauley, *et al.,* "Subsurface Valley and Geoarchaeology of the Eastern Sahara Revealed by Shuttle Radar," in *Science,* 1982, *218*:1004–1020; H. J. Pachur and S. Kröpelin, "Wadi Howar: Paleoclimate Evidence from an Extinct River System in the Southeastern Sahara," in *Science,* 1987, 237:298–300.

10. R. M. Schoch and J. A. West, "Further Evidence Supporting a Pre-2500 B.C. Date for the Great Sphinx of Giza, Egypt," in *GSA Abstracts with Programs,* 2000, *32*(7):A276.

11. For example, Ginkgo Petrified Forest in Oregon (Harold G. Coffin, "The Ginkgo Petrified Forest," in *Origins,* 1974, *1*(2):101–03).

12. T. F. Anderson, "Temperature from Oxygen Isotope Ratios," in Derek E. G. Briggs and Peter R. Crowther (eds.), *Paleobiology: A Synthesis* (Malden, Mass.: Blackwell, 1990), 403–06.

13. Larry Vardiman, "An Analytic Young-Earth Flow Model of Ice Sheet Formation During the 'Ice Age,'" in Walsh, *Proceedings of the Third International Conference on Creationism,* 1994.

14. Wood, "The AGEing Process: Rapid Post-Flood Intrabaraminic Diversification Caused by Altruistic Genetic Elements (AGEs)," in press.

15. Austin, *et al., Grand Canyon: Monument to Catastrophe,* 1994.

Chapter 15

1. Some Christians have identified Peleg's division as the separation of continents. Although a separation of continents or widespread irrigation of the Middle East might be permitted in this passage, the first and primary meaning must refer to the division of languages (given the position of the Genesis 10 genealogy to the Babel narrative, the use of the word *division* throughout Genesis 10 in association with language, families, and nations, and the parallel passage to "the earth was divided" appears to be Genesis 11:1, which says, "The whole earth was of one language, and of one speech"). Furthermore, the division of continents would almost certainly unleash the global catastrophism of Noah's Flood (see chap. 13).

2. Since the purpose of the Genesis 10 genealogy was to list how the languages, families, and nations were divided, it is likely that every person in the final generations were heads of families at the time of Babel. This means they were probably adults having children at the time of Babel.

3. Assuming Joktan was thirty when he began having children, and had all thirteen children within twenty years, and that the youngest child was at least thirty years old when he started having children of his own.

4. Jerry Bergman, "Creation and Creation Myths," in *Creation Research Society Quarterly* 30(4):205–12. Rebecca Conolly and Russell Grigg, "Flood!: Ancient Legends from Various Cultures Around the World Point

to Knowledge of One Cataclysmic Historic Event...," in *Creation Ex Nihilo*, 23(1):26–30.

5.   *e.g.* Kang and Nelson, 1979; Nelson and Broadberry, 1994; Nelson, *et al.,* 1997.

6.   Some Christians have suggested that different races of the present sprang from the wives of the sons of Noah—as if each wife was of a different race. This author does not see this as either an explicit or an implicit claim of Scripture. Plus, it seems possible to explain the origin of races without appealing to this claim. Therefore, this theory is rejected.

7.   See, for example, Stephen Jay Gould, *Mismeasure of Man* (New York, N.Y.: Norton, 1981), 352.

8.   For example, Ham's sons include the following: Cush, the ancestor of the Ethiopians; Mizraim, the ancestor of the Egyptians; and Canaan, the ancestor of the Canaanites. Black, brown, and near-white skin colors are found among Ham's descendants.

9.   Greg Beasley, 1994, A possible creationist perspective on the Tyrolean (Oetztaler) Ice Man, *Creation Ex Nihilo Technical Journal* 8(2):179–91.

10. Cuozzo, John W., 1994, Neandertal children's fossils: Reconstruction and interpretation distorted by assumptions, *Creation Ex Nihilo Technical Journal* 8(2):166–78.

Glossary

AGEing theory—Altruistic Genetic Element theory, a young-age creationist theory of organismal change. In this theory, mobile genetic elements (including viruses) were created by God to facilitate rapid biological change (for example, following the Fall and the Flood) (see Wood).

Amino acid racemization—a method of dating how long ago proteins were in a living organism. Proteins in living organisms are composed of strings of amino acids in a particular ("left-handed") orientation. After the organism dies, the amino acids flip back and forth between "left" and "right" orientations, eventually resulting in 50 percent "left-handed" and 50 percent "right-handed." The rate at which this occurs increases with temperature and rainfall. Under modern climatic conditions and calibrated with C-14 dating, amino acid racemization dates back hundreds of thousands of years. Properly considering post-Flood climate may allow use of this method in young-age creation theory.

Antediluvian Epoch—the period of time between the Fall and the beginning of the Flood.

Anthropic Principle—a regularity of creation originally described by unbelievers whereby the universe and its components intuitively appear to have been designed for man.

Apobaramin (in baraminology and discontinuity systematics)—a group of known organisms and/or fossils that is proposed to be separated from all other known organisms by discontinuities but that may itself be divided by discontinuity. The holobaramin is an apobaramin divided as far as it can be.

Apologetics—Reasoned arguments and/or evidences used to make the Christian faith seem "reasonable" to an unbeliever. Although apologetic arguments can encourage an unbeliever into Christianity, they can also weaken the spiritual life of a believer by displacing true faith.

Arboretum of life, creationist—pictorial representation or analogy of the young-age creationist model of independent (created) origin of a wide variety of different organisms that (after creation) diversified into the many species found within each created group.

Arphaxadian Epoch—the first half millennium or so immediately following the Flood (named after Arphaxad who was born two years after the Flood and died several centuries later).

Babel—the name of the city and tower that was built in defiance of God's command to disperse across the whole earth after the Flood. The insurrection was apparently led by Nimrod and was terminated one to three centuries after the Flood by a confusion of language.

Baramin—"created kind," an organism created by God distinct from all other organisms (a.k.a. "Basic type").

Baraminology—a young-age creationist biosystematics method with the ultimate purpose of identifying, classifying, and studying God's created kinds (baramins).

Basic type—see Baramin.

Biblical hermeneutic—the method by which the Bible is interpreted. Young-age creation theory adopts a historico-grammatical hermeneutic.

Big Bang theory—an evolutionary theory for the origin of the universe and its lightest elements.

Biosystematics—a field of study that names and classifies organisms.

Catastrophic plate tectonics—a synthetic young-age creationist theory of earth history. Similar to plate tectonics theory except that most of the earth's crustal motion occurred during the Flood at meters per second (see Austin, *et al.*, 1994).

Cenozoic Era—see *Tertiary System* and *Quaternary System.*

Chaos theory—a field of physics that studies certain systems (chaotic systems) that are so finely tuned and so affected by so many different factors that we cannot reliably predict their outcome.

Chloroplast—an organelle in a cell where photosynthesis occurs.

Chronogenealogy—a particular type of genealogy that presents not only a complete genealogy but a precise time line of births and deaths. Young-age creation theory suggests the genealogies of Genesis 5 and 11 are chronogenealogies and the only ones in Scripture.

Creation myth—any creation theory developed by man to replace the truth of God's creation (*a la* Rom. 1:21–32). Creation myths include those of the Egyptians and the Canaanites of the second millennium B.C. and evolutionary theories of the second millennium A.D.

Creationism—the belief that a transcendent God is responsible for the origin of the physical world.

Death, biblical—the cessation of biblical life (that is, the departure of the non-physical essence of life from an organism). Biblical death seems to be possible only for organisms that can be biblically alive (that is, man and animals), and in young-age creation theory only postdates the Fall.

Discontinuity systematics—a biosystematic method that identifies the smallest organismal groups surrounded by discontinuity from all other groups.

Doctrine of the Creator—a theological theory that claims God created the physical creation so all people everywhere through all time could come to know and glorify God through it. The doctrine of the Creator provides the only known justification for the presuppositions of science.

Dominion mandate—the divine command (Gen. 1:28) that man was to have dominion over the earth and its organisms.

Edenian Epoch—the period of time between the end of Creation Week and the Fall.

Elegance, explanatory—a characteristic of theories where great complexity is explained in a very simple manner.

Embryological recapitulation—a theory that an organism as it develops from a single cell (its ontogeny) relives (recapitulates) the evolutionary history of that organism from a single cell (its phylogeny). The theory was popularized by Ernst Haekel in the nineteenth century but has fallen into disfavor in most evolutionary circles. The evidence is better explained by creation theory.

Endoplasmic reticulum—an organelle in a cell where proteins are assembled from amino acids and initially folded into their three-dimensional structure.

Epoch, geologic—(in old-age chronology)—the period of time during which a "series" package of rocks was deposited. Subdivisions are known as ages.

Era, geologic—(in old-age chronology)—the period of time during which an "erathem" package of rocks was deposited. Subdivisions are known as periods.

Evolutionism—the belief that the physical world organized itself through natural law and process without intervention by a transcendent God.

Faith—a trust in God's truth given to man as a gift from God when man gives up trying to know, derive, or prove the truth for himself.

Fall—(proper noun) In the strictest sense, the Fall refers to the human spiritual fall caused by Adam's disobedience. In the broader sense, the Fall refers to the group of events (including the curse) that ended the Edenian Epoch and caused all aspects of God's creation to experience pain and suffering.

Firmament (KJV translation of *raqia* better translated "expanse")—the stretched-out heavens ("space") where God placed the sun, moon, and stars.

Flood—(proper noun) the singular period of judgment in the days of Noah. Over one year in length, it destroyed the antediluvian world. In its broadest sense it may have affected the solar system and beyond, and we are still living under its effects today.

Flood basalt—widespread, thick piles of basalt lavas thought to have erupted very quickly from a deep mantle source.

Foundational philosophies—the set of philosophical theories that create the foundation for an academic discipline.

Fountains of the great deep—springs on the land and in the sea before the Flood that were catastrophically broken up on the first day of the Flood to be a source of Flood water (Gen. 7:11). In catastrophic plate tectonics theory, these are thought to be superheated plumes of water hyper-ballistically catapulted into the earth's atmosphere by contact of hot mantle material with ocean water.

Gaia Hypothesis—a theory that suggests that the earth acts like a living organism—adapting to changes and struggling to survive. The evidences explained by the Gaia Hypothesis are better explained by the divine creation of an earth that was supposed to persist through time.

General Relativity—a theory introduced by Albert Einstein in 1915 and confirmed by numerous tests since that time. It suggests that time changes with gravity and speed.

Genetic code—the nucleotide sequences that code for particular amino acids.

Geomagnetism—the earth's magnetic field.

Golgi body—an organelle in a cell that receives proteins from the endoplasmic reticulum and gives them their final structure.

Great synthesis—a sought-for rethinking of the philosophical foundations of all academic disciplines that would ground all of them in a scholarly manner in God's truth.

Historical narrative—a particular type of writing that presents actual events and their real history. Young-age creation theory suggests that Genesis (including the creation account) is historical narrative.

Historico-grammatical hermeneutic—the method of Bible interpretation that accepts Scripture's general perspicuity, assuming the straightforward historical understanding of a passage in the light of its larger context. This is the biblical hermeneutic accepted by young-age creation theory.

Holobaramin (in baraminology and discontinuity systematics)—a group of known organisms and/or fossils that is proposed to be separated from all other known organisms by discontinuities but that is itself not completely divided by discontinuity.

Homoplasy—a similarity between two organisms that seems to suggest a relationship different from that suggested by a particular nested hierarchal classification.

Hybridatabase—an Internet-accessible database of attempted and claimed crosses between different organismal species maintained by the Center for Origins Research and Education at Bryan College.

Ice Advance—the period of time in young-age chronology during which ice built up on several continental regions, then surged over larger areas, and then rapidly melted back.

Ice Age—the period of time in old-age chronology during which ice built up on several continental regions, then moved over larger areas, and finally melted back. See *Ice Advance* for the young-age creation equivalent.

Image of God—a non-physical attribute possessed by human beings from conception that sets them apart from the remainder of creation.

Information theory—a field that studies information—how it comes to be, how it is stored, how it is transferred, and how it is lost.

Intelligent design (ID)—a theory and movement that seeks to develop a secular method of identifying and defending design in the universe. Prominent in this movement are Phillip Johnson and William Dembski.

Intentional ambiguity—the claim that God created the physical creation and authored the Bible in such a way that it was not possible to reason infallibly or prove the existence or attributes of God. This was done so faith is required of man.

Intrabaraminic diversification—change (including the origin of new species) that occurs within a divinely created kind.

Irreducible complexity—a theory made popular in recent times by Michael Behe (*Darwin's Black Box*) that design is indicated in any system that requires the coordinated presence of multiple parts and cannot be derived in a step-wise fashion from systems with fewer parts.

Jussives—Hebrew verb forms (translated "may it be" or "let it be") that are either requests of an inferior (jussives of request) or commands of a superior (jussives of command). Genesis 1 has a number of jussives of command.

Lamb-Humphreys Magnetic Field theory—a theory for how the earth's magnetic field is maintained. It suggests that the earth was created with a bunch of electrons circulating in the molten outer core that have been slowing down by friction since the creation. During the Flood and the Arphaxadian Epoch, circulation in the outer core (caused by catastrophic plate tectonics) resulted in rapid reversals of the earth's magnetic field as perceived at the earth's surface.

Lateral gene transfer—one or more genes copied or transferred from the genetic material of one organism into the genetic material of another organism (not by sexual reproduction).

Life, biblical—a non-physical essence possessed by man and at least most animals. It does not seem to exist in plants, algae, protists, and bacteria.

Magnetic reversal—the flipping of a magnetic field so that magnetic north becomes magnetic south and vice versa.

Maturity, creation with—a theory of young-age creationism that God created many things in a mature form (fulfilling function at the moment of creation), thus appearing as if they had developed when they had not.

Mesozoic Era—see *Secondary Erathem*.

Mitochondrion—an organelle in a cell where energy is extracted from glucose sugar.

Monobaramin (in baraminology and discontinuity systematics)—a group of known organisms and/or fossils that is proposed to be *not* completely divided by a discontinuity but that may or may not be separated from all other organisms by a discontinuity. The holobaramin is the largest a particular monobaramin can be.

Mutational genetic load—the genetic weakness experienced by a species because of the mutations its members carry.

Natural evil—"natural" (that is, not directly human-caused) events that kill or pain "innocents." Natural evil includes biological evils like carnivory, disease, and parasitism, and geological evils like earthquakes, landslides, and volcanoes. Young-age creationism would suggest natural evil does not precede man's sin, whereas old-age creationism would suggest that natural evil preceded man's sin by millions and even billions of years.

Natural selection—a theoretical mechanism whereby less fit organisms are selectively eliminated. Natural selection is a consequence of the overproduction God instituted at the Fall to permit organisms to survive in a world plagued with disease and mutation.

Nested hierarchy—an orderly arrangement where items are classified into successively higher categories and where any item or category finds itself placed into one and only one category of the next highest level of arrangement.

Netted hierarchy—an orderly arrangement where items can be arranged into a number of different nested hierarchies and where any given nested hierarchy has multiple homoplasies.

Old-age creation—theories of creation that maintain both that God is Creator and that the creation is billions of years old. Theories vary on a spectrum from the creation of the universe "pregnant" with the ability to self-evolve (evolutionary creation) to continuous, small-scale intervention (continuous creation also known as theistic evolution) to step-wise, large-scale divine fiat creations scattered through time (progressive creation).

Orchard, creationist—see *Arboretum of life, creationist.*

Order of magnitude—a power of 10. Two numbers where the larger is less than ten times the size of the smaller are within an order of magnitude of one another. A number that is 10 x 10 (*i.e.* $10^2=100$) times larger than another number is 2 orders of magnitude larger (the number 10 is raised to). A number that is 10 x 10 x 10 x 10 x 10 (*i.e.* $10^5=100$) times larger is 5 orders of magnitude larger.

Overproduction—the production of more offspring than will survive long enough to reproduce. In young-age creationism, this only postdates the Fall; in old-age creationism, this was going on billions of years before the sin of man.

Paleozoic Era—see *Primary Erathem.*

Pangaea—the name that old-age geologists have given to a supercontinent that formed during the deposition of upper primary sediments and broke up during deposition of the secondary sediments. In young-age creationism, this supercontinent may not have been above water, forming and breaking up during the Flood.

Parallelism of juxtaposed couplets—a diagnostic characteristic of Hebrew poetry where adjacent lines of text have the same grammatical structure and where parallel words are either synonyms or antonyms.

Pathology—something that does harm to something else (for example, a disease).

Peleg's division—a "division of earth" in the "days of Peleg" (who lived in the second, third, and fourth centuries following Noah's flood). In this book this is understood to primarily refer to Babel's division of tongues.

Period, geologic (in old-age chronology)—the period of time during which a "system" package of rocks was deposited. Subdivisions are known as epochs.

Perspicuous—clear, especially as regards writing. Writing what you mean and meaning what you write. Young-age creation theory suggests God was perspicuous when He authored Scripture.

Phenomenological language—a characteristic of all types of Hebrew literature where things are described as they appear, not necessarily as they are (for example "the sun rises").

Plate tectonics—synthetic old-age geology theory of earth history, including continental drift theory and sea-flood spreading theory. In this theory, the earth's crust has been in constant motion of centimeters per year for all of earth history.

Presuppositions—assumptions that are often unconsciously accepted by practitioners of a discipline and that must be true if pursuing that discipline is to be reasonable. The only known justification for the presuppositions of science is the "Doctrine of the Creator."

Primary Erathem—old name (resurrected here) for the lowest of the four major successive packages of fossiliferous rock layers. It includes the

Cambrian through Permian Systems. In old-age chronology, the interval of time during which it was formed is called the Paleozoic Era. In young-age creation chronology, it was probably produced in the first half of the Flood.

Protein decay—a method of dating how long ago proteins were in a living organism. Proteins in living organisms have particular structures that allow them to accomplish their tasks in cells. After the organism dies, the proteins break down into smaller pieces and alternate shapes. The rate at which this occurs increases with temperature and rainfall. Under modern climatic conditions and calibrated with C-14 dating, protein decay dates back hundreds of thousands of years. Properly considering post-flood climate may allow use of this method in young-age creation theory.

Quaternary System—the uppermost of the four major successive packages of fossiliferous rock layers. It includes the Pleistocene and Holocene Series. In old-age chronology, the interval of time during which it and the underlying Tertiary Systems were formed is called the Cenozoic Era. In young-age creation chronology, it probably represents the period following the Babel dispersion.

Radiometric dating—a method of determining the age of something by using radioactive elements, those that change spontaneously by tossing out component particles.

Residual catastrophism—young-age creation theory of powerful and rapid geologic activity following Noah's flood with decreasing intensity through time.

Rodinia—the name old-age geologists have given to a theoretical supercontinent that began to break up just before the beginning of the deposition of Primary rocks. In young-age creationism, this is the best guess for the continental configuration before the Flood.

Runaway subduction—meter-per-second sinking of ocean crust into the earth's interior in the young-age creationist Flood model (catastrophic plate tectonics).

Scientific creationism—a theory popularized by Henry M. Morris that seeks to develop a non-biblical argument and defense for creation.

Second Law of Thermodynamics—the tendency of every natural process to lose some unretrievable energy. Since the Fall this has resulted in the loss of usable energy and complexity in the entire creation (thus causing it to "wax old"). Before the Fall another law may have countered its large-scale effects.

Secondary Erathem—old name (resurrected here) for the second (from the bottom) of the four major successive packages of fossiliferous rock layers. It includes the Triassic through Cretaceous Systems. In old-age chronology, the interval of time during which it was formed is called the Mesozoic Era. In young-age creation chronology, it was probably produced in the middle of the Flood.

Secular equilibrium—a situation where the total amount of a particular substance stays the same because the rate of loss of the substance equals the rate of production of the substance.

Seismic tomography—a method of inferring the structure of the deep interior of the earth by computer analysis of earthquake waves detected at monitoring stations around the earth.

Stratomorphic intermediate—a fossil that is intermediate in form between two other organisms and at its deepest position in the rocks is above the deepest representative of one group and below the deepest representative of the other group.

Stromatolite—a generally dome-shaped rock structure that contains many sub-parallel layers (often of sediment and organic material). Stromatolites come in a variety of forms, at least some of which can be formed without organisms and most of which are thought to be formed by algae-like colonies of cyanobacteria.

Suboptimal improvisation—a character thought to be less than optimal because it was derived by (inefficient) evolutionary process from some previous organism.

Tertiary System—the third (from the bottom) of the four major successive packages of fossiliferous rock layers. It includes the Paleocene through Pliocene Series. In old-age chronology, the interval of time during which it and the overlying Quaternary System were formed is called the Cenozoic Era. In young-age creation chronology, it was probably produced in the Arphaxadian Epoch.

Thermoluminescence—a method of dating how long ago pottery was fired. When many natural substances are heated (for example, in campfires), some electrons are stimulated into higher energy states, causing them to luminesce as they drop back down in energy. As time passes more and more of these electrons drop down to their lower energy state until all are back to normal. The rate at which this occurs increases with temperature and rainfall. Under modern climatic conditions and calibrated with C-14 dating, thermoluminescence dates back hundreds of thousands of years. Properly considering post-Flood climate may allow use of this method in young-age creation theory.

Transitional forms—In the evolution of one organism from another the forms that must have been evolved through are transitional forms. Stratomorphic intermediates are the best candidates for these hypothetical forms.

Tree of life, evolutionary—pictorial representation or analogy of the evolutionary model of the common origin (by evolutionary branching) of all modern species from a single common ancestor. See *Arboretum of life, creationist* for the young-age creationist alternative.

Waters above—waters located above or beyond the space God created, stretched out, and filled with astronomical objects.

Waters below—presumed to be the oceans of the earth.

Windows of heaven—intense global rain as a water source for the Flood (Gen. 7:11). In catastrophic plate tectonics theory, this was the water from the fountains of the great deep that was not tossed out of the earth's gravitational field. It spread out, cooled by radiation into space, and fell as intense global rain.

Young-age creation—theory of creation history advocated in this book that maintains that God created the entire universe during a six-day Creation Week about six thousand years ago.